Transnational
Religious
Movements

Thank you for choosing a SAGE product!
If you have any comment, observation or feedback,
I would like to personally hear from you.
Please write to me at **contactceo@sagepub.in**

Vivek Mehra, Managing Director and CEO, SAGE India.

Bulk Sales

SAGE India offers special discounts
for purchase of books in bulk.
We also make available special imprints
and excerpts from our books on demand.

For orders and enquiries, write to us at

Marketing Department
SAGE Publications India Pvt Ltd
B1/I-1, Mohan Cooperative Industrial Area
Mathura Road, Post Bag 7
New Delhi 110044, India

E-mail us at **marketing@sagepub.in**

Get to know more about SAGE

Be invited to SAGE events, get on our mailing list.
Write today to **marketing@sagepub.in**

This book is also available as an e-book.

Transnational Religious Movements

Faith's Flows

Jonathan D. James

Los Angeles | London | New Delhi
Singapore | Washington DC | Melbourne

First published in 2017 by

SAGE Publications India Pvt Ltd
B1/I-1 Mohan Cooperative Industrial Area
Mathura Road, New Delhi 110 044, India
www.sagepub.in

SAGE Publications Inc
2455 Teller Road
Thousand Oaks, California 91320, USA

SAGE Publications Ltd
1 Oliver's Yard, 55 City Road
London EC1Y 1SP, United Kingdom

SAGE Publications Asia-Pacific Pte Ltd
3 Church Street
#10-04 Samsung Hub
Singapore 049483

Published by Vivek Mehra for SAGE Publications India Pvt Ltd, typeset in 10.5/12.5 pt Minion Pro by, JMV Design Solutions, Chandigarh 31D and printed at Chaman Enterprises, New Delhi.

Library of Congress Cataloging-in-Publication Data
Name: James, Jonathan D., author.
Title: Transnational religious movements : faith's flows / Jonathan D. James.
Description: Thousand Oaks : SAGE Publications India Pvt Ltd., 2017. | Includes
    bibliographical references and index.
Identifiers: LCCN 2017017025| ISBN 9789386446558 (print (hb)) |
ISBN 9789386446572 (e-pub) | ISBN 9789386446565 (e-book)
Subjects: LCSH: Religions. | Sects. | Cults. | Religion and
    Sociology—History—21st century.
Classification: LCCBL85. J36 2017 | DDC 201/.7—dc23 LC record available at
https://lccn.loc.gov/2017017025

ISBN: 978-93-864-4655-8 (HB)

SAGE Team: Supriya Das, Alekha Chandra Jena, Madhurima Thapa, and Ritu Chopra

Contents

Foreword by Professor Jeffrey Haynes   vii

Acknowledgments   xi

Introduction: Faith's Flows   xiii

1   Transnationalism: Perspectives   1

2   Hillsong Church: Postmodern Parishes, Worldwide Music, and Anointed Acquisitions   15

3   Validating Identity, Spirituality, and Space for BAPS Hindus in India and the Diaspora   37

4   Ciji: Socially Engaged Buddhism, Feminization, and the Politics of Soft Power   59

5   The New Face of Islam in the West: The Case of Islamic Relief   82

6   The Gülen-Hizmet Movement: Reformed Islam or Revitalized Caliphate?   107

7   ISIS: Epistemology, Eschatology, and Empire of a Revolutionary Movement   134

Conclusion: Globalization of Faith, Faith in Globalization   162

Index   182

About the Author   189

Foreword

Transnational religious movements are some of the oldest expressions of interaction between groups of people separated by geographical distance, who share the same religious understanding, values, and norms. Long before the current era of advanced globalization, transnational religious movements helped to make the world a global entity. Christianity and Islam were especially significant in this regard as both saw themselves from the outset of the founding of the faiths as proselytizing religions whose raison d'être was to spread the news of the 'one true faith' to other people.

During the long period of secularization of international relations, from the mid-seventeenth to the late twentieth century, that is, the period between the signing of the Peace of Westphalia (1648) and the closure of the Cold War (late 1980s), transnational religious movements were in some cases active both socially and politically. For example, during the period of dynamic European colonization of Sub-Saharan Africa from the mid-nineteenth century until after World War I, the cross and the sword went hand in hand, just as they had done 700 years earlier during the Spanish and Portuguese colonial intrusions into South America. This is a way of highlighting that the advance of 'secular' Western civilization—for the good of the 'natives', apparently—relied heavily on the support—ideationally, and in some cases administratively and structurally—of religious actors. Chief among these were various 'national' churches, including for Spain and Portugal, the Roman Catholic, and for the English, the Anglican, to further the cause of Western civilization to the benighted reaches of the 'heart of darkness', to use Conrad's evocative phrase (Conrad 2002).

Islam had an earlier phase of expansion in tandem with state power from the mid-seventh century for several hundred years. Within Islam, there was no real or imagined separation of 'church' and state. Islam was the shared body of understanding, knowledge, and values which enabled people of different cultures and ethnicities to trust each other so that trading and other networks could be established, developed, and strengthened. Perhaps inevitably, with two powerful bulls in the field, the two faiths clashed, especially when each was allied to nonreligious state power. International relations was characterized for hundreds of years by this interfaith clash, right up until the late seventeenth century when it became clear that Islam was defeated by Western power, able to utilize superior military, organizational, structural, and technological power, and usher in an era of sustained Western colonization.

Following the end of the Cold War, it became clear that the long period of secularization of international relations was no more. The multifaceted impacts of globalization—with its interactive technological, economic, political, and cultural ramifications—dovetailed with the impact of the demise of the Soviet Union, which, at least momentarily, gave rise to the notion that the West had 'triumphed' in the tense, four-decade-long struggle about values, norms, and outcomes with the USSR.

What was, however, overlooked by many international relations scholars was the social and—in some cases—political importance of many transnational religious movements, manifested in a variety of ways. September 11, 2001 was a high-water mark of IR interest in transnational religious movements; the attack on the World Trade Center twin towers by Al-Qaeda and consequential deaths of nearly 3,000 people put the issue of malign transnational religious movements into stark detail, providing the ammunition for hundreds of reports, journal articles, and books.

But Al-Qaeda and its transnational reach was not the entire story. While the Al-Qaeda attack on the United States on 9/11 was regarded by some as the opening shot in Huntington's projected 'clash of civilizations', others saw the impact of transnational religious movements in a broader context. The most obvious perhaps was that transnational religious movements are capable of enlisting people into networks which may take their chief loyalty. Given that the nation-state was widely thought to be the sole possessor of such power then manifestation of the 'return' of religion to international relations was of major theoretical and perhaps practical significance for our understanding of how the world works and what the role of religion is in IR today.

A key point I want to emphasize in this brief piece is that transnational religious movements are neither 'good' nor 'bad' per se. While this might not come as a surprise for many people reading these words, in my 'home' discipline—international relations—religion is still to this day regarded with suspicion, because of its association for many with violence and conflict, while states are still for many lionized as the key—rather than a key—actor in international relations.

What then does Dr Jonathan D. James' book tell us about the current 'state of play' of our understanding of transnational religious movements? He shows, first, that there is an array of such entities, mainly but not exclusively deriving from the traditions of Christianity and Islam. Other world religions—including, Buddhism, Hinduism, and Judaism—are much less well represented in today's array of transnational religious movements, not least because they did not have strong proselytizing zeal and as a result did not expand—often aggressively, as with Christianity and Islam—from their founding place to various other parts of the world and thus did not set up the context and opportunity for transnational religious movements easily to develop. Having said that, James has two case studies in the book: one on socially engaged Buddhism and the other on a transnational Hindu movement linking followers in the Indian diaspora—which show that when talking about transnational religious movements, we should not overlook faiths, including Buddhism and Hinduism, in today's era of advanced globalization with associated opportunities for communities around the world to engage with each other in religious networks.

Second, James shows empirically that transnational religious movements have a variety of motives and raisons d'être. Some, such as Al-Qaeda or ISIS, are widely, although not uniformly, regarded as thoroughly malign, wreckers of the status quo, and a present and serious danger to peaceful, cooperative international relations. Others such as certain Christian churches are sometimes understood rather ambiguously: on the one hand, pro-development, human rights, and supportive of cooperation between people while, on the other, also seen as denying gender equality.

Finally, and perhaps above all, the transnational religious movements examined in this book can be understood as expressions of a single uniform desire: to link up and work with other like-minded people who live in places which are not easy or convenient to reach by standard transportation. Instead, and this is where globalization comes in so importantly, people can inhabit a network whose members do not have to meet physically to draw inspiration and succor from each other. In sum, Jonathan James' book is a very welcome addition to the small yet growing number of books that focus on transnational religious movements. He has written an illuminating, interesting, and perceptive study, which I believe you will find useful and thought-provoking.

Professor Jeffrey Haynes
Director of Faculty Research, Professor of Politics, and Director of the Centre for the Study of Religion, Conflict and Cooperation
London Metropolitan University

Reference

Conrad, Joseph. 2002. *Heart of Darkness*. San Clemente, CA: Tantor Media.

Acknowledgments

It was during a visit to Vancouver, Canada and Chicago, USA in 2011 that the seeds for this book were planted in my mind. I was amazed beyond words to see both these cities being inhabited by vast numbers of Asians, mainly of Chinese and Indian backgrounds, and how certain suburbs were literally turned into replicas of China and India. I wondered about the religious and spiritual life of these diaspora Asians in the West. Questions such as these flowed through my mind:

- How will faith be sustained in a new country?
- Would the religion in the host country be different from the homeland?
- Would it be influenced by the larger culture?
- What will happen to the next generation of Asians born and raised in the West?

My motivation for this research was to apply critical inquiry and social analysis into the growing number of religious movements around the world. The six case studies I chose are, in the end, my interpretations, as I endeavored to make sense of the religious themes, motivations, goals, and influences from primary sources and the vast array of secondary texts that were made available to me.

It is my hope that future researchers would continue this narrative of how religions function transnationally in today's globalized society.

I wish to offer sincere thanks to CREATEC at Edith Cowan University in Perth, for their support. In particular, I say a big 'thank you' to Professor Lelia Green and Associate Professor Trevor Cullen for their help in approving the partial funding for this project.

I am indebted to Dr John Hall for his conscientious editorial support and general helpfulness.

I owe an intellectual debt to Professor Jeffrey Haynes, an eminent scholar in the field of international relations, religion, and conflict, for his precise and meaningful introductory comments in the foreword.

I thank the Rand Corporation (USA) for giving me permission to reproduce a table in Chapter 5.

On a personal note, I am grateful for the support and prayers of my siblings and their families. I appreciate the fact that writing this book was not a solitary effort and I want to acknowledge the many contributions of my wife, Elizabeth, and my children, Ben and Mel.

In our efforts to trace all the copyright holders, the publisher and I are conscious that we may have omitted some—and if that is the case, we will be pleased to make the necessary arrangements.

Jonathan James
Perth, Australia

Introduction: Faith's Flows

The dramatic global resurgence of religious movements has caught scholars of religion by surprise. According to our Western myth of modernization, the future of religion offered several options, but neither its resurgence nor its ability to shape human beings were among them.
— Martin Riesebrodt (2000)

By 2050, more than 60 percent of the people on earth will be either Christian or Muslim (Pew Research Centre 2015). For the first time in history, "Islam and Christianity would boast roughly equal numbers. Islam, the world's fastest-growing faith, will leap from 1.6 billion (in 2010) to 2.76 billion by 2050" (Pew Research Centre 2015). This demographic study also estimated that by 2050, Muslims will constitute nearly one-third of the world's total projected population of about 9 billion people. As for Christianity, it is expected to grow but not at Islam's explosive rate; Christians will increase from 2.17 billion to 2.92 billion, with a population of more than 31 percent of the world's population (Pew Research Centre 2015).

In this opening chapter, I introduce the book *Transnational Religious Movements: Faith's Flows* by firstly offering a rationale for it. I then cite the main theories that underpin the study, and I proceed to identify five key characteristics of transnational religious entities. I then give an overview of the six case studies in the book and conclude with a summary of the book's main features and significance.

Transnational Religious Movements reveals that despite predictions by sociologists such as Zukerman (2014) that religion will die and atheism will flourish, religion and religious organizations today are actually thriving and poised to make the news—by their acts of goodness or evil and their propensity for social action or subversion. The decline of church attendance in the heartlands of Christianity seems to have blindsided scholars like Zukerman (2014) into making hasty conclusions about the waning of religion in the contemporary world. A careful reading of the world scene reveals a different picture— one that supports the Pew findings (2015). Hence, scholars of world religion caution that "[i]t is myopic and colonial to use a Eurocentric lens to gauge the diverse religious phenomena of humankind and to project the future of religion…. We must adopt a contextual, multiaxial, and transnational approach" (Kwok 2010: para 1).

In the twenty-first century, the world has experienced the dramatic spread of Pentecostal and Charismatic groups within Christianity and the even more dramatic emergence of transnational Islamic networks. Coupled with major movements of people across borders and the revival of new religious groups, these developments have prompted scholars to conclude that there has been a resurgence of deterritorialized communities in our world, that is, the sociocultural displacement of people who have moved to new locations (Giddens 1990).

The book is focused on the reinvention of transnational religious organizations, with an emphasis on representative movements from the four main world religions—Hinduism, Islam, Christianity, and Buddhism. *Transnational Religious Movements* situates religious organizations in the realm of cultural and religious globalization by using comparative and textual analysis as its primary methodology. The book's central argument is based on the premise that religion has always been an important force in society and that the processes of globalization have accentuated its significance.

The book reveals that transnational religious organizations operate in a continuum ranging from apolitical structures to political structures, and from organizations that encourage multiple identities and loyalties to organizations that insist on a singular identity and loyalty. Transnational religious movements also vary in so far as they cooperate with or subvert sovereign states.

Rationale

Transnational religious organizations are an acknowledged reality in our contemporary world; however, there is a dearth of scholarship in this field. The recent rise of transnational radical Islam has caused scholars to reassess the connection between religion and the global and political systems, and much of the new literature in this limited field has been devoted to radicalized and terrorist networks. While this sensational revelation is to be applauded, it should be acknowledged that in many parts of the world, transnational religious movements are engaged in socially cohesive activities such as encouraging dialogue and innovative development. *Transnational Religious Movements* proposes to address the phenomenon of transnational religious organizations by taking a balanced and nuanced approach to the study of six representative transnational religious entities.

While much has been researched on transnational politics and commerce, studies on the transnational experiences of religious life in the four main world religions are sadly lacking. Transnationalism is an important aspect of globalization and therefore it behoves us to consider how people "forge and sustain multi-stranded social relations that link together their societies of origin and settlement" (Basch, Shiller and Blanc 1994: 7). Transnational religious life redefines and extends boundaries. I base my study of the six transnational religious organizations on the premise that a religious-studies approach is useful to understand how these entities carve out new religious spaces and transnationalize everyday life[1] (McAlister 2001; Tweed 1997). Through this study, I intend to continue a conversation with future researchers on the global ethnography of faith and how religion is shaped and recreated by transnational movements in our global world.

Theoretical Underpinnings

Transnationalism in the religious context refers to the fluidity of religion across borders. Religion has a history of operating beyond its native shores. The mission efforts by the Apostle Paul and successive Christian missionaries, the growth of Islam through traders, conquests, and colonies, and the expansion of early Buddhism and Hinduism through trade and 'cultural colonization', all attest to this phenomenon.[2]

In my study of transnational religion, I draw on the theories of Castells (2010), Bourdieu (1991), Baumann (1992), and Vasquez and Marquardt (2003).

Castells' (2010) term 'flows' is critical in understanding globalization and transnational organizations. He distinguishes between the 'space of places' where people's experiences and activities are happening and the 'space of flows' with reference to the movements of messages, people, capital investment, and electronic data (Castells 2010). Castells broadens our vision from spaces to flows in any locality in the contemporary world. Flows (as opposed to spaces) refer to composite movements from one place to another, and they lead us to understand the structure of the economy and culture of transnational organizations that are based on networks (Castells 2010). Whoever controls these flows and the resulting networks holds the power (Castells 2010). In the realm of religion, Castells (2010) maintains that fundamentalist and radical groups—some of which operate as networks and cells—are formed as a direct consequence of the waning of traditional organizations. Hence, these groups, which are on the rise, operate as 'resistance identities' (Lyon 2000: 51).

Tomlinson (2006) supports Castells' theory, stating that networks and flows constitute the heart of globalization:

> [T]here is something going on which is quite simple to describe—and I call this a process of accelerating 'connectivity.' By this I mean that globalization refers to the rapidly developing and ever-densening network of interconnections and interdependencies that characterise it. (Tomlinson 2006: 1)

Bourdieu's (1991) work on the practices people undertake in making sense out of life falls into two categories—structured and fluid. These are life routes that a person takes and follows on a day-by-day basis. The accumulated paths, patterns, practices, and experiences of a person constitute what he terms 'habitus'—the identity and typical social interaction pattern of an individual or group of people in a transnational organization (Bourdieu 1991).

Baumann (1992) builds on Castells' theory by advocating that globalization and transnational organizations operate on the premise of capitalism, but importantly they have incorporated consumption, "[Consumption] is moving steadily into the position of, simultaneously, the cognitive and the moral focus of life, the integrative bond of society and the focus of systemic management" (Baumann 1992: 49). Fenn agrees with this notion theorizing that in today's globalized world, "religion offers at best a consumer-basket of items for the consumption of the religious" (Fenn 1978: 103).

Globalization, which has aided and abetted the phenomenon of transnationalism as we know it today, is not producing a single homogeneous whole. On the contrary, globalization is also bringing about the "unpacking of local cultural complexes, but in the process it creates multifarious local identities and criss-crossing frontiers, so that diversity comes to rule more than ever before in local spaces" (Lehmann 2002: 300).

According to Vasquez and Marquardt (2003), religion is the main instigator of what they call deterritorialization (the displacement of communities) and reterritorialization (the restructuring of cultural practice and identity):

> Religion, we believe, is one of the main protagonists in this unbinding of culture from its traditional referents and boundaries and in its reattachment in new space-time configurations ... giv[ing] rise to hybrid individual and collective identities that fly in the face of the methodological purity and simplicity sought by modernists sociologies of religion. (Vasquez and Marquardt 2003: 35)

My case studies support Levitt's depiction (Levitt 2004) of the ways transnational flows affect religious communities: extended, negotiated, and recreated. Flows come from host nation to the newly settled nation and in the sense of being 'extended'. Also, flows from the host nation are forced to deal with new concepts and constructs and so they are 'negotiated'. Then flows are 'recreated' as they take on board the local dynamics.

In this book, I see transnational religious communities in two ways: diasporic religious communities that have been organized by home countries to take care of their migrant population abroad and 'standalone' world religious organizations that have expansionist policies, extending their services and products to the rest of the world (Rudolph and Piscatori 1997).

Salient Characteristics of Transnational Entities

Transnational religious movements exhibit the following characteristics:

1. Popularity and Far-reaching Influence
The International Society for Krishna Consciousness (ISKCON), also known simply as the Hare Krishna movement, has 600 worldwide

major centers, temples, and rural communities, nearly 100 affiliated vegetarian restaurants, thousands of *Nama-hattas* or local meeting groups, a host of community projects, and millions of congregational members worldwide.[3] It was founded by Bhaktivedanta Swami Prabhupāda in New York City in 1966, but interestingly its worldwide headquarters is located in Mayapur in West Bengal, India.[4] The scale of the popularity of this movement is seen in the amazing way that the names, identities, and icons associated with this group have managed to enter into mainstream popular Western culture.[5] This underscores the phenomenon of the 'Easternization of the West'.

2. Interconnectedness

More and more, we are sensing that religion is not limited to a country or certain countries but linked with networks across transnational borders. Immigration is one of the primary factors for this phenomenon. There are 100,000 Indians, mostly Hindus, living in greater Chicago, known as Chicagoland—with some 90 Hindu temples and Hindu establishments. Devon Avenue in Chicago is an extraordinary sight where there are rows upon rows of Indian restaurants, supermarkets, offices, and businesses owned by Indians. Hindu leaders and temple priests from India visiting the United States make Chicago and New York (where large numbers of Indians make their home) their initial stopping points where seminars, *satsangs*, and mandirs[6] are conducted.

Richmond in Vancouver, Canada has attracted a huge population of Chinese from Hong Kong and Mainland China (the second largest population of American Chinese in North America) because perhaps the name 'Rich' in Richmond is a reference to the materialistic and superstitious nature of these migrants. Buddhist temples and various establishments have sprung up in Richmond and indeed in many parts of Canada to cater for the spiritual needs of the new immigrants. In many parts of North America, the influx of the Chinese diaspora is seen in suburban areas as well.

Using Castells' (2010) theory, we can surmise that both the 'space of places' and the 'space of flows' in Chicago and Richmond have changed quite drastically. Mixed loyalties and a distinct form of religious identity are obviously present. Thus, the religion represents a combination of religious practices and artefacts of the host country and the homelands.

United Muslim Relief (UMR), described as the "fastest growing NGO in the United States," is a nonprofit organization registered with the Internal Revenue Service (IRS), which provides health care, sustainable livelihood, and social services to all people regardless of 'race or religion'.[7] Its website claims that UMR is not just for Muslims "although inspired by our Islamic ethos, we are open-minded and pluralistic."[8] However, on closer study, it appears that relief works are targeted to Muslim nations or nations with large Muslim populations, such as Syria, Pakistan, and Bangladesh. UMR's main charitable activities for 2012 took place in Syria.[9] Hence, Muslims living in war-torn lands are being connected transnationally through agencies such as UMR.

3. Sustainable Principles and Contemporary Technology

Great Enlightenment Lotus Society (GELS), a Buddhist transnational organization based in Taiwan, with offices in the United States and Canada, is a multifaceted entity that has its own health product company (Heartland), an educational foundation with various study groups, income-generation projects including an organic agricultural foundation, and a host of subsidiaries.[10] State-of-the-art technologies are used in GELS for the dissemination of Buddhist teaching, practices, and products to its more than 70,000 members.[11]

The Hizmet movement, an Islamic transnational organization, is an example of a religious movement successfully engaged in several entrepreneurial activities, particularly in the fields of education and media (Pandya and Gallagher 2012). Religious-based entrepreneurship is also rampant in the Christian world and uses the free-market economy model (Levitt 2001).

Levitt (2001) found that technology is the glue that keeps transnational religious organizations intact: "New technologies heighten the immediacy and intensity of migrants' contact with their sending communities, allowing them to be active in everyday life in fundamentally different ways than in the past" (Levitt 2001: 10). Religious events, celebrations, and festivals are relayed through modern technology and social media instantly and simultaneously to multiple locations around the globe.

Babb (1997) describes the extraordinary place of technology in merging the medium with the message in the purist Hindu group, the 'Swadhyayees':

> At first glance the most significant use to which these tapes are put to use would seem to be recruitment to the movement ... the real significance

lies in the role they play in ... 'social cohesion'.... The tapes are part of the ritual observances of the movement ... in India and abroad ... devotees believe that viewing these tapes is a true devotional encounter with a sacred being. The tapes themselves are regarded as sacred objects. (Babb 1997: 15)

The Facebook page of the ISKCON Vrindavan branch has more than 19,395 'likes', and this page is used both for donations and as a way to connect with devotees and impart daily devotionals and darshans— spiritual blessings through reflection or meditation upon a Hindu icon, deity, or holy man.[12]

4.   Spiritual Capital

French sociologist Bourdieu (1991), in his analysis of society, described layers or fields, with schemas that he called 'habitus'. For Bourdieu, it is in the fields and habitus that capital (goods or resources) are accessed and utilized as Jenkins (1992) explains his theory:

> [A] field is structured internally in terms of power relations. Positions stand in relationships of dominion, subordination or equivalence (homology to each other by virtue of the access they afford to the goods and resources (capital) which are at stake in the field. These goods can be principally differentiated into ... economic capital, social capital ... cultural ... and symbolic. (Jenkins 1992: 85)

Thus, spiritual capital is the sum of the total value of spiritual beliefs, artefacts, and practices for individuals, groups, and society. And proponents equate spiritual capital to other forms of capital, such as intellectual capital, financial capital, and social capital. Some scholars, such as Barro (2004), see spiritual capital as an aspect of the power and influence generated by religious beliefs and practices of institutions and entities. The Metanexus Institute in the United States defines spiritual capital as the "effects of spiritual and religious practices, beliefs, networks and institutions that have a measurable impact on individuals, communities and societies."[13] Transnational religious organizations thrive and prosper mainly because of the ease of accessing religious and spiritual capital. As Levitt (2001) suggests, these organizational members "have access to social and institutional resources that imbue them with the potential to remain active in two worlds" (Levitt 2001: 6).

The production and distribution of the Bible by various entities such as the Bible Society and the Bible League, across nations in the languages of the world, is an example of the flows of transnational religious capital. For example, in 2014, the American Bible Society spent more than $50 million for overseas outreach (Wuthnow and Offutt 2008).

The *Swadhyayees* (devotees of a Hindu movement known as the Swadhyay Parivar) believe in inner purification through self-learning and watching spiritual videotapes and lectures by their leader with English subtitles mailed to thousands of people around the world from their headquarters in Mumbai, India (Levitt 2001).

Spiritual capital goes beyond texts and discourse; they are also icons, myths, traditions, stories, and experiential and religious feelings, including visions and enlightenment. Therefore, groups such as the Hindu-based ISKCON offer on their media-savvy website a daily darshan (beholding a deity so that you receive an immediate blessing), videos of bhakti yoga, news of study groups in every major city in the United States and the United Kingdom, and live chat and bhakti music.[14]

5. Political Economy
Political economy is the study of how an entity is governed or managed, taking into account both political and economic indicators as well as issues concerning ownership and influence (Weingast and Witman 2008).

In 2001, the then President of the United States, George W. Bush, introduced a 'faith-based' initiative as an agenda item for his administration. Bush planned to further the cause of charitable organizations through funding from the federal government "… publicly subsidized religious charities would be allowed to engage in employment discrimination based on religion, and public funds could be used to pay for construction and repair of buildings used for religious worship."[15] Funding was made available to both home-based missions and to organizations with foreign mission interests. This move sparked *Hindutva* forces[16] in India to speculate that the United States was engaged in a conspiracy to Christianize India.

In 2001, some 65,000 non-US citizens were engaged in Christian work outside the United States with full sponsorship from protestant agencies in the United States (Wuthnow and Offutt 2008).

van der Veer (1995) reveals that religious migrant communities especially in the West strongly influence political outcomes and policies in their homelands. Prashad (1997) reinforced this finding by disclosing that Indians living and working in the United States sent an estimated $350,000 for the support of Hindu nationalistic ventures in India between 1992 and 1993. Hindu televangelism in India, unlike Christian televangelism, operates on donations and sales with no overt fundraising on the airwaves, and diaspora Indians are the main donors for these TV programs both in India and abroad (James 2010).

Ernst & Young, a large multinational accounting firm, estimated that the asset values of Sharia-compliant Islamic banks had grown at an annual rate of 17.6 percent from 2009 to 2013, with the predicted rate placed at 19.7 percent a year through to 2018.[17] At that time, the estimated total asset value of Islamic banks was $2 trillion, and Islamic financial institutions were doing business in 105 countries.[18] According to Warde (2010), the five dominant Islamic banking countries are Iran ($345 billion in assets), Saudi Arabia ($258 billion), Malaysia ($142 billion), Kuwait ($118 billion), and UAE ($112 billion; Warde 2010). According to the 2013–14 World Islamic Banking Competitiveness Report, Qatar, Indonesia, Saudi Arabia, Malaysia, UAE, and Turkey represented 78 percent of the international Islamic banking assets and they constituted "the driving factors behind the next big wave in Islamic finance" (Nazim and Bellens 2015).

Concern that there is a relationship between Islamic charities and the support of Islamist organizations is worthy of note especially if the supported transnational organizations have radical agendas. This is especially so in the light of actions taken by US authorities in shutting down a US charity—The Holy Land Foundation (HLF) shortly after 9/11. Authorities found that donations of US$12 million from the HLF were channeled to Hamas suicide bombers "under the guise of humanitarian relief."[19]

Some transnational religious organizations purportedly stay out of politics. For example, Fethullah Gülen, the founder of Hizmet, an Islamic development agency, does not directly take part in Turkish partisan politics, though he has been known to carefully frame his messages on civic society with political implications. He promotes the democratic system but has not joined a parliamentary party.[20] It is a known fact that Gülen has influenced Turkish politicians but what is not known is whether his organization receives any kickbacks from political parties.[21] The Turkish government has blamed the Hizmet organization for the recent coup in Turkey in July 2016 even though Gülen now lives as a recluse in the United States and has vehemently denied the charges.

Cases: Chapter Summaries

Six religious organizations representing the four world religions— Hinduism, Islam, Christianity, and Buddhism—have been chosen as case studies and are reported in the respective chapters of the book. Prior to the six case studies, Chapter 1 gives an overview of transnational studies and how this discipline developed as religious organizations become more pronounced in the international scene. In each case study, the following rubrics are used to convey to readers the unique aspects of each transnational organization: an historical overview, typology, transnational practices, the content and direction of the organizational 'flows', and the future of the organization.

1.   Chapter 1: Transnationalism: Perspectives

Transnational studies, based on the disciplines of sociology and international relations, were developed because of the upsurge of nonstate actors in the global theater of nation-states. However, scholars did not make room for the study of religious transnational organizations as the disciplines of sociology and international relations were largely propelled by the secularization theory, which assumed that religions would fade away as modernization and globalization increased. The contemporary resurgence of religion as a global phenomenon has caused scholars to rethink this false notion and depict religion according to new perspectives like the constructivist paradigm and the 'cosmopolitan worldview'.

2.   Chapter 2: Hillsong Church: Postmodern Parishes, Worldwide Music, and Anointed Acquisitions (Christian)

Hillsong Church is a Pentecostal mega church located in Sydney, New South Wales, Australia and affiliated with the Assemblies of God (AoG) denomination, a 100-year-old church denomination with a central-ized hierarchy. Hillsong's AoG institutional underpinning is largely downplayed because it operates as a 'stand-alone' Christian entity with a growing transnational flavor—with branches currently in the United States, the United Kingdom, Ukraine, Sweden, France, Amsterdam, Russia, Argentina, and Brazil.[22] Over 30,000 people attend the weekly services in Sydney, Australia.

It is indeed music and song that have shaped Hillsong in the public consciousness and its expansion across the world. Hillsong Music has topped Australian charts, with its albums having achieved gold and platinum sales status—a controversial practice because these albums are released at the annual conferences which attract about 30,000 delegates, providing an automatic way to reach the Australian Recording Industry Association (ARIA) charts[23] which are based on sales. Worship leaders are also important at Hillsong. The worship teams operate like rock bands, presenting an entertainment gospel led by a dynamic senior pastor, Brian Houston, and his acolytes who practice Charismatic theology and more recently an ambivalent 'gay-welcoming' approach in the midst of the current controversial same-sex marriage debate.[24] Hillsong is also well known for its prosperity teach-ing and its annual Hillsong Conference, which attracts the worldwide fraternity of Charismatic speakers as well as international pop artists such as Justin Bieber. Recent moves to take over overseas churches and bring them to the fold of Hillsong have provoked criticism about its political economy from media observers and Church leaders.

3.   Chapter 3: Validating Identity, Spirituality, and Space for BAPS Hindus in India and the Diaspora (Hindu)
Bochasanwasi Shri Akshar Purushottam Swaminarayan Sanstha (BAPS) is a Hindu organization inaugurated in 1995 by Pramukh Swami Maharaj. BAPS is a purist group within Hinduism and its website explains the dimensions of its faith philosophy:

[BAP's] universal work through a worldwide network of over 3,850 centers has received many national and international awards and affili-ation with the United Nations. Today, a million or more Swaminarayan followers begin their day with puja and meditation, lead upright, honest lives and donate regular hours in serving others. No alcohol, no addic-tions, no adultery, no meat, no impurity of body and mind are their five lifetime vows. Such pure morality and spirituality forms the foundation of the humanitarian services performed by BAPS.[25]

Given that this is an organization that glorifies simplicity and purist ideals, its ostentatious building project (and its quest for celebrity endorsements) is rather surprising—BAPS is commonly known for its Swaminarayan Mandir (also called the Neasden Temple), a Hindu temple in the London borough of Brent in North West London. Built entirely with traditional materials and technology, Neasden's Swaminarayan Mandir has been described as Britain's first authentic Hindu temple.[26] It is also considered to be Europe's first traditional Hindu stone temple and is listed in the 2000 edition of the Guinness World Records as the biggest temple outside India.

> The Shri Swaminarayan Temple in Neasden, London, UK, is the largest Hindu temple outside India.... It was built by His Holiness Pramukh Swami Maharaj, a 92-year-old Indian sadhu (holy man), and is made of 2,828 tonnes of Bulgarian limestone and 2,000 tonnes of Italian marble, which was first shipped to India to be carved by a team of 1,526 sculptors. The temple cost £12 million to build.[27]

Temple building seems to consume BAPS as it is intent on building more and more temples and beating their own records. For instance, the biggest BAPS temple outside India is currently located (in 2016) in a 162-acre property in New Jersey, USA.

4. Chapter 4: Ciji: Socially Engaged Buddhism, Feminization, and the Politics of Soft Power (Buddhist)

The Buddhist Compassionate Relief and Merit Society—*Ciji Gongde Hui*, also referred to as Tzu Chi (or Ciji) has 5 million members, with its headquarters in Taiwan. Ciji was established

> to help the poor and relieve suffering. Over time, the Foundation's mission started with Charity and extended into Medicine, Education, and Humanistic Culture. [Ciji] provides aid to over 90 nations. Its volunteers selflessly contribute through a mindset of gratitude, expressing their sincerest care and support to each and every individual in need.[28]

In 1984, Ciji was registered as a nonprofit 501(c) (3)[29] organization in the United States as the Tzu Chi Foundation. There are now more than

60 offices and facilities in the United States with over 100,000 volunteers and donors working to enhance Buddhism in local communities. The primary leadership is given by the founder, the Venerable Zhengyan, a charismatic nun, and a group of female nuns—a remarkable gender-empowering feature of this form of practical Buddhism.

Ciji's primary target group is the diaspora Chinese, especially those of Taiwanese origin. The spiritual capital that is transmitted and cherished by the group consists of the teachings of Buddha, the tenets of Mahayana Buddhism, and importantly the life of the founder herself and her mystical sermons, which allude to a more 'this world' attitude—unlike traditional Buddhism's 'other worldliness'.

5.   Chapter 5: The New Face of Islam in the West: The Case of Islamic Relief (Muslim)

Islamic Relief Worldwide (not to be confused with International Islamic Relief Organization [IIRO], a terrorist-linked agency), launched originally in the United Kingdom and well established in the United States (as Islamic Relief Worldwide USA [IRUSA]) is a nonprofit organization providing health care, sustainable livelihood, and social services to all people regardless of "race, political affiliation, gender or belief" (IRW website).[30] However, on closer study, it appears that relief works are targeted to Muslim nations or nations with large Muslim populations, such as Syria, Pakistan, and Bangladesh. Islamic Relief's (IR) main charitable activities in recent years took place in Syria (IRW website).[31] With its caption 'Faith in Action' and its values based on the Quran and the Sunnah, IR demonstrates that while cultural and ideological dimensions of IR are useful in Muslim contexts, IR has successfully created a new public sphere or *Umma*, which had redefined and secularized Islam in the West. Islamic Relief has worked hard to gain recognition from well-respected international agencies and beneficiaries, such as United Nations International Children's Emergency Fund (UNICEF) and World Health Organization (WHO).[32] It is, therefore, not surprising that IRW annual records show that in 2014 its income reached nearly US$400 million (IRW website).[33]

The agency is not without controversy about its links with radicalized Islam. The recent announcement that the Hong Kong and Shanghai Banking Corporation (HSBC) has cut links with IR over the issue of IR's ties with terror groups has been a blow to IR and many

Muslim charities (Ghosh 2016). Hence, the flows of funding are affecting the goodwill of this well-respected transnational organization.

6. Chapter 6: The Gülen-Hizmet Movement: Reformed Islam or Revitalized Caliphate? (Cultural Islam)
The Gülen-Hizmet Movement (GHM) founded by Turkish cleric, Fethullah Gülen, is a good example of the integration of Islam and modernity. GHM enjoyed close links with various Turkish governments including the current Adalet ve Kalkinma Partisi (AKP)-led government until recently when the AKP government accused GHM of instigating a major coup in Turkey in early 2016. Gülen now lives in the United States and is the spiritual and administrative leader of a vast network of schools, universities, cultural centers, and civic organizations in many parts of the world. GHM's claim that it is a counter entity to radical Islam has been welcomed in many parts of the West, but some scholars have questioned this assertion because of GHM's deep political links and promotion of Sunni Islam especially among students at various levels of its educational entities.

7. Chapter 7: ISIS: Epistemology, Eschatology, and Empire of a Revolutionary Movement (Theocratic Islam)
ISIS stands for the Islamic State of Iraq and Syria. It is an extremist rebel group operating in the territories of Iraq and Syria as well as Libya, Egypt, and other countries on the Arabian Peninsula (Wood 2015). It is important to understand that ISIS does not represent the larger Islamic faith as the use of the word 'extremist' or 'fundamentalist' in Islam denotes a departure from the original doctrine of the religion. The following subsets are seen within Islam: radical fundamentalism (largely political); scriptural fundamentalism (e.g., Jama'a al Tabligh); traditionalists (mainstream Shiites); liberal secularists (e.g., secular parties in Turkey and Indonesia); modernists (e.g., Muhammadiyah), and authoritarian secularists (e.g., Ba'ath Party).[34] ISIS belongs to the first group.

In the past, ISIS has had various associations with other fundamentalist rebel groups from the area, but in June 2014 it declared itself the ISIS. This involved a new paradigm in Islam—the launch of a caliphate which is the revival of the former theocratic form of Islam—wherein the Islamic religion is the foundation for the nation and empire (Wood 2015). The world has not experienced an Islamic caliphate for the last 500 years.

ISIS has built a global brand to rival Western corporations through the use of technology, social media, videos, and celebrity warriors such as 'Jihadi John' and has influenced and gained support from 'lone-wolf operatives', such as the terrorist in the Lindt café shooting in Sydney, Australia and from terrorist groups, such as Abu Sayyaf in Southern Philippines and Boko Haram in Nigeria.

ISIS is a prime example of theocratic Islam which operates as a caliphate and looks to conquer territory by all means, including force and expansion of its radicalized Islamic agenda.

8.   Conclusion: Globalization of Faith, Faith in Globalization
The concluding chapter outlines six salient characteristics of the six case studies, drawing attention to the fact that transnational religious organizations are inextricably linked with the globalization phenomenon.

Conclusion

Transnational Religious Movements reveals that the contemporary world has become the contested site of extensive transnational linkages brought about by religious organizations. Transnational religion is redefining the issues of identity, belonging, and loyalty and in the process influencing the religious thinking and practices of people worldwide. These organizations are symptomatic of modern-day dynamics—globalization, migration, technology, and consumption, as well as the deeply ingrained role that religion plays in the lives of communities of people.

Transnational religious organizations can strengthen communities and nations or subvert them.

Transnational Religious Movements describes the whole gamut of transnational organizations—those without political leanings and those that are clearly political and striving to form a theocratic state.

The book contributes to the burgeoning literature on transnational religion by examining in detail the practices and strategies of six representative organizations drawn from the four major world religions. It describes how these movements are organized, structured, and institutionalized in many parts of the world, thereby fleshing out the shape of religion and its interactions in our globalized world. The detailed studies on world religious organizations counteract the mistaken notion that globalization increases uniformity, producing a singular, global culture.

This book will aid governments, nongovernment agencies, the media, and individuals as they endeavor to negotiate carefully and circumspectly with the growing variety of religious organizations and their multiple agendas.

Notes

1. The religious-studies approach is a critical approach to the understanding of religious beliefs, institutions, and behavior based on multidisciplinary and cross-cultural perspectives.
2. The Srivijaya Empire was mainly a commercial empire that had religious significance during the seventh and thirteenth centuries. Historians allude to traders and priests who were used during this time to bring Hinduism and its ally—Buddhism to Indonesia and other parts of Southeast Asia.
3. See http://www.iskcon.org/
4. Ibid.
5. The Hare Krishna mantra appears in a number of popular songs, namely in former Beatles singer George Harrison's hit song: 'My Sweet Lord'. Later, Paul McCartney produced a single with an icon on the album cover of Lord Krishna riding a swan.
6. *Satsang* is a Sanskrit word which means 'gathering of the truth' and is a reference to a Hindu worship meeting in a temple or any place of worship. Mandir is another word for a Hindu temple or a worship place.
7. See http://umrelief.org/
8. Ibid.
9. Ibid.
10. See http://gebisociety.org/
11. Ibid.
12. See https://www.facebook.com/pages/ISKCON-Vrindavan/494797313939237
13. See www/spiritualcapitalresearchprogram.com/what_is.asp
14. See http://www.iskcon.org/
15. See https://www.au.org/resources/publications/the-faith-based-initiative
16. *Hindutva* is a reference to 'Hinduness', but more than a cultural connotation, it is also part of the political ideology (mainly of the current ruling party in India—the BJP) that tends to define all of Indian culture in terms of Hindu values.
17. See http://www.economist.com/news/finance-and-economics/21617014-market-islamic-financial-products-growing-fast-big-interest-no-interest

18. Ibid.
19. See https://www.justice.gov/opa/pr/federal-judge-hands-downs-sentences-holy-land-foundation-case (para 2).
20. See http://www.Gülenmovement.us/political-implications-of-the-hizmet-Gülen-movement.html on 2 August 2015.
21. Ibid.
22. See https://hillsong.com/
23. The charts are a weekly record of the highest selling singles and albums in various musical genres within Australia.
24. See http://www.breathecast.com/articles/hillsong-ny-homosexuals-leadership-church-carl-lentz-misunderstood-reach-none-30518/
25. See http://www.baps.org/About-BAPS.aspx
26. Ibid.
27. See http://www.triposo.com/poi/BAPS_Shri_Swaminarayan_Mandir_London
28. See http://tw.tzuchi.org/en/index.php?option=com_content&view=article&id=293&Itemid=283
29. A 501 c (3) organization is an IRS approved organization in the United States. Donations to these corporations are exempt from income tax.
30. See http://www.islamic-relief.org/ (accessed on 10 September 2015).
31. See http://www.islamic-relief.org/category/appeals/emergencies/syria-crisis-appeal/ (accessed on 10 September 2015).
32. UNICEF is an organization affiliated with the United Nations (UN) and is head-quartered in New York City, USA. WHO is another UN-affiliated organization.
33. See note 31.
34. See http://www.rand.org/content/dam/rand/pubs/monographs/2004/RAND_MG246.pdf (7–14).

References

Babb, L. A. 1997. "Introduction." In *Media and the Transformation of Religion in South Asia*, edited by Lawrence A. Babb and Susan S. Wadley, 1–20. New Delhi: University of Pennsylvania Press.

Barro, R. J. 2004. "Spirit of Capitalism: Religion and Economic Development." *Harvard International Review* 25(4): 64–67.

Basch, L. G., N. G. Shiller and C. S. Blanc. 1994. *Nations Unbound: Transnational Projects Postcolonial Predicaments, and Deterritorialized Nation-states*. Langhorne, PA: Gordon and Breach.

Baumann, Z. 1992. *Intimations of Postmodernity*. London: Routledge.

Bourdieu, P. 1991. "Genesis and Structures of the Religious Field." *Comparative Social Research* 13: 1–43.

Castells, M. 2010. *The Rise of the Network Society: The Age, Economy, Society and Culture*. Malden, MA: Wiley-Blackwell.

Fenn, R. 1978. *Toward a Theory of Secularization*. Storrs, CT: SFSSR.

Ghosh, A. 2016. *HSBC Snaps Ties with Islamic Relief Over 'Terror' Fears*. Accessed on 2 June 2016 from http://www.ibtimes.co.uk/hsbc-snaps-ties-islamic-relief-over-terror-fears-1535825

Giddens, A. 1990. *The Consequences of Modernity*. Cambridge: Polity Press.

James, J. D. 2010. *McDonaldisation, Masala McGospel and Om Economics: Televangelism in Contemporary India*. New Delhi: SAGE Publications.

Jenkins, R. 1992. *Pierre Bourdieu*. London: Routledge.

Kwok, P. L. "A Transnational Approach to Religion." Accessed on 7 July 2015 from http://www.patheos.com/Resources/Additional-Resources/Transnational-Approach-to-Religion.html

Lehmann, D. 2002. "Religion and Globalisation." In *Religion in the Modern World: Traditions and Transformations*, edited by Linda Woodhead, Paul Fletcher, Hiroko Kawanami and David Smith, 407–428. London: Routledge.

Levitt, P. 2001, 1 July. "Between God, Ethnicity, And Country: An Approach to The Study of Transnational Religion." *Transnational Migration Conference*, Working Paper No. WPTC-01-13. Princeton University, NJ, USA.

———. 2004. "Redefining the Boundaries of Belonging: The Institutional Character of Transnational Religious Life." *Sociology of Religion* 65(1): 1–18.

Lyon, D. 2000. *Jesus in Disneyland: Religion in Postmodern Times*. Cambridge: Polity Press.

McAlister, M. 2001. "The Madonna of 115th Street Revisited: Voodo and Haitian Catholicism in the Age of Transnationalism." In *Gatherings in Diaspora*, edited by Warner and Whitter, 123–162. Berkeley, CA: University of California Press.

Money Jihad. 2015. *Islamic Relief gave $118 K to terror-linked groups*. Accessed on 1 July 2015 from https://moneyjihad.wordpress.com/2014/09/21/islamic-relief-gave-118k-to-terror-linked-groups/

Nazim, A. and Jan Bellens. 2015. *World Islamic Banking Competitiveness Report, 2014–2015*. Bahrain: EY Global Centre of Excellence. Accessed on 2 August 2015 from http://www.ey.com/Publication/vwLUAssets/EY_-_World_Islamic_Banking_Competitiveness_Report_2013%E2%80%9314/$FILE/EY-World-Islamic-Banking-Competitiveness-Report-2013-14.pdf

Pandya, S. and N. Gallagher, eds. 2012. *The Gülen Hizmet Movement and Its Transnational Activities: Case Studies of Altruistic Activism in Contemporary Islam*. Boca Raton, FL: BrownWalker Press.

Pew Research Centre. 2015. "The Future of World Religions: Population Growth Projections, 2010–2050". Pew Research Centre. Accessed on 29 July 2015 from http://www.pewforum.org/2015/04/02/religious-projections-2010-2050/

Prashad, V. 1997, February. "Culture Vultures." *Communalism Combat* 30(February): 9–15.

Riesebrodt, M. 2000. "Fundamentalism and the Resurgence of Religion." *Numen* 47(3): 266–87.

Rudolph, S. H. and J. Piscatori, eds. 1997. *Transnational Religion and Fading States*. Boulder, CO: Westview Press.

Tomlinson, D. 2006. *Globalization and Culture*. Accessed on 2 August 2015 from http://citeseerx.ist.psu.edu/viewdoc/download?doi=10.1.1.465.9581&rep=rep1&type=pdf

Tweed, T. 1997. *Our Lady of Exile: Diasporic Religion at a Cuban Catholic Shrine in Miami*. New York, NY: Oxford University Press.

van der Veer, P. 1995. *Nation and Migration*. Philadelphia, PA: University of Pennsylvania Press.

Vasquez, M. A. and M. F. Marquardt. 2003. *Globalizing the Sacred: Religion Across the Americas*. New Brunswick, NJ: Rutgers University Press.

Warde, I. 2010. *Islamic Finance in the Global Economy*. Edinburgh: Edinburgh University Press.

Weingast, B. R. and D. Witman, eds. 2008. *The Oxford Handbook of Political Economy*. Oxford: Oxford University Press.

Wood, G. 2015 (March issue). "What ISIS Really Wants?" *The Atlantic*. Accessed on 30 June 2015 from http://www.theatlantic.com/features/archive/2015/02/what-isis-really-wants/384980/

Wuthnow, R. and S. Offutt. 2008. "Transnational Religious Connections." *Sociology of Religion* 69(2): 209–32.

Zukerman, P. 2014. *Living the Secular Life: New Answers to Old Questions*. New York, NY: Penguin Press.

1

Transnationalism: Perspectives

Introduction

In August 2000, 1,000 religious and spiritual leaders congregated in the UN headquarters in New York for the Millennium World Peace Summit. In the opening address, the then Secretary-General of the UN, Kofi Annan affirmed the need for governments to protect religious freedom and reinforced the summit's commitment to global religious tolerance[1] (Reilly 2000). However, the purpose of this much-publicized gathering of religious leaders was undermined by the absence of the Dalai Lama. His absence was mainly due to protests from the Chinese government and Chinese religious leaders.[2] When the news reached the public of the Dalai Lama's exclusion, protests broke out both within and without the conference, and a barrage of correspondence from both religious and secular leaders caused the organizers to issue a late invitation to the Dalai Lama. The Dalai Lama graciously declined the invitation, but sent a message to be read at the summit. And when the Dalai Lama's address was read, members of the Chinese delegation staged a 'walkout' in an act of further protest[3] (Reilly 2000).

The aforementioned cluster of incidents invites attention to several issues about transnational religion and its interplay with governments in today's globalized society:[4]

1. Religion, as a nonstate actor, has entered the world's global theater.
2. Even though they recognize the role and importance of religion, governments are still, by and large, motivated by political and economic interests.
3. Nevertheless, religion is a key aspect of human behavior worldwide, along with politics.

In this chapter, I reflect on the theoretical foundations of religion and politics in the modern world. Specifically, I introduce the discipline of transnationalism and consider the entry of religion into transnational studies and international relations within the milieu of secularization. I reveal how scholars from both disciplines—international relations and sociology—have used the secularization theory in their study of religion. I conclude by outlining the main paradigms of international relations insofar as they reflect on religious organizations and transnational religion.

Transnationalism

In the 'old world' (prior to the fifteenth century), empires and nations were free to exercise governance and the rule of law over their territories without any interference from other actors. However, the contemporary world is inhabited by nonstate actors and international organizations along with nation-states. In keeping with this trend, a new field of inquiry—transnational studies—has emerged from the broad disciplines of the social sciences and international relations. Transnationalism refers to the sociopolitical and economic activities that take place between and beyond the boundaries of nation-states. Transnationalism specifically speaks of nonstate organizations, interest groups, and entities that are part of civil society operating across the world. Lipschutz (1992: 390) defined transnational civil society as the "self-conscious constructions of networks of knowledge and action by decentered local actors that cross reified boundaries of space as though they were not there." Transnational studies' scholars consider the dynamics of the interaction between new nonstate actors and nation-states (Keohane and Nye 1972; Tarrow 2001). And they have noticed more interplay between state and nonstate actors today because nation-states have become more aware of the significance of the actions and ideologies of domestic and external players (Keohane and Nye 1972; Young 1997). Correspondingly, this interplay has reduced the relative importance of state actors (Della Porta and Tarrow 2005). For example, recently, Japan's whaling activities in Antarctica were found to contravene the International Whaling Commission (IWC). Besides IWC's actions, the Sea Shepherd Conservation Society (a transnational activist organization) used protests and other activities to curb Japan's whaling activities.

Rosenau (1999) argued that the perception of viewing states as sole actors does not give the full picture of contemporary global governance and the role regimes play. Increasingly, regimes are made up of non-state actors (Young 1997). According to Young (1997), regimes need to contend with state interests and global civil society interests. For example, one of Mexico's public interest law groups, the Asociación Jalisciense de Apoyo a GruposIndígenas, resorted to both national and international laws to gain an unprecedented restitution from the state government of at least one quarter of the land that was in dispute (Chavez and Arcos 1999).

This birth of international organizations and nongovernmental actors in the global arena has recalibrated international politics because it has affected the distribution of power. Keohane and Nye (1972) defined politics as a relationship in which at least one actor consciously employs resources, both material and symbolic, including laws to enforce punishment, and influences behavior among actors. Bealey (1999) defined state sovereignty this way: a state becomes sovereign when other states give it due recognition. State sovereignty, according to Bealey (1999: 306), is "a claim to authority, originally by sovereign monarchs but by states since the treaty of Westphalia in 1648."[5] However, in Bealey's (1999) terms of reference for states, there is no mention of nonstate actors.

Historically, when religion and state were still one, Christian and Muslim transnational religious communities were in existence well before the emergence of centralized secular states (Haynes 2001). For example, before the signing of the Westphalia treaty in 1648, Islam had expanded its territory in all directions through trade, proselytization, and conquest for almost a millennium. Likewise, Christendom, a term used in medieval times to refer to the spread of Christianity, had brought several European cultures under the norms and beliefs of the Word of God—the Bible—by the fifteenth century.

Secularization and International Relations

The fundamental premise of secularization theory is that as society advances in modernity and scientific achievement, religion will recede and ultimately fade into obscurity (Swatos and Christiano 1999). Casanova (1994) introduced three aspects of secularization:

1. **Differentiation:** This basically refers to the collapse of religious hegemonies and the formation of secular spheres such as the

military, education, politics, etc. with faith becoming one of these spheres. This is the main component of secularization.

2. **Privatization:** This follows from differentiation and is a reference to the relegation of religion to the private sphere. A second consideration of privatization is that religion has become a private matter, seldom discussed in the public sphere.

3. **Decline:** This refers to the withering of organized religion and membership within faith organizations.

One factor that has contributed to secularization, as pointed out by van der Veer (2001), is the issue of migrant religious communities and their political loyalty to the host nation-state:

> The European wars of religion of the sixteenth and seventeenth centuries were fought around the question of political loyalty: Can one be loyal to the state when one is not following the religion of the state? As Hobbes and other political thinkers realized, it was the nature of the state that was at issue here. One outcome of the political revolutions in America and France of the late eighteenth century was that political loyalty could rest on citizenship instead of membership in the state church. This development led ultimately to the 'secular' idea, for example in nineteenth-century Britain, of the enfranchisement of the Roman Catholics and of dissenting minorities. (van der Veer 2001: 16)

One of the strongest forces religions have had to contend with in the modern world is religious pluralism. Religious pluralism began after the Reformation when the Roman Catholic Church splintered into various religious systems and denominations.[6] According to Berger and Luckmann (1967: 48), religious traditions with multiple denominations are less able to legitimize social reality than those where one religious system enjoys the monopoly. When various religious systems become options for people in any society, traditional faith (the faith of the fathers) is obscured within the structure of society. According to Berger and Luckmann (1967: 107), historically, "this pluralism was first combated by extermination, then by segregation, and finally by secularization, that is, the removal of sectors of society from the domination of religious institutions and symbols."

Thomas (2005) explained secularization by referring to the early sixteenth and seventeenth centuries when states took over the intellectual and social functions of religion, thereby postulating the modern notion of religion as merely a set of beliefs or doctrines. The Treaty of Westphalia regularized and solidified this shift. According to Thomas (2005: 25),

> For the state to be born, religion had to become privatized and nationalized. The state used the invention of religion to legitimate the transfer of the ultimate loyalty of people from religion to the state as part of the consolidation of its power—the process of state-building and nation-building, which we have come to call internal sovereignty.

According to Thomas (2005) and Fox and Sandler (2004), Western scholars had constructed a myth regarding the relationship between religion and government based on the practical 'lessons' of the wars of religion and the subsequent Peace Treaty of Westphalia in 1648. These lessons were

1. When religion and government integrate, invariably, violence and oppression will be the outcome.
2. The modern secular state and the privatization of religion are needed to safeguard society from potential conflict and destruction (Thomas 2005).

Thomas (2005) asserted that Western scholars and governments conceived this modern notion of religion inappropriately: as a privatized reality; certainly this construction went counter to the way religion was seen in many non-Western nations, that is, as a more encompassing 'way of life'. Armstrong (2014) recounted the novelty of secularism:

> We now take the secular state so much for granted that it is hard for us to appreciate its novelty, since before the modern period, there were no 'secular' institutions and no 'secular' states in our sense of the word. Their creation required the development of an entirely different understanding of religion, one that was unique to the modern west. No other culture has had anything remotely like it, and before the 18th century, it would have been incomprehensible even to European Catholics. (para 5)

As mentioned previously, Thomas (2005) believed that this myth was based on the wrong assertion of seeing religion merely as a set of beliefs or doctrines to be studied or accepted independently, rather than as a creed founded within a community of believers (that is, religion is a social and cultural reality). The term for 'religion' in Arabic, Hindu, and Hebrew worldviews has a much larger and inclusive meaning whereby religion is not encouraged to retreat from the political arena (Armstrong 2014). This faulty Western assumption accounts for the West's inability to grapple with the religious wars in the Balkans (1991–2001) and the ongoing sectarian tensions in the Middle East, because of the Western understanding of religion as a separate entity rather than as a holistic reality.

The notion of secularization described previously has influenced scholarship on religion and world affairs, particularly in the realm of international relations. The consequences of holding on to the Westphalian myth described by Thomas (2005) and Berger (1999) are similar to the effects of the secularization thesis as outlined previously. Arguably, Western scholars have continued to apply an essentially Western perspective to non-Western states, societies, and religions. In my case studies (Chapters 2–7), it is clear that while secularization has affected European and American governments and society in some measure, religion is still a core element of culture in most societies of the world. This misperception by Western scholars has led to an indifferent attitude toward religion in the West and an incorrect extrapolation that religion does not equate to anything of appreciable value in modern societies (Fox and Sandler 2004; Thomas 2005). All this means that the West is, by and large, unable to deal with the primacy of faith in domestic politics and world affairs in several foreign countries.

The discipline of international relations was birthed in such a milieu (soon after World War I), dictated by the aftermath of war and the new notion of secular nation-states (Wiener and Schrire 2009). The precept for this model was that modern countries have no need for religion to legitimize their right to govern because their state legitimacy is founded on the fundamental principles of nationalism and democracy. Some scholars went so far as to assert that both politicized religion and nationalism would ultimately die out (Appleby 1994), and that territorial states would replace man's spiritual and identity needs (Connolly 1988). Furthermore, Shils (1978: 4–10) predicted that with "new core encompassing institutions, identity, and service functions would replace the former diffused zone of [religious] authority."

The Rise of Transnational Movements

With the rise of globalization and modern technology in the 1970s, transnational organizations such as the UN, World Bank, and the Organization of the Petroleum Exporting Countries (OPEC) have become significant actors. Nevertheless, nation-states are still recognized as significant players and sometimes, the most important ones in international relations (Keohane and Nye 1972; Tarrow 2001; Walker 1994). National governments arguably play a vital role in framing and implementing national policy and overseeing transnational actions and relationships (Tarrow 2001). Risse-Kappen (1995), Rosenau (1999), and Walker (1994) asserted that the focus should not be whether one actor has dominance over the other but on understanding and the influence of nonstate actors.

Tarrow (2001) named three categories of nonreligious transnational actors besides national governments:

1. Transnational social movements (TSMs) are organizations that have social or political bases outside of the nation-state where the movement has its focus. For example, the Latin American activism that gave birth to the social movement called World Social Forum (WSF), in its first meeting which took place in Sao Paulo (Brazil) in 2001, revealed that social movements are not mere street demonstrations but quests for global social justice with a twofold agenda: attacking the capitalist principles of market liberalization and arguing against alternative measures for the trade agreement in the Americas (Milani and Keraghel 2006). In the same vein, the protests against economic globalization by global conferences organized by WTO, International Monetary Fund (IMF), Group of Twenty (G-20), and the Free Trade Area of the Americas (FTAA)[7] held in various cities such as Seattle (USA), Prague (Czech Republic), Nice (France), and Genoa (Italy) gained notoriety as the world saw the creation of a strong voice with an antiglobalization agenda that challenged the global status quo.

2. International nongovernment organizations (INGOs) are defined as entities where members of two or more countries, who operate outside of government parameters, promote international goals and provide services to citizens of other states

(Tarrow 2001). Examples of INGOs are Oxfam, World Vision, Amnesty International, and Greenpeace. The difference between TSMs and INGOs is that the former tend to be involved in more contentious activities, whereas the later participate in more routine acts of poverty alleviation or development according to their stated goals and objectives (Tarrow 2001).

3. Transnational activist networks (TANs) are nonformal networks of INGOs and TSMs who work together for periods of time with other entities: local, transnational, governments, and nonstate actors. TANs encourage local bodies to adopt their goals and norms and taper their vision and strategy toward international politics. TANs are networks of advocates (people who are dedicated to taking affirmative action on a specific cause) from various organizational walks of life. Members of TANs hope that in the long term, people from different countries will become aware of their activist networks and TSMs will be birthed. Examples of TANs are the Sea Shepherd Conservation Society (aforementioned), World Advocacy, Center for Individual Rights, and International Women's Tribune Center.

Interestingly, the aforementioned three categories do not make mention of transnational religious actors.

Transnational Religion as a New Actor

Transnational studies' scholars have generally ignored the role of religious organizations. The major topics addressed by transnational studies include economic globalization, political processes, migration issues, terrorism, violence, organized crime, and culture. The current integration processes taking place around the world through formal organizations such as the European Union (EU) have also been featured in transnational studies (Kivisto 2001; Robinson 1998).

Religious movements' entrance into the foray of transnationalism and consequently international relations has raised some confusion because religion and international relations are founded on two different assumptions: first, Western modernity is premised on the understanding that the world of government and international relations is basically a secular one; second, religion has always had a universalistic tendency to operate beyond national borders. This tendency is especially true at least in two world religions: Christianity and Islam. Because of these two assumptions, scholars of international relations have had difficulty coming to terms with the reality and significance of religions in transnational contexts.

The Resurgence of Religion

Sociologists, like scholars in international relations, have also contributed to the marked absence of a scholarly approach to transnational religious entities. In 1967, sociologist Peter Berger predicted that as the world continued to modernize and people placed more faith in science and reason, religion would no longer be a force in society. Thus, secularization would be a reality and religion would no longer dominate the world's societies. Because this prediction has not been realized and religion remains vibrant in many parts of the world, Berger (1999: 22) recalled his earlier prediction and admitted his mistake: "The world today ... is as furiously religious as it ever was, and in some places more so than ever. This means that a whole body of literature by historians and social scientists loosely labelled 'secularization theory' is essentially mistaken." In his revised thinking, Berger (1999: 26) also asserted that religion, in every age, has played a key role in the life of the individual and society:

> Men are congenitally compelled to impose a meaningful order upon reality....
> The sacred cosmos, which transcends and includes man in its ordering of reality ... provides man's ultimate shield against the terror of anomy.

In my discussion of the six religious organizations (Chapters 2–7), I show that religion also serves to give meaning and legitimization to society. My depiction is in keeping with Berger's description: "Religion legitimates social institutions by bestowing upon them an ultimately valid ontological status, that is, by *locating* them within a sacred and cosmic frame of reference" (Berger 1999: 33). International studies' scholar Kubálková (2003: 93) provided another perspective on the role of religion:

> [Religion is] a system of rules (mainly instructive rules) and related prac-
> tices which act to explain the meaning of existence, including identity,
> ideas about self, and one's position in the world, thus motivating and
> guiding the behaviour of those who accept the validity of these rules
> on faith and who internalize them fully.

The twenty-first century has seen both the revitalization of many forms of spirituality and an unprecedented movement of people across the world's borders. The resurgence of religious politics in the post–Cold War era, seen in the worldwide explosion of Pentecostal and Charismatic Christianity, Islamic networks, and the formation of deterritorialized global faith communities, is a call for a new under-standing of faith in today's world.

Arguably, transnational religion has the potential to have two broad effects. Positively, it can encourage cooperation, increase stability, and foster reconciliation. Negatively, it can engender violence, creating divisions and disrupting the status quo, thereby challenging the state's legitimate authority and even weakening transnational religion. It is a well-known fact that adherents of religion can enhance peace and promote humanitarian intervention and postwar reconciliation; on the other hand, religious zealots can be highly destructive (as we will see in Chapter 7), for example, ISIS' participation in suicide bombings and ethnic cleansing.

Various Approaches to Religious Organizations in International Relations

With religion very much part of the arena of international politics, scholars have viewed the phenomenon variously according to their disciplines. Realism is the foundational paradigm of international rela-tions. Realists tend to overlook religion as a significant transnational influence in the international realm. Realists believe that states are the primary actors in international relations (Viotti and Kauppi 1999), and therefore reduce religious conflict to a minor aspect of security. Security theory (also called international security and global security) refers to the need for specific steps and measures to be initiated by states and larger organizations, such as the UN, North Atlantic Treaty Organization (NATO), and the EU, to ensure the safety and security of its citizens[8] (Buzan and Hansen 2007). These measures include treaties, conventions, military action, and diplomatic agreements.

Alternatively, the liberal paradigm acknowledges the significance of transnational actors, whereas realists look at nations as billiard balls about to collide into each other; the liberals look at nations as a piece of latticework or a gigantic cobweb, where intricate and interdependent relations are at play (Kent 2008). Liberals put a lot of faith in umbrella organizations, such as the UN, NATO, or EU, to resolve member conflicts. While this is commendable, liberals have marginalized the discipline of religious studies and therefore have failed to see the impact and inherent significance of religion. Many liberal scholars still hold to the secularization theory. The liberal paradigm pays adequate attention to TSMs, INGOs, and TANs but fails to notice transnational religious organizations.

The constructivist paradigm on transnational religion is a post–Cold War addition to the existing paradigms in international relations. Constructivism has its roots in several disciplines, including sociology. While constructivism is still in its infancy as a discipline within international relations, it offers important alternatives to the existing paradigms, fostering a greater sense of understanding of transnational religion. Constructivists see reality as something constructed through human interaction with ideologies and discourses. Thus, human behavior and actions are regulated and influenced by the socially constructed reality of society.

Constructivist theory is often attributed to the seminal writings of Peter Berger and Thomas and Luckmann, as reflected in their book *The Social Construction of Reality* (1967). The importance constructivists like Berger and Luckmann (1967) have placed on societal norms and relationships enables scholars to comprehend the phenomena of transnational religion in the international system more so than the realist and the liberal paradigms. My case studies of religious organizations in Chapters 2–7 will utilize the constructivist lens to view the raison d'être of the six religious organizations.

A useful offshoot of the constructivist paradigm is the 'cosmopolitan worldview', which places groups of individuals and organizations at the center of the analysis rather than states. This model was developed when the number of INGOs increased from 2,000 in 1972 to more than 5,000 within two decades (Haynes 2001).

In the conclusion of the book, I draw attention to a new perspective that is emerging: transmodernism, a periodization of our age that transcends both modernism and postmodernism and embraces both modern perspectives and religion.

Conclusion

Transnational studies is a by-product of the growing presence of nonstate actors such as TSMs, INGOs, and TANs in our global world. Religion and spirituality have reentered the world's stage as powerful and pervasive forces of meaning and activism together with these nonreligious, nonstate actors. Scholars from sociological studies and international relations have had to alter their prior thinking and this shift is reflected in the evolution of new designs like the constructivist paradigm and the cosmopolitan model to accurately appraise the role of transnational faiths in our contemporary world. Other paradigms would, no doubt, come into place to cope with the global resurgence of religion and religious movements.

Notes

1. See http://www.millenniumpeacesummit.org/
2. The Dalai Lama is the spiritual leader of Tibetan Buddhism and Tibetan people. The current Dalai Lama was exiled from Tibet in 1959 after a failed Tibetan uprising against the Chinese occupation. He led the Tibetan government in exile for many years but entrusted his political authority to the relevant democratic institutions. Despite more than 50 years of China's oppressive occupation, Tibetans remain greatly devoted to their spiritual leader.
3. See http://www.millenniumpeacesummit.org/
4. There are at least four noteworthy elements in this episode:
   i.   The omission due to the Chinese protests.
   ii. The protests about the omission.
   iii. The change of mind and the last-minute invitation.
   iv. The reading of the Dalai Lama's address and the walkout.
5. The Treaty of Westphalia (1648), named after a region in Western Germany, ended the 30-year war in Europe that started when Austria tried to impose Roman Catholicism on Protestant residents in Bohemia. Although the war was largely fought in Germany, the Swedes, Swiss, Danes, Russians, Dutch etc. were

somehow drawn into this destructive conflict involving religion, politics, and commerce.

6. After the Reformation of the Roman Catholic Church in 1517, Lutheranism began. This was soon to be followed by Anabaptism, Calvinism, Anglicanism, Baptist teachings, Quaker theology, Pietism, and Wesleyanism, to name a few.

7. WTO is based in Geneva, Switzerland. IMF is based in Washington, DC, USA. G-20 is an international forum of 20 of the world's leading economies. FTAA is a trade agreement that would eventually include 31 countries under the North American Free Trade Agreement (NAFTA).

8. NATO is a regional grouping currently comprising 28 countries committed to the security of the North Atlantic area. The EU, with headquarters in Brussels, Belgium, is a politico-economic union of European member states with an estimated population of over 500 million people.

References

Appleby, R. S. 1994. *Religious Fundamentalism and Global Conflict*. Ithaca, NY: Foreign Policy Association.

Armstrong, K. 2014. "The Myth of Religious Violence." *The Guardian* (Australia Edition). Thursday, 25 September. Accessed on 2 September 2016 from https://www.theguardian.com/world/2014/sep/25/-sp-karen-armstrong-religious-violence-myth-secular

Bealey, F. 1999. "State Sovereignty." In *The Blackwell Dictionary of Political Science: A User's Guide to Its Terms*, edited by F. Bealey, 130–43. Oxford: Blackwell.

Berger, P. and T. Luckmann. 1967. *The Social Construction of Reality: A Treatise in the Sociology of Knowledge*. Garden City, NY: Anchor.

Berger, P. 1999. *The Desecularization of the World*. Washington, DC: Ethics and Public Policy Center.

Buzan, B. and L. Hansen. 2007. *International Security*. London: SAGE Publications.

Casanova, J. 1994. *Public Religions in the Modern World*. Chicago, IL: University of Chicago Press.

Chavez, C. and A. Arcos. 1999. "The Wixaritari Today." *Cultural Survival Quarterly* 23(1): 56–77.

Connolly, W. E. 1988. *Political Theory and Modernity*. Oxford: Basil Blackwell Ltd.

Della Porta, D. and S. Tarrow. 2005. "Transnational Processes and Social Activism: An Introduction." In *Transnational Protest and Global Activism*, edited by D. Della Porta and S. Tarrow, 1–20. Lanham, MD: Rowman and Littlefield.

Fox, J. and S. Sandler. 2004. *Bringing Religion into International Relations*. New York, NY: Palgrave Macmillan.

Haynes, J. 2001. "Transnational Religious Actors and International Politics." *Third World Quarterly* 22(2): 143–58.

Kent, J. M. 2008. *The Challenge of Transnational Religion to International Relations*. Thesis submitted to Baylor University. Accessed on 1 August 2016 from https://

baylor-ir.tdl.org/baylor-ir/bitstream/handle/2104/5156/jennifer_kent_masters. pdf?sequence=1

Keohane, R and J. Nye. 1972. "Transnational Relations and World Politics: An Introduction." *International Organization* 25(3): 329–49.

Kivisto, P. 2001. "Theorizing Transnational Migration: A Critical Review of Current Efforts." *Ethnic and Racial Studies* 24(4): 549–77.

Kubálková, V. 2003. "Towards an International Political Theology." In *Religion in International Relations: Return from Exile*, edited by F. Petito and P. Hatzopoulos, 79–106. New York, NY: Palgrave.

Lipschutz, R. 1992. "Reconstructing World Politics: The Emergence of Global Civil Society." *Millennium* 21(3): 389–401.

Milani, C. and C. Keraghel. 2006. "The International Agenda for Sustainable Development: International Contestatory Movements." In *Participation for Sustainability in Trade*, edited by S. Thoyer and B. Martimort-Asso, 93–110. London: Ashgate Publishers.

Reilly, W. M. 2000. "World Summit of Religion Opens at UN." *GPF Forum*. Accessed on 10 October 2016 from https://www.globalpolicy.org/component/content/article/227/29721.html

Risse-Kappen, T. 1995. "Bringing Transnational Relations Back in: Introduction and Structure of Governance and Transnational relations: What Have We Learned?" In *Bringing Transnational Relations Back In: Non-state Actors, Domestic Structures and International Institutions*, edited by T. Risse-Kappen, 3–36. Cambridge: Cambridge University Press.

Robinson, W. I. 1998. "Beyond Nation-State Paradigms: Globalization, Sociology, and the Challenge of Transnational Studies." *Sociological Forum* 13(4): 561–94. DOI: 10.1023/A:1022806016167.

Rosenau, J. 1999. *Toward Ontology for Global Governance in Approaches to Global Governance Theory*. New York, NY: SUNY Press.

Shils, E. 1978. *Tradition*. Chicago, IL: University of Chicago Press.

Swatos, W. and K. Christiano. 1999. "Secularization Theory: The Course of a Concept." *Sociology of Religion* 60(3): 209–28.

Tarrow, S. 2001. "Transnational Politics: Contentions and Institutions in International Politics." *Annual Review of Political Science* June: 1–23. DOI: 10.1146/annurev. polisci.4.1.1.

Thomas, S. M. 2005. *The Global Resurgence of Religion and the Transformation of International Relations*. New York, NY: Palgrave Macmillan.

van der Veer, P. 2001. *Imperial Encounters: Religion and Modernity in India and Britain*. Princeton, NJ: Princeton University Press.

Viotti, P. and M. Kauppi. 1999. *International Relations Theory: Realism, Pluralism, Globalism*. Boston, MA: Allyn & Bacon.

Walker, R. J. 1994. "Social Movements/World Politics." *Millennium* 23(3): 669–700.

Wiener, J. and R. A. Schrire. 2009. *International Relations: Volume 1*. Oxford: EOLSS Publishers.

Young, O. 1997. *Rights, Rules and Resources in World Affairs and Global Governance: Toward a Theory of Decentralized World Order in Global Governance*. Cambridge, MA: MIT Press.

2

Hillsong Church: Postmodern Parishes, Worldwide Music, and Anointed Acquisitions

They copy the image of themselves projected on their smooth screens to the accompaniment of inane music.
—R. S. Thomas (1913–2000; Philips 1986)

Introduction

Hillsong is clearly the largest mega church in Australia, with over 30,000 attendees in the various Sydney campuses alone, and in the last few years it is making its presence felt internationally with an estimated 100,000 attendees worldwide and some 10 million followers on social media. Brian and Bobbie Houston founded the church in Sydney in 1983, then known as the Hills Christian Life Centre with just 45 people. The music and worship songs created by the church, primarily through high profile worship pastors Geoff Bullock and later Darlene Zschech,[1] revolutionized the church's music ministry to such an extent that the name of the church was changed to Hillsong in 1999. For more than 15 years, Hillsong was known for the creation of its own brand of worship songs and the development of a distinctive worship style with a Sydney focus; although during this time its music influenced churches all around the world, including the United States and Europe. Today, the church has gone worldwide, with branches in 13 countries, and it is actively pursuing a strategy to seek other branches, networks, and even acquisitions of churches with low attendances.

Why is there such avid interest about Hillsong in Australia? Whereas nearly 80 percent of Americans identify themselves as Christians, and 37 percent say they regularly go to church services, the number of people attending church in Australia is less than 10 percent of the population (Bentley 2012).[2] So Hillsong seems out of place in the secular context of Australia. Australia is not generally known for mega churches and neither is the nation in the cusp of a religious revival akin to the time in the United States when the religious right was responsible for the election of George W. Bush into the White House.

Is Hillsong catering to a new consciousness—the felt needs of postmodern people? And, conversely, are the mainline, traditional churches in Australia and around the world failing to respond to the needs and aspirations of people in postmodern society in a way that Hillsong and other neo-Pentecostal churches are doing?

Criticisms of Hillsong are rampant—from the media, ex-Hillsong attendees, and the fraternity of Christians and church leaders. Most of the criticisms of Hillsong stem from people who hold the essentialist view of what a church ought to be (Fore 1987; Postman 1985). Critics who use this view typically cite the Bible (or their interpretation of it) to frame their argument on the measure of a church. Interestingly, some of this criticism comes from the Anglican Church, which has the monopoly on Australian Church membership with the largest number of Christian followers in Australia. Whilst critiques based on essentialist ideas should not be taken lightly or dismissed, in this chapter, I argue that the reason for Hillsong's meteoric rise is due to the fact that while mainline churches, by and large, are endeavoring to keep true to the text of scripture in their operation of the church, Hillsong, on the other hand, is concerned about being true to the context of the times. Hillsong takes pains to relate to the postmodern world, albeit sometimes at the expense of being true to the text of the Bible and even—to the founder of the Christian faith. I assess Hillsong's contemporary and contextual approach by focusing on the following aspects of the movement: the institutional location of the church, its theology and rhetoric, the objectification of the body and the senses, the postmodern nature of this phenomenon, its political economy, and its expansionistic outlook.

The Institutional Location of the Church

Brian Houston, Hillsong's senior pastor, had a background in the Salvation Army and the Methodist holiness church, and so in all likelihood he learned the discipline and precise planning that characterized these two church denominations in establishing Hillsong (Bentley

2012). Every service at Hillsong is planned and orchestrated with the precision of a rock concert or a Broadway musical. Hillsong is also influenced by the seeker-friendly movement of churches conceived in California, USA. These churches deliberately locate in new suburban centers where there are very few existing churches (Sargeant 2000).

In keeping with this seeker-friendly strategy, the original Hillsong is located in a north-western Sydney suburb in a 21-acre property in Baulkham Hills. Hence, Hillsong's name celebrates the fact that it is like a city on a hill (obviously, a New Testament reference to Matthew 5:14; The Holy Bible 1985)[3] as well as the fact that the church is all about song and music.

In addition to being on a hillside, the site is located in a business center in the fast-growing 'technology corridor', home of global companies such as Microsoft, Toshiba, Sony, Hyundai, Siemens, Fuji Xerox, and Foxtel (Maddox 2013). From the Baulkham Hills location as its base, the church has expanded into inner suburbia. Its second site was established in Waterloo in 2009, near the city and is surrounded by some of Sydney's elitist design outlets and brasserie-style eateries. A third site was launched recently in the inner suburb of Campbelltown. Shuttle courtesy buses transport attendees from Sydney's Central Train Station (30 km away) to Baulkham Hills, the main church site.

Further to its three churches, Hillsong has several 'extension centers' in which it conducts specialized services to reach out to the migrant communities: Blacktown (Filipino); Burwood and Castle Hill (Asian); Dulwich Hill (Spanish); Merrylands (Spanish); Minchinbury, Miranda, and Parramatta (Chinese); Ryde, St Mary's (Mandarin/English); and St Leonards (Cantonese/English; Connell 2006). Thus, Hillsong conducts church services in 30 locations across Sydney. But the largest is the original site in Baulkham Hills, which has a 3,500-seat auditorium, built in 1990 at a cost of AU$25 million, plus a separate 800-seat youth meeting hall, Sunday school rooms, play areas, and a children's day care center. As mentioned previously, Hillsong follows the seeker-friendly church movement design of churches without any of the symbolism of traditional churches—crosses, stained-glass windows, pews, and podiums.[4] This multipurpose design is conducive to the churches being leased out regularly to secular outfits for various entertainment functions, including the National Youth Rock Eisteddfod and business conferences. Hillsong's architects (Noel Bell, Ridley Smith and Partners) have claimed that Hillsong Baulkham Hills is one of the most significant church buildings in Australia—second only to the iconic St Mary's Cathedral (Catholic) in Sydney, which was built in the 1880s (Connell 2006).

Beyond the state of New South Wales, Hillsong has also opened up campuses in Queensland (Brisbane, Gold Coast, Mount Gravatt, and Noosa) and Victoria (Melbourne).[5]

And beyond Australia, Hillsong has deliberately adopted a city focus—with branches in London (UK), New York City and Los Angeles (USA), Stockholm (Sweden), Amsterdam (Holland), Moscow (Russia), Paris (France), Konstanz (Germany), Kiev (Ukraine), Copenhagen (Denmark), Sao Paulo (Brazil), Barcelona (Spain), Buenos Aires (Argentina), and Cape Town (South Africa).[6]

Hillsong is part of the AoG denomination known in Australia as the Australian Christian Churches (ACC), which is affiliated with the World Assemblies of God Fellowship that was established some 100 years ago in Hot Springs, Arkansas (USA). The AoG denomination is hierarchical with a superintendent who fills a role similar to that of a bishop and an administrative structure that serves a national organization, including a theological college and other affiliated agencies. Much of this institutional underpinning is ignored in the discussions about Hillsong primarily because Hillsong has in fact outgrown fraternal relationships such as the ACC.[7] Hillsong, therefore, portrays itself as an autonomous body comprising a dynamic senior pastor and his acolytes practicing neo-Pentecostal theology, including the prosperity gospel and speaking in tongues. The worship leaders who lead worship are given the status of pastors, but they appear more as entertainers and performers, using song, television, and media technology in their delivery of the Christian message. Indeed, it is song that best represents the spirit of Hillsong.

Arguably, the very essence of Hillsong is also its weakness. As a neo-Pentecostal movement, with loose links with the ACC, it is somewhat divorced from traditional theology and is seen to be at times vacillating and shallow in its interpretation of the Bible.[8] When confronted by problems, Hillsong has little historical and theological tradition to fall back on. And, when confronted by scandals of a financial or sexual nature[9] (as sometimes happens), neo-Pentecostal churches may crumble into insignificance because the senior pastor is probably involved in either or both scandals, and there is no one else with the status or charisma to replace or rebuke him or her (James and Shoesmith 2006). The recent closure of a neo-Pentecostal church in Western Australia, owing to the senior pastor's fall from grace, is a case in point (Martin 2015).

Its Theology and Rhetoric

Hillsong, as a part of the neo-Pentecostal churches, espouses a three-part theological position upon which the Hillsong church, its music industry, and its network of churches are built: (a) the prosperity gospel, (b) the emphasis on the Holy Spirit, and (c) an eschatology (doctrine of end times) that promotes that the coming Kingdom is here and now (not just in the future). I will now elaborate on these aspects.

Hillsong believes in the prosperity gospel and has built its theology from verses in the Bible (mostly out of context and without distinguishing the metaphorical from the literal) which claim that it is the right of every Christian to have health, wealth, and happiness. It is due to their hermeneutics which is pneumatic based, that is, the belief that the Holy Spirit allows each individual to make his or her own interpretation of any scripture, and, therefore, hermeneutical issues such as the context of history, culture, language, and grammar are downplayed.

Brian Houston, in one of his earlier landmark books *You Need More Money: Discovering God's Amazing Financial Plan for Your Life* (1999), made the claim that "the scriptures ... [are] full of promises of prosperity" (Houston 1999: 10). He summarized the goal of his book rather pointedly: "If you and I can change our thinking and develop a healthy attitude towards money, I believe we can all walk in the blessing and prosperity that God intends for us. We will never have a problem with money again" (Houston 1999: 3). And in a related matter, Houston exhorted: "If you are struggling with your health, know that it is the will of God to see you whole and healthy. Health is one of the promises of God for our lives" (Houston 1999: 31).

Using the biblical text: "For you know the grace of our Lord Jesus Christ that though he was rich, yet for your sake he became poor, so that you by his poverty might become rich" (2 Corinthians 8: 9), Houston commented:

> I've heard people misinterpret this scripture to support their belief that it is biblical to be poor. They only read half of it, that "though He was rich,

yet for your sakes He became poor." They completely miss the crucial point because if you read on, the reason why He became poor was that "you, through his poverty, might become rich." (Houston 1999: 12–13)

Such highly contentious interpretations seldom go unchallenged by other Christian leaders. For example, Rosner (2004) of the Anglican Theological School in Sydney argued that Houston's exegesis of the Bible is faulty.

> Houston is right to declare that Jesus became poor so that we might become rich, but he does not seem to realise that 'rich' here is not meant to be taken literally. Instructively, the letter to the Laodiceans in Revelation has both the literal and metaphorical senses of riches in neighbouring verses. Jesus tells the literally rich they are spiritually poor, and need to become spiritually (or really) rich…. Jesus is talking about being 'rich towards God', which, as the parable of the Rich Fool (Luke 12: 13–21) shows, has no connection to material riches, except perhaps inversely. Earlier in 2 Corinthians, Paul describes his own ministry in similar terms: he was "(materially) poor, yet making many (*really*) rich" (6: 10). Along with … many other powerful images, getting rich (*by buying gold!*) is a metaphor for salvation and is not meant to be taken literally.
>
> The consequences of misreading the Bible on the subject of poverty and riches are grave. To claim that the benefits of peace with God include health and wealth is an insult to tens of millions of Christians in the Majority World, who are not and may never be affluent … [it] ignores the Bible's clear teaching on the dangers of greed and the freedom contentment brings (Rosner 2004: para 15)

Besides prosperity teaching, Hillsong gives undue emphasis on the Holy Spirit—the third person of the Trinity, who is portrayed almost as a genie in the fable 'Aladdin's Lamp'—one who comes immediately to the bidding of Christians. Neo-Pentecostal churches believe that there is a two-stage experience in becoming a Christian: first, one comes to Jesus Christ for salvation; second, the Holy Spirit comes into one's life (as a believer). The second stage manifests itself through speaking in tongues, as well as other supernatural phenomena. Thus, the invisible Holy Spirit is made almost tangible at Hillsong through the preaching, music, and atmosphere of the worship services wherein the pastors routinely emphasize the importance of the congregation having an encounter with the Holy Spirit. The Hillsong musical composition

'Holy Spirit Rain Down' exemplifies the special place given to the Holy Spirit in the life and worship of the church.

> Holy Spirit, rain down, rain down
> Oh, Comforter and Friend
> How we need Your touch again
> Holy Spirit, rain down, rain down
> Let Your power fall
> Let Your voice be heard
> Come and change our hearts
> As we stand on Your word[10]

Hillsong, like other Pentecostals, separates the Holy Spirit from Christ and this also has incurred strong criticism from Christian leaders such as Gaffin (1998: 48–50).

Worship of any one of the three at once entails worship of all three and worship of the indivisible Trinity. An undue emphasis on one person, whether it be the focus on Jesus in pietism or the concentration on the Holy Spirit in charismatic circles, is a distortion.

The third aspect of the theology is Hillsong's eschatology that the Kingdom mentioned in the Bible and the inheritance promised to the Christian in the afterlife are a present blessing. Hillsong's view on the Kingdom is part of the dominion theology that originated in the United States. Dominion theology claims that when Adam sinned, the authority of this world was lost to Satan, and God was looking to a group of Christians to take over this authority: 'a covenant people' who will be His 'extension' or 'expression' in the earth to take dominion back from Satan (Burke 2001; Leslie 2010). Hillsong clearly considers itself the covenant people who are chosen to take back the authority. Houston (1999) teaches that wealth gives us 'the ability to have dominion' and that money is equated with 'dominion Certificates' (Houston 1999: 19, 51).

Walter's (2008) study of Hillsong theology found that Hillsong had virtually changed the basics of the classical evangelical interpretation of many of the aspects of the gospel, such as Christ's death on the cross (cited in Payne and Cheng 2008). The death of Christ was not substitutionary, Hillsong believes, in the sense that Christ became the substitute for the people of the world. Jesus' death and resurrection is "usually quoted either as an example (of overcoming difficulty and living with purpose) or explained as the source of healing and empowerment for living an abundant and healthy life" (cited in Payne and Cheng 2008: 16). Also, 'negative' aspects of the gospel such as sin have been omitted in the preaching, and when they are mentioned, sin is treated as acts of immorality or worse still—it involves "negative thinking and attitudes that destroy God's purpose in our lives" (cited in Payne and Cheng 2007: 16). Hence, the Hillsong gospel runs the risk of both moving away from classical evangelical Christianity and from classical and historic Pentecostal teaching.

Houston readily admits that Hillsong is not that concerned with doctrines and the specifics of theology: "We believe a basic charismatic/Pentecostal theology, but we don't build strong on theology.... We make it about Jesus, about the grace of God, and we try to have a net so it's broad, not narrow" (Bailey 2013). Hillsong's commitment to identify with the postmodern age is so great that it has accommodated to the spirit of the age (Corney 2005). Corney (2004) describes this as 'liberal reductionism' where a church allows "the spirit of the age to influence its interpretation of the Gospel" (Corney 2004: 4).

Summing up, Hillsong is built on these three aspects of theology. And with these three foundations, Hillsong pastors advocate that people can: experience the infinite God (usually through the Spirit) and feel his presence; can show the world the greatness of God and make a difference; and prove God's reality in this world by our health, wealth, looks, and success in our business and ministries.

Objectification of the Body and Senses

Hillsong's three-part theology reveals the objectification of the body and the senses in the church's emphasis and practice. In the broad sweep of religious history, most world religions focus on the immaterial world rather than the material world because there is a sense of paradox between immateriality and monumentality (the building of large objects, be it for worship or for other purposes). Meskel's studies showed that it is "through monumentality [that] the divine could be apprehended" (cited in Miller 1999: para 30). Tilley argued that material objects actually "embody ideologies and powers which form an essential part of their nature" (Tilley 1991: 149). The Catholic Church's legacy of building large and iconic cathedrals and worship centers since its inception attest to this fact. Miller (1999) expanded this argument by pointing out that material culture goes beyond objects and artefacts to include the "ephemeral, the imaginary, the biological; within a larger conceptualization of culture" (Miller 1999: para 5).

Objectification theory is related to the theory of materiality and has been primarily centered on studies of how the human body (especially females) is objectified, that is, they are made to be larger than life (and viewed as parts rather than as a whole) and treated as the object of pleasure by the gaze of men. According to Tilley (2006: 60), "the object world is absolutely central to an understanding of individual persons and societies."

A random sampling of web searches that I undertook on aspects of contemporary culture revealed the flagrant use of the body (especially the female) in advertising, news, entertainment, cultural, and medical information. This trend is no doubt aided and abetted by the interpenetration and congruence of new and mobile media technologies freely available in today's market. The phenomenon just described, known by scholars as objectification, posits that girls and women are raised in a culture mainly by our media to "internalize an observer's perspective as a primary view of their physical selves" (Fredrickson and Roberts 1997: 173). Even medical and educational texts of women in contemporary culture resort to using images of women with 'Hollywood' looks and figures. Several conclusions stem out of objectification studies, namely that the body is treated as a commodity. Also, the lines between mainstream culture (and what is acceptable) and pornography are indeed very porous. Additionally, the role of the female has shifted from the maternal, nurturing one to that which exists simply of giving pleasure in this image-driven society.

Through the framework of materiality and objectification theories, I argue that Hillsong is seeking to understand the infinite God by an expansionistic outlook involving building big churches and establishing branches and networks throughout the world. Furthermore, Hillsong is objectifying the human body (males and females) by catering to the health and wealth teaching—based on the belief that healing, prosperity, and success are the fundamental rights of every Christian. Hillsong's teachings suggest that success is the goal of the abundant

Christian life, which Christ promises in the New Testament in passages such as John 10:10[11] (The Holy Bible 1985).

This body emphasis is seen in several levels. Females are made to be attractive (physically and spiritually) to their husbands and would-be husbands; hence, 'Colour' conferences for women and girls are held regularly to "champion the young girls of this generation."[12] The Hillsong Colour website says: "From the very beginning, Colour Conference was birthed through a strong sense from God to create a conference for young women, girded about by older women. This conference champions the young girls of this generation."[13] Bobbie Houston, wife of the senior pastor of Hillsong, says:

> [T]here's a wealth of fabulous potential within the feminine heart and I think down through history it's been quenched at times … the secular world doesn't have an issue with women and I think really the church needs to come of age sometimes and just grow up and realize that there's a wealth of wonder and goodness and potential and all sorts of things within the feminine heart and that together we can actually make the church more beautiful and more vibrant and more relevant to society. (Menzie 2014: para 5)

Bobbie Houston's comments reveal that Hillsong seeks to adopt some aspects of the secular world and is attempting to win new seekers, such as young women, to become members of the fellowship by appealing to their outward looks, grooming, and of course their inner spiritual life.

The website announces that the 2016 conferences will be held in "five fabulous world class cities: Gorgeous Sydney, Beautiful Cape Town, Charming London, Historic Kiev, and announcing New York City."[14]

What Brian Houston does for the whole church, Bobbie Houston has made a commitment to do for women:

> I am personally committed to the health and wellbeing of the women in our church. So I have a responsibility to teach them, to hopefully example what a woman of God could look like.[15]

The Colour Sisterhood is a name given to a group of women and girls who sign up to make a difference. These women and girls are encouraged to contribute their donations and time to change society through community projects.[16]

In a blog titled *Super Working Mum*, one of the attendees of the 2015 Colour Conference shared how she was in the company of 10,000 women at the Sydney Arena and how Christian celebrity speakers with Hollywood looks such as Beth Moore and Dawn Chere ministered to the women. The blog describes Dawn Chere as "a sweet fashionable power house of God" and how when Beth Moore walked on the stage, the blogger felt strongly in her heart "I want to have what she has."[17] This phrase is an obvious reference to the title of the book written by Bobbie Houston, which in turn was unashamedly taken from a scene in a 1989 movie *When Harry met Sally* in which Sally, who is at a restaurant, pretends to have a sexual climax and an onlooking customer says to the waitress "I'll have what she's having." Thus, bodily and sexual expression is celebrated, bringing an end to age-old church repressions and making way for freedoms hitherto unheard of in the Christian church. So, the sense of sight, sound, touch, and feeling dominates Hillsong's worship, the website, the books, and the publicity material. In doing so, Hillsong has reversed classical Christianity's focus on the spiritual and the heavenly to the fleshly and the worldly.

Through the Shine program, Hillsong runs courses for young women aged between 15 and 18 on etiquette, deportment, hairstyles, nail care, and grooming. This program runs in some 20 public and private schools and community and religious groups in New South Wales, Australia. The promotional material from Hillsong refers to young women's "created uniqueness … [and that] through skin care, natural make-up, hair care, nail care girls discover their value and created uniqueness."[18] Some experts and parents have expressed concerns about the program as it is run by underqualified leaders and the fact that no allowance is made for troubled young women who may feel unduly pressured by such motivational teachings (Bibby 2008).

Hillsong courses include titles such as 'Back in Shape Body-shaping Exercise Guide', 'Keeping Up Appearances', and '21-Day Fat-blasting Starter Plan' (Maddox 2013). In this milieu, the body is to be groomed well and clothed with the finest of garments, free of sickness and experiencing success and prosperity. Besides this, the body's senses must be catered for in this life and in the worship services at the church. Thus, the Hillsong culture is premised on the critical need for sensate impressions to entertain, inform, educate, and give pleasure. The term 'sensate' refers to the intense use of visual images to summon the attention of all the human senses so that individuals can participate fully in the experience of the moment.

At Hillsong, music is featured at all worship services, and the worship is staged like a rock concert with the full complement of singers and musicians and sometimes with smoke machines to give additional stage effects. So important is music that there is an almost continuous flow of music throughout the service, even during the prayer time and announcements. At worship, the music is loud, and worship leaders encourage the congregation to lift up their hands, sway, and move with the rhythmic tunes. Hillsong's objectification of the body and the senses is integral to the place given to music at the worship service. Music is almost treated as another sacrament of the church, on par with communion and baptism. The worship leaders and pastors are seen to be the embodiment of God himself as Hillsong's goal seems to be to translate the infinite God into a tangible and palpable entity. This translation and reification (of God's presence) underpins much of the Hillsong philosophy of ministry and the construction of its worship services.

The Postmodern Nature of This Phenomenon

Postmodernism entails questioning the values, ideas, and construction of the modern era especially in the fields of arts and culture. According to Palmer (2014):

> Modernism insists on a clear divide between art and popular culture....
> But like modernism, postmodernism does not designate any one style of
> art or culture. On the contrary, it is often associated with pluralism and
> an abandonment of conventional ideas of originality and authorship in
> favour of a pastiche.... (Palmer 2014: paras 7–8, 22)

Pastiche is an Italian term for medley, and in postmodernism we see the blending and intertextuality of somewhat discursive and discordant themes, ideas, and techniques that may not necessarily fit neatly. Issues of cultural identity are also important in postmodernism in contrast to modernism which, according to Palmer, apparently celebrated patriarchy, racism, and heterosexuality (Palmer 2014). Applying these theoretical concepts to the Hillsong phenomena, we can see the pastiche of music, popular culture, technology, taboo topics, material-ism, and conspicuous consumption blended in with Hillsong's theology and practice. In terms of cultural identity, we can detect the move to make the gospel positive with biblical verses that are selectively quoted (Yip 2015) and hard-to-understand theologies and doctrines omitted in favor of an open and seeker-friendly service for all (women are received into leadership positions) including a somewhat ambiguous gay welcoming approach.[19]

Crawford (cited in O'Malley 2013), an advertising consultant from the advertising/public relations giant BBDO Sydney,[20] argued that Hillsong preaches the prosperity gospel because it is a win-win solution; people benefit from it and the church benefits as well. Therefore, Hillsong's strategy is based on this thinking: rather than going against the modern, materialistic world in which we live, Hillsong intentionally works within contemporary society. Hillsong's message seems to be: enjoy life now and if you buy into this brand of faith, your finances and health will be sustained both in this life and the life to come. This message is pack-aged in a well-coordinated, oftentimes dramatic and theatrical service, delivered by passionate, articulate pastors with understandable and contemporary illustrations and language drawn from sports, popular culture, and video clips. The word 'cool' is heard frequently.

Clearly, music is used as the centerpiece of the whole Hillsong empire. Professor Ari Y. Kelman (cited in O'Malley 2013: para 10) of Stanford University explains music's significance at Hillsong.

> Back in 1995, Christian worship music was already a big deal in the US, but for a decade or so the same songs had dominated its charts. That was when an Australian, Darlene Zschech, a professional jingle writer and member of Hillsong, wrote Shout to the Lord. The significance of the song can't be overstated.... It broke the old guard's stranglehold on the Christian charts, and helped turn Hillsong into a phenomenon that now produces and sells its music through its in-house label around the world.

Kelman's assertion is confirmed by the fact that close to 20 percent of all church songs in the United States originates from Hillsong, and the multi-genre music industry of Hillsong ranges from soft pop to hard rock (cited in O'Malley 2013). The Hillsong United band (known variously as Hillsong United or simply United) originated as a part of Hillsong's youth ministry made up of promising worship leaders who also wrote original compositions. Their debut extended play, *One*, which was released alongside the Hillsong Worship album Touching Heaven Changing Earth, launched a new chapter in Hillsong's music. Since then, Hillsong United has released eleven annual live albums and four studio albums, with performances at church services and concerts worldwide. Their single Oceans (Where Feet May Fail) from their third studio album Zion reached No. 1 on the American Billboard Christian Songs chart at the end of 2013 and remained in the chart for two years (Harowitz 2015). The song also charted on the Billboard Hot 100 in March 2014, peaking at No. 83 (Harowitz 2015).

United was the first Christian group to achieve sell-out performances at Los Angeles' prestigious Staples Center, and additionally it has also sold out in the following notable venues in the United States: Seattle's ShoWare Center, New York's Radio City Music Hall, Chicago's Sears Centre Arena, Denver's Red Rocks Amphitheatre, and Los Angeles' Hollywood Bowl (Williams 2015).

Hillsong Music Australia (HMA) is the record label of Hillsong churches. All the current albums are produced under this label and distributed by HMA as well as by secular distributors such as Capitol Music Group and Universal Music Group.[21] HMA has sold more than 16 million albums worldwide and earns US$100 million a year.[22]

Hillsong uses state-of-the-art technology and employs full-time audiovisual and design staff. Each Sunday service at Baulkham Hills is an extravaganza with a multiplicity of giant screens. On the screens, the congregation sees on display the lyrics of the worship songs (thus doing away with cumbersome hymnals and sheets) and the 'larger than life' images of the worship leaders, pastors, and musicians are oftentimes superimposed over the lyrics. When I visited the Baulkham Hills church, I noticed that at critical times the pastors and worship leaders would deliberately look into the cameras so as to engage with the screen and TV audiences. As a worshipper, it was difficult, if not impossible to not engage with the screens because of the sheer size of the worship facility and technology. The American poet R. S. Thomas (1986), whose verse appears before the introduction to this chapter, was not particularly referring to Hillsong when he wrote the striking poem about the technological takeover of contemporary society, but his words resonate with Hillsong's mediated worship.

The aforementioned analysis of Hillsong by Crawford is that it has a ready-made audience—primarily through its music: "it's difficult to sell something to anyone if they're not listening" (cited in O'Malley 2013). Crawford went on to comment that, just as the producers of the men's aftershave Old Spice "took masculinity and re-framed it for the younger generation, Hillsong did a similar thing with Christianity—[re-imagining] Christianity to a younger, contemporary and postmodern culture" (cited in O'Malley 2013).

Its Political Economy

Hillsong is supported by church offerings, product sales (especially music), book sales, conference fees (its annual conference draws 30,000 delegates from all over the world), concert ticket sales, and membership and training fees. As a church, Hillsong's income is tax-free according to the Australian law, an issue that many critics point out is a loophole that needs to be tightened up by the government.

Over the years, the church has influenced the congregation's stand on political campaigns and political parties. The ACC of which Hillsong is a member, was instrumental in forming the federal political party—Family First—which was launched in 2000 by the then President of the ACC, Bob Evans, pastor–politician.

Well-known politicians, including the former Australian Prime Minister John Howard and the Federal Treasurer Peter Costello, and a selection of senators and parliamentarians from all sides of the political scenario, have either visited the church, participated at the annual Hillsong conferences, or had an audience with the Hillsong leadership. Interestingly, the church has survived the Royal commission on sex abuse, allegations of financial matters, vote rigging in the TV reality show *Australian Idol*, and other scandals.

Hillsong also has close connections with several businesses, including Gloria Jean's—the Australian version of Starbucks. Gloria Jeans was founded by Nabi Saleh who is an elder and board member of Hillsong church. An in-house publication of Hillsong businesses, *Hillsong Emerge*, lists hundreds of businesses ranging from banks to restaurants (Sargeant 2000). And through its international network,

Hillsong attracts Hollywood celebrities such as Justin Bieber and NBA star Kevin Durant (who was baptized by Hillsong's New York Pastor Lentz) and other high profile entertainers.[23]

Its Expansionist Outlook

As mentioned early in the Chapter, in recent years, Hillsong has enlarged its parish to the world as reflected in Hillsong's vision statement: "… to reach and influence the world by building a large Christ-centered, Bible-based church, changing mindsets and empowering people to lead and impact in every sphere of life."[24]

According to the Hillsong website, the "Hillsong Leadership Network is not a denominational movement, is not a spiritual covering, and is not designed to replace nor compete with existing affiliations."[25] There are two ways to join the Hillsong network—as an associate member which gives churches, individuals, and organizations access to certain resources (at no cost); and as a Church/Ministry member which costs AU$500 annually, for which members receive "the full benefits of the Hillsong Leadership Network including Open House events, Luncheon & High Tea, relational opportunities, discounted registration to conferences, resource discounts and more."[26] Professor Flory of the Center for Religion and Civic Culture at the University of Southern California claimed that this loose international network of alliances works particularly well for Hillsong (O'Malley 2013). The network leads to the mentoring of churches and in the process some eventually come under the umbrella of Hillsong.

Hillsong is fulfilling its worldwide vision with its music and by sharing its philosophy of ministry (primarily through its annual conferences). But Hillsong is also deliberately building its own branches, with 13 churches worldwide to date. Most of these churches are launched by traditional 'Church planting' methods, that is, Hillsong representatives are sent to start churches overseas or sometimes overseas pastors are encouraged to start churches on behalf of Hillsong. Lately, Hillsong has taken another approach—it finds churches overseas that are dying and negotiates with the local pastors ways and means whereby Hillsong can assist or takeover the church's ministry. The business of acquisitions and strategic partnerships sometimes begins at the Hillsong

International College where pastors from all over the world come to the Sydney campus to study about ministry in postmodern times with its specializations of music, worship, pastoral ministry, and dance.

One of the members of a church in Norway bemoans how Hillsong came and took over the local church in Norway allegedly with little consultation with the church members:

> But a year later, around the time we were joining the Hillsong family, the Easter service was very different. First of all, our pastor did not preach, even though he was present. The pastor from Stockholm Hillsong preached. I just didn't understand why the Hillsong pastor wouldn't want to be preaching at his own church on Easter morning. And why would our pastor move over on such an important Sunday? This is the big Sunday they encourage everyone to invite guests and people that maybe don't normally go to church. If I had invited anyone to church that Sunday, they wouldn't have gotten an impression of our own pastor. **The sermon was so unmemorable. I can't even remember the main points.**
>
> But worst of all, was that they had a trapeze artist swinging from silk scarves hanging from the stage ceiling as the praise and worship band played. **It was a total show!** It did not at all help me to think about the real reason of 'Resurrection Sunday'.[27]

The various Hillsong churches around the world are purported to be independent but on closer examination they are part of a strong network of churches with Hillsong at the helm of the movement: "[these churches] are less than an autonomous church. Each of them draws from the experience, branding, style, theology and practices of the Australian church, although indigenous pastors preach and teach" (Stetzer 2014: para 7).

Future of the Hillsong Movement

As mentioned at the outset, Hillsong is part of the neo-Pentecostal movement with loose links with the AoG. However, in its 30 years of existence, it has become more of a celebrity church possessing proven ministry insights to offer to churches in the Western world and beyond.

One of the issues it may face in the future is institutionalism. Even though Hillsong is a stand-alone church, in many ways as time progresses and as its branches grow, it will be tempted to become more institutionalized. Institutionalism is always a challenge and brings with it the problems of bureaucracy and traditionalism.

Succession of leadership is another issue. Hillsong is led by Brian and Bobbie Houston who are variously called senior pastors, presidents, executive producers, and other such titles for their multilevel ministries. Joel Houston, their son, may in all likelihood be groomed for leadership, but it's left to be seen how Hillsong deals with its succession of leadership when the time approaches.

Also, there is always the real danger (as revealed in recent studies on mega churches) that in hard economic times or health crises some of the currently jubilant congregation members may become disillusioned with the prosperity and health gospel (Smith and Campos 2015).

There may be new contenders on the scene—new-style Pentecostal churches which come up with more upbeat music and engaging church dynamics. In fact, in a small way, this is already happening with the rise of Jesus Culture, a church that started in Redding, California. Jesus Culture also specializes in music (with its own record label) and is growing in influence.

Alternatively, established churches that have a more traditional and classical theology may take the initiative in launching creative ministries and composing songs equal to or better than Hillsong's. Sovereign Grace in the United States is doing just that. So it will be interesting to watch how Hillsong responds to this expanding worldwide contestation.

Conclusion

Hillsong began as a fascinating movement with a loose affiliation with the Pentecostal AoG church denomination, but it has evolved into a prestigious and landmark mega church in the Western world. In this chapter, I have identified the institutional location of Hillsong and described its theology—notably that Hillsong has moved away from classical evangelical theology and from classical Pentecostalism which is its heritage. The theology of Hillsong has brought about a new social and cultural phenomenon in the contemporary church—the objectification of the body and the senses primarily through the focus on prosperity theology and the place given to the Holy Spirit, to the exclusion of God the Father and the Son, Jesus.

Hillsong has catered for contemporary society and has been ostentatiously linked with politicians, businesses, and celebrities.

Its expansion has been impressive, but there are indications that Hillsong is beginning to face the issues of competition, institutionalization, and succession.

The chapter shows that Hillsong is true to the context of the times, at some expense of the text, while the mainline churches are true to the text of the scripture oftentimes overlooking the context of the times. Time will tell how Hillsong and mainline churches maintain the delicate balance between text and context and whether they interact to form new alliances or remain in a state of continual contestation.

Notes

1. Geoff was the worship pastor and convener of the annual conferences from 1987–95. Darlene took over as worship pastor with an illustrious singing and recording career from 1996–2007.
2. For more information on the status of Christianity and other religions in Australia, see Bentley (2012). This is a publication of the Christian Research Association (CRA). Also, see http://www.cbsnews.com/news/new-york-city-hillsong-megachurch-draws-thousands-every-sunday/
3. "You are the light of the world. A city built on a hill cannot be hidden" (Matthew 5:14).
4. For more details on the nature of contemporary mega churches, see James (2015).
5. See http://hillsong.com/australia
6. See http://hillsong.com/
7. Brian Houston was also the national president of the Pentecostal churches (AoG) known in Australia as ACC from 1997 to 2009.
8. For more details of two gay men who had a part in Hillsong and the repercussions following that, seehttp://www.christianpost.com/news/gay-couple-at-center-of-hillsong-controversy-say-theyve-been-open-and-forthright-about-relationship-from-the-get-go-142563/
9. Hillsong had to appear before the Australian Royal Commission on child sex abuse over allegations that Brian Houston's father Frank had abused young boys previously. For more information, see https://www.thesaturdaypaper.com.au/news/law-crime/2014/10/18/hillsong-the-royal-commission-child-sex-abuse/14135508001136
10. See http://www.azlyrics.com/lyrics/hillsonglive/holyspiritraindown.html

11. "The thief comes only to steal and kill and destroy; I came that they may have life, and have it abundantly."
12. See http://hillsong.com/colour/history/
13. Ibid.
14. Ibid.
15. See http://www.abc.net.au/austory/content/2005/s1427576.htm (para 28).
16. http://hillsong.com/colour/history/
17. See http://www.superworkingmum.com/my-experience-hillsong-colour-conference/
18. See http://www.shinetoday.com.au/
19. See http://www.christianpost.com/news/gay-couple-at-center-of-hillsong-controversy-say-theyve-been-open-and-forthright-about-relationship-from-the-get-go-142563/
20. In 1891, a small agency named Batten Company opened in a single room on Park Row in New York City. In subsequent years, it thrived and in 1928, it merged with Barton, Durstine, and Osborn. Thus, BBDO was born. Today, BBDO Worldwide employs 15,000 people in 289 agencies across 81 countries. (https://bbdo.com/about).
21. https://hillsongstore.com.au/
22. See http://www.cbsnews.com/news/new-york-city-hillsong-megachurch-draws-thousands-every-sunday/
23. See http://www.cbsnews.com/news/new-york-city-hillsong-megachurch-draws-thousands-every-sunday/
24. See http://hillsong.com/
25. See http://hillsong.com/network/
26. See http://hillsong.com/leadership/
27. See https://hillsongchurchwatch.com/tag/roman-catholicism/

References

Bailey, S. P. 2013. "Australia's Hillsong Church Has Astonishingly Powerful Global Influence." *Huffpost*. 11 May. US Edition. Accessed on 15 July 2015 from http://www.huffingtonpost.com/2013/11/05/australia-hillsong-church-influence_n_4214660.html

Bentley, P. 2012. "The City is my Parish? Understanding the Hillsong Model." *Pointers* 22(3): 12–16.

Bibby, P. 2008. *Hillsong Hits Schools with Beauty Gospel*. Accessed on 5 September 2015 from http://www.smh.com.au/news/national/hillsong-hits-schools-with-beauty-gospel/2008/07/25/1216492732905.html

Burke, D. 2001. *5 Facts About Dominionism*. Accessed on 5 September 2015 from http://www.huffingtonpost.com/2011/09/01/5-facts-about-dominionism_n_945601.html

Connell, J. 2006. "Hillsong: A Megachurch in the Sydney Suburbs." *Australian Geographer* 36(3): 315–22.

Corney, P. 2004. "In the Ruins of the Church." *Working Together: Australian Evangelical Alliance* (4): 4–5.

———. 2005. "Religion and Politics in Australia: Reviving the Connection." *Working Together: Australian Evangelical Alliance* (3): 1–14.

Fore, W. F. 1987. *Television and Religion: The Shaping of Faith, Values and Culture.* New Haven, CT: SBS Press.

Fredrickson, B. and T. Roberts. 1997. "Objectification Theory: Towards Understanding Women's Lived Experiences and Mental Health Risks." *Psychology of Women Quarterly* 21(2): 173–206.

Gaffin, R. Jr. 1998. "Challenges of the Charismatic Movement in the Reformed Tradition." *Ordained Servant* (7): 48–57.

Harowitz, S. J. 2015. *Jesus is the Ultimate Crossover: Christian Act Hillsong United on Why Their Message Is for Everybody.* Accessed on 2 June 2016 from http://www.billboard.com/articles/news/6575880/hillsong-united-exclusive-interview-christian-music-jesus-crossover

Houston, B. 1999. *You Need More Money: Discovering God's Amazing Financial Plan for your Life.* Sydney: Trust Media Distribution.

James, J. D. and B. Shoesmith. 2006, 16 April. *Hillsong, Benny Hinn and the Message of Health and Wealth: Looking at Technology and Religion.* Conference (Pubtalk). Perth: Murdoch University.

James, J. D. 2015. "A Moving Faith: An Introduction." In *A Moving Faith: Mega Churches Go South,* edited by J. D. James, 1–17. New Delhi and Washington, DC: SAGE Publications.

Leslie, S. 2010. *What Is Dominionism?* Accessed on 5 July 2015 from http://apprising.org/2011/01/26/what-is-dominionism/

Maddox, M. 2013. "Prosper, Consume and Be Saved." *Critical Research on Religion* 1(1): 108–15.

Martin, L. 2015. *WA Branch of Acts Christian Church to Close After Local Leader David Volmer Linked to Pedophile Ring.* Accessed on 1 December 2015 from http://www.abc.net.au/news/2015-07-30/wa-church-to-close-after-leader-charged-with-sexual-offences/6660980

Menzie, N. 2014. *Pastor Bobbie Houston Explains Why Hillsong Does Not 'Sideline the Girls'.* Accessed on 5 September 2015 from http://www.christianpost.com/news/pastor-bobbie-houston-explains-why-hillsong-church-does-not-sideline-the-girls-128563/

Miller, D. 1999. *Materiality: An Introduction.* Accessed on 11 September 2015 from www.ucl.ac.uk/anthropology/people/academic_staff/d.miller/mil-8

O'Malley, N. 2013. *The Rise and Rise of Hillsong.* Accessed on 20 September 2015 from http://www.smh.com.au/national/the-rise-and-rise-of-hillsong-20130907-2tbzx.html

Palmer, D. 2014. *Explainer: What Is Postmodernism?* Accessed on 7 September 3025 from http://theconversation.com/explainer-what-is-postmodernism-20791

Payne, T. and G. Cheng. 2007, January. "The Surprising Face of Hillsong." *The Briefing* 340(January): 11–19.

Philips, D. Z. 1986. *R. S. Thomas, Poet of the Hidden God: Meaning and Mediation in the Poetry of R. S. Thomas.* Eugene, OR: Pickwick Publishers.

Postman, N. 1985. *Amusing Ourselves to Death: Public Discourse in the Age of Show Business*. London: Penguin.

Rosner, B. 2004. *Want to Be Really Rich?* Accessed on 7 September 2015 from http://sydneyanglicans.net/blogs/indepth/1486a

Sargeant, S. 2000. "House of Worship Aussie Style." *Entertainment Design* 37(August): 6–8.

Smith, D. A. and L. S. Campos. 2015. "Concentrations of Faith: Mega Churches in Brazil." In *A Moving Faith: Mega Churches Go South*, edited by J. D. James, 169–90. Washington, DC and New Delhi: SAGE Publications.

Stetzer, E. 2014, 24 June. *Hillsong Church at a Glance*. Accessed on 6 November 2015 from http://www.christianitytoday.com/edstetzer/2014/june/closer-look-at-hillsong-church.html

The Holy Bible. 1985. *New American Standard Version (NASB)*. La Habra, CA: The Lockman Foundation.

Tilley, C. 1991. *Material Culture and Text: The Art of Ambiguity*. London: Routledge.

——. 2006. "Objectification: Things and Words." In *Handbook of Material Culture*, edited by C. Tilley, W. Keane, S. Kuchler, M Rowlands, and P. Spyer, 60–62. London: SAGE Publications.

Yip, J. 2015. "Marketing the Sacred: The Case of Hillsong Church, Australia." In *A Moving Faith: Mega Churches Go South*, edited by J. D. James, 106–26. New Delhi and Washington, DC: SAGE Publications.

Williams, L. 2015. *10 Things You Didn't Know About Hillsong UNITED*. Accessed on 10 September 2015 from http://www.gospelmusic.org/blog-10-things-you-didnt-know-about-hillsong-united/

3

Validating Identity, Spirituality, and Space for BAPS Hindus in India and the Diaspora

Introduction

In December 2007, Michael Witty, a senior representative of *The Guinness Book of World Records*, travelled to New Delhi and Ahmedabad (Gujarat) in India to speak at events associated with the Hindu entity called Bochasanwasi Shri Akshar Purushottam Swaminarayan Sanstha (BAPS). After attending the dedication of a BAPS facility in New Delhi, regarded as the largest Hindu temple in the world, Witty moved on to the next BAPS function in Ahmedabad where he remarked:

> [H]aving seen the BAPS organization in London, Delhi and here [Ahmedabad], the volunteers who have given up time for free, [I believe] BAPS does not need Guinness Book of World Records, Guinness Book of World Records needs BAPS. (Kim 2009: 362)

In this chapter, I discuss how BAPS, a sectarian and schismatic branch of Hinduism, has successfully developed in India over the last 120 years and has now expanded into a worldwide movement serving Hindus in India and the diaspora. I start with a brief overview of Hinduism's main theological schools and locate BAPS in the overall scheme of Hinduism. I then identify some of the key elements of this movement by looking at its institutional and regional underpinnings. I argue that the primary motivation for BAPS' growth and expansion is twofold.

First, its revised theological position on reincarnation, which paves the way for devotees to become perfect and attain moksha—release from the endless cycle of rebirths.

Second, its perceived need to define and validate itself as an acceptable faith organization within mainstream Hinduism.

I demonstrate how BAPS validates itself through its own forms of spirituality and the establishment of mega temples. I also show the shifting constructs and contexts that BAPS negotiates and reveal how the movement has cleverly blended neo-Hindu spirituality with capitalism and materiality, as evidenced in its massive temple-building projects.

Hinduism[1]

Hinduism, unlike other world religions, is a faith without a single founder. Neither can followers of the faith point to a definitive text or a central spiritual hierarchy. Recent studies on Hinduism have, therefore, introduced the concept of 'Hinduisms' (Knott 1998; Oddie 2006; Zavos 2012) as a means of explaining the breadth and variety of this faith. However, traditionally, and in practice, Hinduism has been understood as a faith with four broad theological schools—Shaivism, Shaktism, Smartism, and Vaishnavism.

1. In Shaivism, Shiva is the Supreme Being who is creator, preserver, destroyer, and revealer. Shaivism is also known as *Pantha* in Sanskrit. This form of Hinduism is practiced in India and Southeast Asia, especially Indonesia and Cambodia. Devotees strive to become one with Shiva through temple worship and the practice of yoga.[2]
2. Shaktism consists of the worship of Shakti or Devi—the Hindu Mother God. It is popular in the Indian states of Bengal and Assam.[3]
3. Smartism is different from the other schools because it is not bound to the worship of any particular deity. For this reason, Smartism is sometimes referred to as the 'liberal' school within Hinduism. Smartism is usually passed on through one's family, and when a woman marries a Smartist she usually converts to her husband's faith.[4]
4. Vaishnavism is based on the veneration of Vishnu and his 10 avatars including Rama and Krishna. Vishnu is the Supreme Lord in the Hindu *Trimurti* (three images of trinity). Adherents are nonascetic, monastic, and devoted to meditative and ecstatic chanting. Devotional or bhakti worship is prevalent in the Vaishna denomination and its religious texts are based on the Vedas, Upanishads, and the Puranas.[5]

Swaminarayan Hinduism is one of the sects of Vaishnava Hinduism. It was founded by Swami or Swaminarayan (1781–1830), a religious reformer in the Indian state of Gujarat. Swaminarayan Hinduism regards Swaminarayan as the ultimate and perfect manifestation of

God and an incarnation of Vishnu (New World Encyclopedia 2015a). BAPS devotees believe that Swaminarayan is superior to all previous avatars (manifestations of the divine in human beings) but, as we shall see in the forgoing section, BAPS takes this doctrine further.

Prior to his death, Swaminarayan decided to establish a line of acharyas or spiritual overseers as his successors. After his death, several divisions occurred, each with a different perspective on the issue of leadership succession (New World Encyclopedia 2015a).

BAPS—A Schism Within This Sect

BAPS schismatic sect within Swaminarayan Hinduism (Figure 3.1) and the history of the organization bears witness to this fact. BAPS began when Shastriji Maharaj (born in 1865 as Dungar Patel) felt a strong leaning to promote a mode of worship that was based on the teachings of Swaminarayan who focused on devotional Hinduism called bhakti (Kim 2009). Maharaj's early efforts to propagate his interpretation of the faith were met with opposition from Vaishnava teachers and others hostile to Swaminarayan's bhakti teachings (Dave 2013; Kim 2009). In an effort to continue the practice of the Swami's teachings amidst growing opposition, some of the devotees attempted to revise Swaminarayan's teachings, omitting the disagreeable elements. However, in time, Maharaj was bold enough to reveal the fullness of Swaminarayan's teachings, which asserted that Swaminarayan and his closest devotee, Gunatitanand Swami, were essentially *Purushottam* (divine being) and *Akshar* (the abode of the divine being), respectively (Kim 2009). This controversial teaching about this doctrine was met with opposition from devotees and leaders who belonged to the Vartal[6] diocese (Kim 2009; Williams 2001). As the opposition mounted, physical violence took place and eventually Shastriji Maharaj and his followers were forced to leave the Vartal group (one of the two dioceses in Gujarat). This was the inauspicious beginning of the new movement—BAPS.

The theological basis of BAPS rests on the doctrine of *Akshar Purushottam* whereby followers worship Swaminarayan as God (*Purushottam*), and Swaminarayan's choicest devotee Gunatitanand Swami as *Akshar*—the divine abode of God. The concept of *Akshar* has been interpreted variously by Swaminarayan denominations.

Figure 3.1:

Where BAPS fits into the scheme of Hinduism

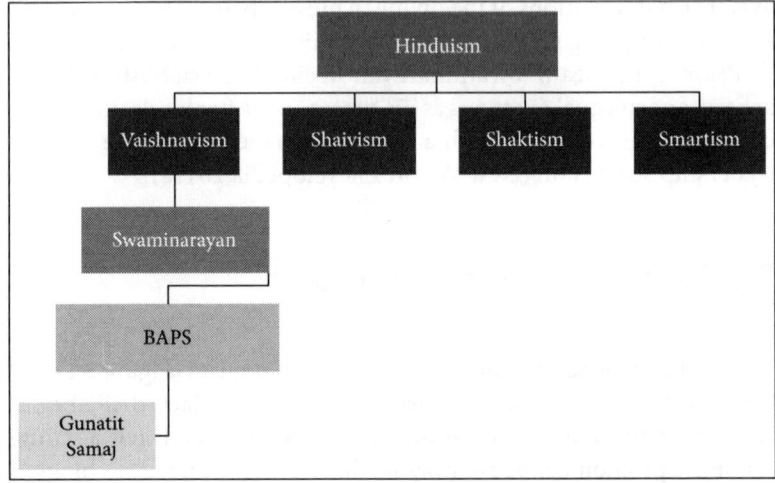

Source: James (2016).

The Swaminarayan *Sampraday*, the regional decision-making body in the cities of Vadtal, and Ahmedabad believes *Akshar* to be the divine abode of the supreme entity *Purushottam* (Kurien 2007). The BAPS denomination goes a step further to teach that *Akshar* is "an eternally existing spiritual reality having two forms, **the impersonal and the personal**" (Williams 2001: 8). Furthermore, BAPS claims that Gunatitanand Swami, the successor of Swaminarayan, was believed to be the first personal manifestation of *Akshar* and he started a spiritual line of 'perfect devotees' who provide "authentication of office through Gunatitanand Swami and back to Swaminarayan himself" (Williams 2001: 86). The Vadtal and Ahmedabad dioceses of the Swaminarayan Sampraday do not subscribe to this teaching (Williams 2001: 55–60). BAPS believes that the entity of *Akshar* continues in this world through a succession of 'perfect devotees', namely the spiritual leaders or gurus of the organization (Figure 3.2). These leaders are believed to continue spiritual succession through Gunatitanand Swami who is traced to Swaminarayan himself.[7] Therefore, Pramukh Swami Maharaj (born in 1921), the current leader of BAPS, is regarded as the personification of *Akshar*, and Swaminarayan is present on earth through Pramukh Swami Maharaj. The living guru, and the continuing manifestation of God in the guru leaders, is what BAPS is all about.

Figure 3.2:

The spiritual hierarchy of BAPS

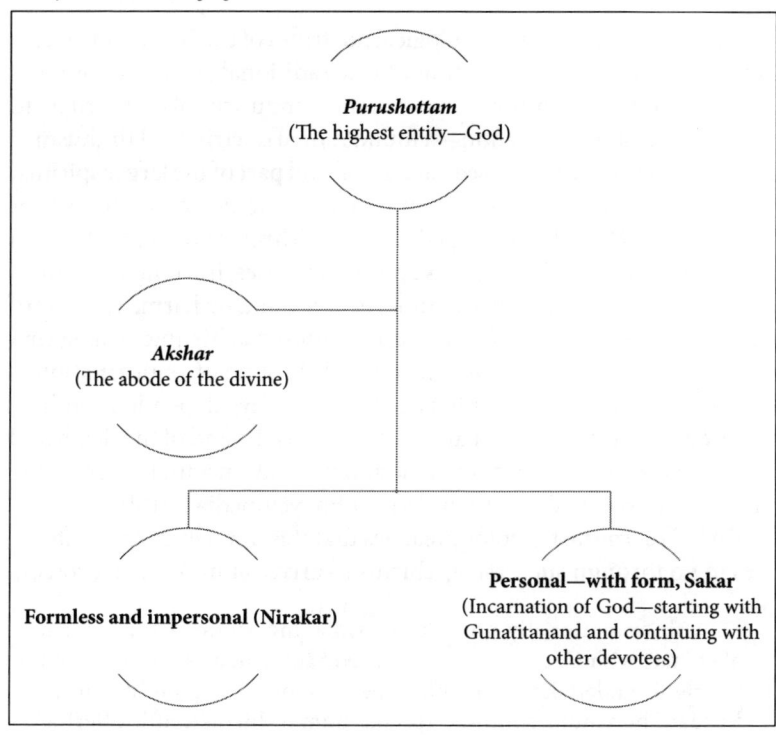

Source: James (2016).

Hence, *Akshar Purushottam* is the main doctrine and forms the two middle names of BAPS (Bochasanwasi Shri Akshar Purushottam Swaminarayan Sanstha).

Gunatit Samaj, a splinter group from BAPS, was established in 1966 (Figure 3.1); this group believes that Gunatitanand, the closest devotee of Swaminarayan, is the true successor of the movement. Gunatit Samaj also had a major disagreement with BAPS on the place of women in the temple activities. BAPS is male-dominated and has clear rules separating women from men in temple activities, such as: Sadhus are strongly advised not to even look at women. Gunatit Samaj, now a worldwide movement in its own right, has a more inclusive approach to women joining its ranks as ascetics and close devotees unlike BAPS (Williams 2001).

Revised Theology and Practices

One of the distinguishing theological doctrines of the BAPS movement is based on a new interpretation of the traditional Hindu teaching of reincarnation. For centuries, most of the Hindu schools subscribed to the doctrine of reincarnation—a foundational doctrine of Hinduism—in which the soul, which is seen as eternal and part of the larger spiritual realm, returns to the physical realm in a new body—either human or animal (New World Encyclopedia 2015b). Through reincarnation, an individual soul will undergo this cycle many times, learning new things and growing each time. In a lifetime, people build up karma (the law of cause and effect), based on their actions within that lifetime. This karma affects their future lives and existence. This cycle of reincarnation is called samsara and its next incarnation is always dependent on how the previous life was lived (karma). Moksha is the end of the death and rebirth cycle, and it signifies release and unification with Brahma—the ultimate source of all life (New World Encyclopedia 2015b).

BAPS' revisionist theology teaches that it is not necessary for devotees to go through successive rebirths to arrive at moksha. Devotees:

> ... with exceptionally good karmas, having attained some form of contact with God or the God-realized Sādhu, maybe released from having to undertake birth within the cycle of 8.4 million life forms. Instead, he would continue to take human births until, offering devotion to God, he earns the pleasure of God or the God-realised Sādhu and attains moksha.[8]

In one of his speeches, Pramukh Swami Maharaj, the current BAPS leader, said:

> On the path of moksha, serving at the wrong place is like trying to pass through a wall by banging one's head against it. It is not possible. But if one uses the door one can easily pass through; the God-realized Sadhu is the doorway to moksha. Pleasing such a Sadhu pleases God. Serving such a Sadhu bears fruit because he has no worldly desires, no wish for worldly fame or glory. (BAPS Swaminarayan Sanstha 2000c)

Therefore, BAPS believes that followers can transcend what it considers the miserable and perpetual cycle of rebirth. This is the attraction of BAPS.

Swaminarayan taught that the mind is often swayed by desires that would impede the devotee's release from samsara—the endless cycle of rebirths (Kim 2013). But if the mind and body were reshaped through discipline and useful action, the devotee will be freed from the cares of this world thus enabling moksha—release from the cycle of rebirths (Kim 2013). The teaching of *Akshar* plays a critical role in the overall scheme of ultimate liberation (Dave 2012). Swaminarayan's manifestation as *Purushottam* through the personal form of *Akshar* means that all BAPS devotees would be guided and helped both in this life and in the final release of their souls from the endless cycle of rebirths (Kim 2013).

To ensure this release from rebirth, devotees must adhere to the prescribed practices. *Nitya Puja* (daily prayer) is a daily devotional worship that entails a prayer ritual performed every morning. Devotees may recite a Sanskrit verse and invite Swaminarayan and *Akshar* to be present at their puja. This practice helps devotees to clear their minds, resulting in a calming effect on them. *Seva*, a stint of voluntary work for the benefit the community, is another BAPS requirement for devotees. Both these practices are pleasing to *Akshar* and *Purushottam*. Whereas social and relief efforts are encouraged, most of the voluntary work by BAPS members seems to be focused on the building of BAPS temples worldwide. Volunteers take time off and travel to overseas locations to help build in their area of expertise. BAPS has built a record number of mandirs, which are Hindu places of worship and centers for social and cultural activities. The BAPS Shri Swaminarayan Mandir was completed in Atlanta, Georgia in August 2007 within a record time of 17 months, primarily because of the sacred *seva* (service) of volunteers 'utilizing 1.3 million volunteer hours'.[9]

BAPS has registered its charitable arm as a nongovernmental organization (NGO) affiliated with the UN, and it holds general consultative status with the United Nations Economic and Social Council.[10]

The Institutional Location in Gujarat

Swaminarayan was born with the name Ghanshyam Pande in Chhapaiya, Uttar Pradesh, India in 1781. In 1792, he began his pilgrimage across India, and later settled in the state of Gujarat around 1799. In 1800, he was initiated into the Uddhav Sampraday[11] by his guru Ramanand Swami and was given the name Sahajanand Swami. In 1802, his guru handed over the leadership of the Uddhav Sampraday to him. Through this office, Swaminarayan introduced reformed teachings on Hinduism. After his death, the Swaminarayan Sampraday continued in two dioceses and splits took place within the organization and BAPS is one of the groups that emerged from such a split.

BAPS is described as a socio-spiritual organization, with 3,850 centers worldwide and more than 1 million followers:

> ... with its roots in the Vedas ... [BAPS is] founded on the pillars of practical spirituality, the BAPS reaches out far and wide to address the spiritual, moral and social challenges and issues faced in our world....[12]

It was founded in 1907 in Bochasan, Gujarat and was restricted to servicing Gujaratis until it expanded its spiritual operations to East Africa in 1969 because of the large numbers of Gujarati immigrants there.[13]

Its main nexus remains as Bochasan in Gujarat where the first stone temple was built; however, the world BAPS movement is administered from Ahmedabad in Gujarat, India by a board of trustees, with the spiritual head holding the twin roles of administrative president and religious head.

For many Indians, historically, Gujarat emanates a lot of religious sentiments. It was in this state that communal violence erupted between Hindus and Muslims and spiraled out of control, with clashes lasting for months. What was even more troubling was the fact that the violence reeked of the state government's involvement in favor of the Hindu majority (Jaffrelot 2007). Gujarat, a stronghold of the ruling BJP party, has also been seen as a testing ground for the nation of India especially in the context of the controversial issue of communalism and the BJP's vision of a Hindu *rashtra* (Hindu nation; Sinha 2014).[14]

Vijayakumar (2015) argued that BAPS temples are sites for a grand revision of Hindu devotional practices and their underlying meanings, which are informed by the historical reality of centuries of colonial and Islamic rule that in part led to India's partition. However, this assertion needs further substantiation. In fact, it would appear that BAPS has distanced itself from these past issues of communalism and nationalism to stay focused on the spirituality of its Hindu reformed faith.

Gujarat is also home to the Patel caste[15]—mainly landed peasants who prospered in farming to such an extent that they now control almost all the vital segments of the state's economy in trade, industry, and business enterprise. Gujaratis, like the Patel families, have also travelled and migrated to the West; and hence, the formation of BAPS in the countries outside of India mainly follows Gujarati migration patterns. BAPS' entry to countries beyond India started when Gujaratis immigrated to the former British colonies in Africa—Kenya, Tanzania, and Uganda (Dwyer 2004). Invariably, BAPS communities were started there in the late 1950s and soon temples were built. After the Africanization policy in the late 1960s, many Gujaratis began migrating to the United Kingdom, Canada, and then later to the United States; hence, BAPS began to blossom in these new lands (Dwyer 2004). The wealth and business acumen of Gujarati families, like the Patels, is a key reason for the rapid growth, expansion, and massive building programs of the movement worldwide.

Therefore, it is fair to say that BAPS originated as a regional sect, then it became a national entity, and now it is a transnational movement.

Most of the 1 million followers worldwide are of Gujarati background and 970 are guru leaders—men called sadhus—who have taken vows of celibacy (Figure 3.3). Rigorous study, culminating in examinations, is required before sadhus can be formally initiated into leadership.

BAPS is a purist group and has strict prohibitions. For example, all adherents take a lifetime vow, which includes "No alcohol, No addictions, No adultery, No meat, No impurity of body and mind as their five vows. Such pure morality and spirituality forms the foundation of the humanitarian services performed by BAPS."[16]

At the apex of the BAPS organizational structure (Figure 3.3) is the current spiritual and administrative leader Pramukh Swami Maharaj. Below him are the 970[17] sadhus, followed by volunteer followers (around 55,000). At the base of the organizational pyramid are the devotees who carefully negotiate a purist lifestyle. Devotees called *satsangis* meet to sing *bhajans* (spiritual hymns) and listen to lessons based on two texts—Vachanamrut and Swamini Vato. There is also a BAPS code of conduct contained in a book called *Shikshapatri*, which consists of 212 verses with injunctions that include dietary rules, such as avoiding garlic, onions, intoxicants, and the like.[18] Life in a BAPS

Figure 3.3:

The organization of BAPS

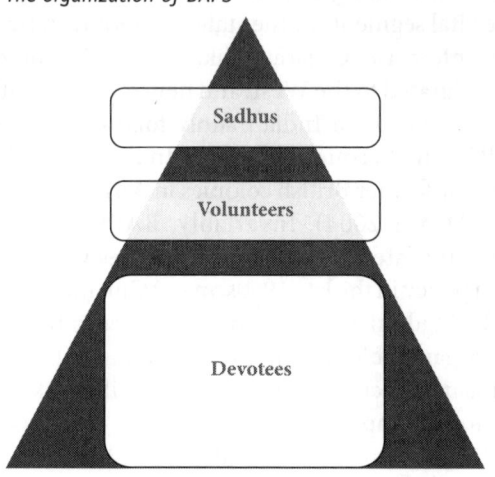

Source: James (2016).

community also includes strict rules of engagement between males and females, and behavior at home and at the temples. The Gujarati language is important for active participation in temple worship, although teachings and texts are also available in Hindi and English—especially for devotees outside of India.

Anyone who attends the weekly assemblies at the nearest mandir (temple), or participates in the daily *arti* (worship) and follows the precepts and codes of conduct prescribed by Swaminarayan is considered to be a follower of BAPS.[19]

In answer to a question on whether women can take the role of sadhus (a male-dominated office), the current spiritual leader, Pramukh Swami Maharaj answered:

> No, Lord Swaminarayan has not given any such *agna* [ruling], so we do not accept ladies as *sahdvis*. However, they may be initiated as *sankhya yogis*. These are mostly widows or women who wish not to marry and … who remain in the *agna* [spiritual covering] of their parents or brothers and stay in the ladies' temple to spend their days engrossed in bhakti [devotion]. But as *sankhya yogis*, not *sadhvis*.[20]

BAPS's Hinduism is monotheistic and exclusive: there is only one divine being, one continuing revelation through the living BAPS leader and one way for followers to attain eternal bliss according to Swaminarayan.

> There can be only one such Satpurush [living incarnation of God]. Shriji Maharaj manifests only through Aksharbraman and eternal Aksharbraman is only one. God's manifestation is naturally, therefore, though one. A King may have more than one son, but only one ... inherits the throne. (Akshar Puroshottam Upasana 2012: 96)

Opulence and Materiality

In the twenty-first century, BAPS temples have increasingly become postmodern sites of capitalism, consumption and tourism, as well as places to reinforce neo-Hindu beliefs and practices for devotees. The Swaminarayan Akshardham complex (SAC) in New Delhi, supposedly the biggest temple in the world, attracts more than 2,000 visitors and tourists on a week day and more than 5,000 on weekends (Brosius 2010). Interestingly, the BAPS leaders who built SAC by the banks of the historic Yamuna river failed to get the usual clearances from the local environment Ministry: "serious concerns were set aside ... the state bent backwards and broke its own laws" (Nanda 2009: 135). However, no penalties were imposed, and SAC's opening of the temple was unhindered. The lack of environmental clearance and penalty could be due to the fact that the authorities view the temple as a commercial enterprise. It is no secret that SAC is treated as a tourist destination by the Delhi Tourism who describe it as a monument that:

> ... epitomizes 10,000 years of Indian culture in all its breathtaking grandeur, beauty, wisdom and bliss. It brilliantly showcases the essence of India's ancient architecture, traditions and timeless spiritual messages.... The Swaminarayan Akshardham complex was built in only five years through the blessings of HDH Pramukh Swami Maharaj ... and the colossal devotional efforts of 11,000 artisans and thousands of BAPS volunteers....[21]

Seventy percent of visitors are followers of Hindu beliefs including the BAPS faith. The SAC is located in 60 acres of land with a temple, buildings, themed landscaped gardens, a musical fountain, a cafeteria, shops, and an IMAX theatre. The temple charges an entrance fee and on top of that there are ticketed events such as exhibitions, demonstrations, tours, as well as the large food court and picnic grounds. In the week days, there are lectures and classes.

Visitors to SAC worship, gain more information of Swaminarayan through multimedia presentations, and witness the musical fountain at sunset and sunrise; both these times are considered holy times for Hindus and so the fountain is intentionally built to fit in with Hindu practices and beliefs (James 2010).

However, SAC has not been accepted by all. For example, it has invited critical responses from scholars such as Vijayakumar (2015), who questions this new kind of religious experience that blends Western high tech media with ancient devotionalism and turns "sacred spaces into 'spectacles' through an uninhibited adoption of entertainment technology and an unmistakable touch of Disney" (Vijayakumar 2015: 1).

Temples are significant for every Hindu but for BAPS members the temple takes on additional significance, pointing to identity and legitimacy. Festivals are the times when the temples become 'larger than life' sites. The temples are filled to capacity during festivals such as Vasant Panchami, a Hindu festival celebrating the advent of spring but for BAPS, this festival has added significance, as it points to the time when Swaminarayan compiled the sacred code—*Shikshapatri*. During the Diwali festival,[22] these temples are transformed into Indian cultural centers where week-long celebrations showcase Hindu art, images, and color in a spectacular manner using multimedia presentations. BAPS temples reinforce the faith and reify neo-Hinduism[23] at home as well as outside India. When the BAPS Bochasan temple celebrated its centenary as the first BAPS temple in Gujarat in April 2007, a grand Vedic *yagna* (worship according to the Vedas, the Hindu scriptures) was held in Bochasan, graced by the presence of the BAPS leader Pramukh Swami and some 20,000 devotees.[24]

Most of the BAPS temples are made of marble and handcrafted in the most intricate design and religious artistry. In London, half a million pilgrims and tourists visit the magnificent BAPS Neasden Temple every year. Built in 1995, this BAPS temple was constructed entirely from marble and limestone.[25]

The first traditional Hindu mandir in Africa was built by BAPS in Nairobi, Kenya. It boasts of being constructed entirely from intricately carved wood.[26] BAPS continues to break its own records in its large-scale temple-building projects. Currently the world's largest Hindu temple outside of India is a BAPS temple in Robbinsville, New Jersey (USA). It is a 162-acre complex built with the help of 2,000 artisans in Rajasthan (India) who handcrafted the designs in Italian and Rajasthani marble. The finished pieces were then assembled in New Jersey by a team of master craftsmen (Wang 2014; Yagniki 2014). Previous to this, the largest temple was a BAPS temple built in the Bible Belt region of Atlanta, Georgia (USA) occupying 30 acres at a cost of US$90 million.

The affluence and wealth of the BAPS movement has invited scholarly concerns about its underlying motivations (Brosius 2010, 2012). Certainly there is a definite disjunction between the current display of wealth and materiality and the original BAPS teachings. Swaminarayan's teachings are clear that his followers are to take the five vows and to "forswear all worldly goods and all concerns of this world. They are not even to possess any article made of metal...." (Williams 2001: 20–21). Brosius (2012) pointed out that village visitors to SAC in New Delhi were overwhelmed by the flagrant display of modern technology at the temple—for some, this was the first time they saw change machines (for money) or lawn-watering machines.

The conspicuous materiality of the temples has situated BAPS as a prestigious sociocultural faith community and one definitely associated with middle class wealth. This, according to Brosius (2012), encourages a modern-day form of sensitization, a term used by the sociologist Srinivas (1952) to refer to the lower classes in India who desire to move up in the social and economic ladder by joining appropriate groups.

Brosius acknowledged that BAPS attracts people of all classes, but he argued that some come into the movement to draw on the "well-oiled social and professional networks of the members" (Brosius 2010: 166). And there is no doubt that the global network of the movement has created a transnational religious grouping known not only for its faith but for its socioeconomic status and opportunity.

From his study of the movement in Fiji, Kelly (1988) defended BAPS' infatuation with materiality, by asserting that bhakti devotionalism and capitalism are 'two influential grammars' and that Gujaratis 'relate to God through capital' (Kelly 1988: 5). However, the opulence and the magnitude of the temple-building projects continue to disturb both Hindu devotees and scholars alike.

A Habitus for Diaspora Hindus

Foucault (1926–84) concluded that power in society was 'ubiquitous' and beyond agency or structure, and Bourdieu (1930–2002) saw power as cultural creations using symbolic representations to relegitimize itself (Gaventa 2003). According to the latter, the principal means for the creation of power is what he calls 'habitus' or socialized norms that reinforce behavior and thinking. Habitus is "the way society becomes deposited in persons in the form of lasting dispositions, or trained capacities and structured propensities to think, feel and act in determinant ways, which then guide them" (Navarro 2006: 16). Habitus is enduring and transferrable from one context to another; "it is not fixed or permanent, and can be changed under unexpected situations or over a long historical period" (Navarro 2006: 16).

Arguably, BAPS' habitus is primarily defined by the devotional life of its devotees who enter into a lifelong worship experience out of intense gratitude to the living guru who takes the form of *Akshar* and is linked to Swaminarayan who is *Purushottam* or the divine being. From Gujarat, the Hindu reformed movement has transported its ideas and practices to major cities in the world where BAPS followers are found. So, American Hindu Indians from all sectors of society meet weekly in one of the 100 mandirs (temples) in the United States to gain the path of bliss.

> The central religious tenet for BAPS satsangis is bhakti, or devotion to God. Bhakti, when combined with dharma, gnan (spiritual knowledge), and vairagya (detachment), leads to one becoming an ideal devotee, or an ekantik bhakta. This is achieved in the BAPS Swaminarayan Sanstha by devoting oneself to God as per the example set by the guru. The guru is the ideal bhakta of God; hence, the guru guides spiritual aspirants on the path to spiritual bliss, a state that he enjoys continuously.[27]

BAPS devotees are also encouraged to participate in the early morning puja, a prayer time that particularly includes Swaminarayan and his living *Akshar*, Pramukh Swami Maharaj.

> The word 'puja' comes from the Sanskrit word 'puj', meaning to worship or to adore. A devotee can communicate with God during daily puja and convey one's concerns and feelings directly to God. Puja helps an individual concentrate on the divine murti of God and his Gunatit sadhu.[28]

Arranged marriages still prevail within the BAPS community but in the case of the diaspora BAPS families, parents may not have to look to India for brides for their sons because the community of Indians in the West may provide what they need. Social gatherings organized by the temples cater for this. However, strict observance is upheld in temple worship where males and females are seated separately even in the Western countries. Ballard's (1994) study of diaspora Indians revealed the concept of what he termed *Desh Pardesh*—the activity of Indian groups reconstructing their own norms and habitus from their homelands in newly settled areas, to give them a sense of belonging, self-respect, and acceptance.

BAPS members are involved in social service (*seva*) and as noted in the previous section, I pointed out how *seva* has been linked to BAPS' view of reincarnation. However, social service is also a form of transnational citizenship in the diverse areas where BAPS operates, thus enhancing globalized partnerships (Brosius 2010, 2012).

Whereas BAPS' authenticity was contested in India, especially in the early days of its formation, it is now accepted in the West and furthermore it is presented as mainline Hinduism to non-Hindus and even some diaspora Hindus. Peach and Gale (2003) have shown how Western landscapes are changing, primarily because the value of Western tolerance has brought about a new engagement with the exotic and mystical aspects of Eastern religions.

The first wave of Indian migration to the United States took place in the 1960s when migrants sought to congregate in large cities such as Chicago, Houston, and New York. The early Indian immigrant generation focused on India, and Hindu meetings were held in the homes of Hindus. However, the second generation of Hindus seems to be motivated by the urge to articulate their faith as a way of life to Americans. Their desire is not so much to win converts (Hinduism is not known for its 'missionary' intent) but "it's about making their faith less exotic to others while making it more meaningful to their own modern American lives" (Gilgoff 2011).

Therefore, BAPS' purist Hinduism is still observed by Hindu Indians in America—at home, in the temple, and in social and recreational spheres of life. BAPS Hindus are still Hindu in faith but they are also engaged with the broader American culture and in the process forging a distinctly American Hindu identity that is interwoven into the national fabric.

Negotiating Other Cultures and Systems

From colonial days, Swaminarayan was an astute student of cultures, and he made regular contacts with colonial rulers, including the Governor of Gujarat and the Bishop of the Anglican Church.[29] He kept records of all correspondence, especially letters of commendation from British officials. This practice of keeping records has continued.

BAPS' foray into global contexts has gained recognition, commendations, and awards from secular, media, and government officials and has successfully positioned the movement positively in the public sphere. On 8 July 2000, representatives from the Guinness World Records presented the current leader of BAPS, Pramukh Swami Maharaj, with certificates marking his entries into the world famous record book (BAPS 2000a).

In October 2000, Pramukh Swami Maharaj was warmly welcomed to the US House of Representatives and just prior to that, he addressed the UN-sponsored Millennium Peace summit at the UN headquarters in New York (BAPS Swaminarayan Sanstha 2000b). In November 2005, the former president of India A. P. J. Abdul Kalam, the former prime minister Dr Manmohan Singh, and the former leader of opposition Lal Krishna Advani, together with the BAPS leader Pramukh Swami Maharaj, inaugurated Swaminarayan Akshardham in New Delhi, India.[30] In 2007, Pramukh Swami Maharaj was awarded the Guinness World Record for a single individual inaugurating the largest number of Hindu temples worldwide (Kim 2016).

BAPS has negotiated the discursive practices of local councils in Western nations where its plan to build BAPS temples was many a times contested by local residents and government officials. Kim (2012) documented how BAPS' failed attempt to receive temple-building approval from the East Windsor Council in the United States enabled the leadership to take great pains in submitting the application for the Robbinsville temple in New Jersey, USA. BAPS was armed with a team of lawyers, experts in engineering, architecture, environment, traffic, and BAPS Hinduism. Kim remarked that even the engineering and other experts not related to Hinduism made reference to the religious aspects of the BAPS movement (Kim 2012). They focused on similarities of their faith with Western conceptions of faith in an effort to be more appealing: "BAPS translated its Hindu tradition to fit the contours of a universalized conception of religion" in dealing with the Robbinsville Planning Board (Kim 2012: 419). All this reflects a potpourri of cross-cultural skills (legal, political, cultural, and regional) that BAPS has amassed at negotiating new public spheres.

Conclusion

From one temple in Gujarat, BAPS has become a global movement reaching millions of people around the world with more than 800 mandirs and 3,850 centers.

BAPS is a reformed Hindu movement, which traces its roots to the illustrious Hindu reformer Swaminarayan. BAPS is a subset of the Swaminarayan organization, based on its controversial belief that since Swaminarayan's death, he has become *Purushottam* (God) and his successors are *Akshar* or the incarnation of God. Swaminarayan adapted the best of the religious traditions known to him to create "a new ... sacred world [revitalizing] the experience of sacred person, sacred space and sacred time" (Williams 2001: 100–01).

Since its inception in 1907, BAPS has had to define itself not only to its followers but to its contenders—the Vaishna Hindu School, other Hindu organizations, the colonial administration, and also more recently, to government officials and the general public in Western countries where BAPS has rapidly established itself. Its prolific and massive temple-building projects are in part motivated by the need to authenticate itself in the face of its new ideological framework within Hinduism. The wealth of the Gujarati followers enables BAPS' dreams to be fulfilled as a transnational Hindu organization. BAPS members' high involvement in social and voluntary work could be attributed to BAPS' doctrine that sacred works can save devotees from the endless cycle of rebirths and bring moksha.

Despite having attained the status of a transnational movement, BAPS' organizational philosophy and structure may need to be continually changed and sharpened to reach and sustain its worldwide membership. Meaning-making in diasporic contexts is a continuous struggle to ensure that the movement is reproducing itself in its changing environments.

BAPS has successfully established a Hindu habitus for its followers in India and in the West for the diaspora Indians. The key challenge for BAPS is that its intersection with capitalism and materiality may mean that over time, the spiritual foundations of the movement slowly erode and BAPS becomes merely what it is now categorizes itself as 'a worldwide civic and religious movement' and 'a socio-spiritual group' (Kim 2012: 419).

Another possible challenge BAPS will face in the coming years is whether it can sustain its purist Hindu teachings as new generations of Hindus are born in the United States, Canada, the United Kingdom, and other Western nations; in all likelihood, future Hindus will become immersed with the prevailing cultures of the day and lose their connection to Gujarat—the spiritual headquarters of BAPS. If so, McCarthy Brown's (2008) description of what she terms the 'cosmologistical problem'—practicing religion which is linked to a place when the followers are no longer in that place—may be relevant to the BAPS movement.

Notes

1. Knott's definition of Hinduism is becoming more accepted in religious studies circles.

> Hinduism defies our desire to define and categorize it. It is both a dynamic phenomenon of the modern world, evolving from the combined imaginations of many individuals and groups, Hindu and non-Hindu, and the sum of its many parts—its traditions, myths, Institutions, rituals, and ideas—its many Hinduisms. It has the power and diversity to capture the imaginations of Hindus and non-Hindus alike,

and the capacity to challenge all preconceived ideas about what a religion is. (Knott 1998: 117)

2. See https://www.himalayanacademy.com/readlearn/basics/four-sects
3. Ibid.
4. Ibid.
5. The Vedas are the primary texts of Hinduism. There are four main Vedas and they contain hymns, incantations, and rituals for Hindu living. The Upanishads are a continuation of the Vedic tradition. This is where the teaching on the possibility of the soul's unification with Brahman is mentioned. The Puranas are post-Vedic texts. They contain narratives of the history of the universe from creation to destruction. Also, see https://www.himalayanacademy.com/readlearn/basics/four-sects
6. Vartal is a town in Gujarat where BAPS has deep and historic connections.
7. See http://www.swaminarayan.org/lordswaminarayan/
8. See http://www.swaminarayan.org/faq/bapsgeneral.htm#3 (para 9).
9. This BAPS temple is constructed with three types of stone—Turkish Limestone, Italian marble, and Indian pink sandstone. "More than 34,000 individual pieces were carved by hand in India, shipped to the USA and assembled in Lilburn like a giant 3-D puzzle." See http://www.baps.org/Global-Network/North-America/Atlanta/Visitor-Info.aspx
10. BAPS Charities (formerly BAPS Care International) is an international nonreligious, charitable organization. Its focus on service to society is stated in the organization's vision statement that "every individual deserves the right to a peaceful, dignified, and healthy way of life. And by improving the quality of life of the individual, we are bettering families, communities, our world, and our future" (See: http://www.bapscharities.org/, accessed on 5 May 2016).

    BAPS Charities carries out this vision through a several development programs which include health, education, the environment, and natural disaster recovery.
11. *Sampraday* can be translated as a spiritual order, tradition, or a religious system. It relates to a succession of masters and disciples, which ensures stability to the religious order.
12. See http://www.baps.org/Spiritual-Living.aspx
13. See http://www.baps.org/About-BAPS/TheFounder%E2%80%93BhagwanSwaminarayan/Life/Timeline.aspx
14. The concept of a *rashtra* is usually related to the *Hindutva* vision of an India for Hindus only. However, Sinha (2014) argues that the connotation is actually inclusive in its origin and does not necessarily allude to a Hindu theocratic state. The etymology of the *rashtra* is from the Hindu legendary Bharat, the son of Shakuntala and Dushyant. Therefore, in terms of epistemology, the term 'Bharat' is more religious than Hindu (see Sinha 2014).
15. The founder of BAPS Shastriji Maharaj was of the Patel caste. His birth name was Dungar Patel.
16. See http://www.baps.org/Spiritual-Living.aspx
17. This was the number of sadhus in 2014. As examinations are held regularly, more sadhus are initiated upon the successful completion of all the requirements.

18. The Shikshapatri is a key scripture to all followers of Swaminarayan followers and the BAPS community. It is considered the basis of the sect. The Shikshapatri was written in Vadtal in 1826. It is a dharma text, providing detailed instructions on how to live a spiritually uplifting life. Originally written in Gujarati, it is available in Hindi and English. There is also a digital version.
19. See http://www.swaminarayan.org/faq/bapsgeneral.htm#3
20. The place of women is a contested topic in BAPS. Although there is strong evidence for concluding that women and men are not equal, the concept of inequality in BAPS does not necessarily indicate subordination or domination by one gender over the other. Women often find ways to negotiate their own forms of power in different roles which at time seem equally as important as those forms of power traditionally held by men (Rudert 2004). BAPS has taken pains to shed off these negative perceptions by hosting women's conventions and other such activities. See http://www.swaminarayan.org/pramukhswami/searchingquestions/156.htm
21. See http://www.indiatourismecatalog.com/india_states_travel_guide/delhi/delhi_akshardham.html
22. Diwali, also spelt in two other ways: Diwali or Deepavali, is an ancient Hindu festival known as the festival of lights. It is usually celebrated in autumn in the Northern hemisphere and in spring in the Southern hemisphere.
23. Neo-Hinduism is a label that has been in use since the 1950s. Earlier labelling of 'Neo-Hindu' was already in existence prior to the 1950s but it was used more in a pejorative way. In 1893, critics of Swami Vivekananda questioned his faithfulness to Hindu traditions by calling his methods neo-Hindu. Contemporary scholars use the term variously, but in essence the term depicts the blending of Hinduism with modern concepts and ideas, that is, new religious movements that have arisen within Hinduism.
24. See http://www.swaminarayan.org/lordswaminarayan/
25. See http://www.sacred-destinations.com/england/london-neasden-temple
26. See http://www.baps.org/Global-Network/North-America/Atlanta/Visitor-Info.aspx
27. See http://www.baps.org/Spiritual-Living.aspx (para 3).
28. See http://www.baps.org/cultureandheritage/Traditions/HinduPractices/Puja.aspx (para 1).
29. Bishop Heber and Sir John Malcolm were some of the first colonial leaders to be acquainted with Swaminarayan. Swaminarayan also influenced Professor Monier Williams of Oxford University and later India's great social reformer and activist—Mahatma Gandhi (*Swaminarayan Bliss* 2009: 32). *Swaminarayan Bliss* is a collection of archived articles available from https://www.swaminarayan.org/publications/magazine/bliss/archive.htm
30. See http://www.hinduismtoday.com/modules/smartsection/item.php?itemid=1481 (para 1).

References

Akshar Purushottam Upasana . 2012. *Akshar Purushottam Upasana* (3rd edition). Ahmedabad: BAPS.

Ballard, R. 1994. *Desh Pardesh: The South Asian Presence in Britain.* London: C. Hurst.

BAPS Swaminarayan Sanstha. 2000a. *Guinness World Records Honors HDH.* Accessed on 10 May 2016 from http://www.baps.org/News/2000/Guinness-World-Records-Honors-HDH-Pramukh-Swami-Maharaj-for-Two-World-Records-3288.aspx

———. 2000b. *Millennium World Summit.* Accessed on 19 May 2016 from http://www.swaminarayan.org/news/2000/08/peacesummit/

———. 2000c. *Swami Addresses Peace Summit.* Accessed on 1 May 2016 from http://www.baps.org/About-BAPS/TheCurrentSpiritualGuru-PramukhSwamiMaharaj/Speeches.aspx

Brosius, C. 2010. *India's Middle Class: New Forms of Urban Leisure, Consumption and Prosperity.* London: Routledge.

———. 2012. "The Perfect World of BAPS: Media and Urban Dramaturgies in a Globalised Context." In *Public Hinduisms,* edited by J. Zavos, P. Kanungo, D. S. Reddy, M. Warrier, and R. B. Williams, 440–62. New Delhi: SAGE Publications.

Dave, K. 2012. *Akshar Purushottam Upasana as Revealed by Bhagwan Swaminarayan.* Ahmedabad: Swaminarayan Aksharpith.

Dwyer, R. 2004. "The Swaminarayan Movement." In *South Asians in the Diaspora: Histories and Religious Traditions,* edited by K. A. Jacobsen and P. Kumar, 180–99. Leiden: Brill.

Gaventa, J. 2003. *Power After Lukes: An Overview of Theories of Power Since Lukes and Their Application to Development.* Unpublished paper. Brighton: Participation Group, Institute of Development Studies.

Gilgoff, D. 2011. "In Texas, Young Hindus Want to Americanize Ancient Faith." *CNN Religion Blog.* Accessed on 7 May 2016 from http://religion.blogs.cnn.com/2011/07/10/in-texas-young-hindus-want-to-americanize-ancient-faith/

Jaffrelot, C. 2007. *Hindu Nationalism: A Reader.* New Jersey: Princeton University Press.

James, J. D. 2010. *McDonaldisation, Masala McGospel and Om Economics: Televangelism in Contemporary India.* New Delhi: SAGE Publications.

Kelly, J. 1988. *Bhakti and the Spirit of Capitalism: The Ontology of the Indians of Fiji.* PhD. Dissertation. Chicago, IL: University of Chicago.

Kim, H. H. 2009. "Public Engagement and Personal Desires: BAPS Swaminarayan Temples and Their Contributions to the Discourses on Religion." *International Journal of Hindu Studies* 13(3): 357–90.

———. 2012. "The BAPS Swaminarayan Temple Organization and its Publics." In *Public Hinduisms,* edited by J. Zavos, P. Kanungo, D. S. Reddy, M. Warrier, and R. Williams, 417–39. New Delhi: SAGE Publications.

———. 2013. "Devotional Expressions in the BAPS Swaminarayan Community." In *Contemporary Hinduism,* edited by P. P. Kumar. London: Routledge.

———. 2016. "Transnational Movements." In *Hinduism in the Modern World,* edited by B. A. Hatcher, 48–64. New York, NY: Routledge.

Knott, K. 1998. *Hinduism: A Very Short Introduction*. Oxford: Oxford University Press.

Kurien, P. 2007. *A Place at the Multicultural Table: The Development of American Hinduism*. New Brunswick, NJ: Rutgers University Press.

McCarthy Brown, K. 2008. "Staying Grounded in a High-rise Building: Ecological Dissonance and Ritual Accommodation in Haitian Vodou." In *Gods of the City: Religion and American Landscape*, edited by R. A. Orsi, 79–102. Bloomington, IN: Indiana University Press.

Nanda, M. 2009. *The God Market: How Globalization is Making India More Hindu*. New York, NY: Monthly Review Press.

Navarro, Z. 2006. "In Search of a Cultural Interpretation of Power: The Contribution of Pierre Bourdieu." *IDS Bulletin* 37(6): 11–22.

New World Encyclopedia. 2015a. *Swaminarayan*. Accessed on 5 May 2016 from http://www.newworldencyclopedia.org/entry/Swaminarayan

———. 2015b. *Reincarnation*. Accessed on 6 May 2016 from http://www.newworldencyclopedia.org/entry/Reincarnation

Oddie, G. A. 2006. *Imagined Hinduism: British Missionary Constructions of Hinduism, 1793–1900*. Thousand Oaks, CA: SAGE Publications.

Peach, C. and R. Gale. 2003. "Muslims, Hindus, and Sikhs in the New Religious Landscape of England." *The Geographical Review* 93(4): 469–90.

Rudert, A. 2004. "Inherent Faith and Negotiated Power: Swaminarayan Women in the United States." Dissertation, Cornell University. New York: Cornell University. Accessed on 19 May 2017 from https://ecommons.cornell.edu/handle/1813/106

Sinha, R. 2014. "Hindu Rashtra Reflects Inclusion Not Theocracy." *The New Indian Express*. Accessed on 19 May 2017 from https://bharatabharati.wordpress.com/2014/07/29/a-hindu-rashtra-is-not-a-theocracy-rakesh-sinha/

Srinivas, M. N. 1952. *Religion and Society Among the Coorgs of South India*. Oxford: Oxford University Press.

Vijayakumar, S. 2015. "Birth of a Hindu-national Temple: Convergence of Religion and Politics of Swaminarayan Akshardham." *2014–15 Colloquium Series*. University of Berkeley, California. Accessed on 5 May 2016 from http://www.tourismstudies.org/news_archive/VijayakumarShirvani2014.htm

Wang, F. K. 2014. *World's Largest Hindu Temple Being Built in New Jersey*. Accessed on 10 May 2016 from http://www.nbcnews.com/news/asian-america/worlds-largest-hindu-temple-being-built-new-jersey-n166616

Williams, R. B. 2001. *An Introduction to Swaminarayan Hinduism*. Cambridge: Cambridge University Press.

———. 2012. "Representations of Swaminarayan Hinduism." In *Public Hinduisms*, edited by J. Zavos, P. Kanungo, D. S. Reddy, M. Warrier, and R. B. Williams, 176–89. New Delhi: SAGE Publications.

Yagniki, B. 2014. *162 Acre Akshardham Coming up in New Jersey*. Accessed on 10 May 2016 from http://timesofindia.indiatimes.com/NRI/US-Canada-News/162-acre-Akshardham-coming-up-in-New-Jersey/articleshow/38836679.cms

Zavos, J. 2012. "Transnational Religious Organizations and Flexible Citizenship in Britain and India." In *Citizenship and the Flow of Ideas in the Era of Globalisation*, edited by S. Mitra. New Delhi: Samskriti.

4

Ciji: Socially Engaged Buddhism, Feminization, and the Politics of Soft Power

Introduction

Ciji (also known as Tzu Chi) is a Buddhist 'benevolent society' established in Taiwan, with offices in Southeast Asia, China, Japan, the United States, Canada, Australia, and New Zealand and claims 10 million followers worldwide.[1] Its importance resides in the fact that largely because of Ciji, Buddhism has become a mainstream force in Taiwan and even politicians court the movement's leaders especially during elections.

In this chapter, I describe how this Buddhist charity in Taiwan, founded by a nun, the Venerable Zhengyan (also known as Chen Yan), has grown into a worldwide organization and how Ciji has reinterpreted Buddhism, feminized the faith, and positively changed the formerly strained political dynamics between Taiwan and Mainland China.

I begin with a brief overview of Buddhism and its representative schools, then go on to trace the founding of Ciji and the growth of the movement. Finally, I explore Ciji's reinterpretation of Buddhism, its spiritual capital, and how Ciji is using soft power to enhance Taiwan–China relations.

Overview of Buddhism

Ciji, which literally means 'compassion relief', is one of the three largest Buddhist movements based in Taiwan and also popular among the Taiwanese diaspora in Malaysia, the United States, Canada, and the United Kingdom (Huang 2008). The other two movements are Buddha's Light Mountain (or Fagushan led by Master Xingyun) and the Dharma Drum Mountain (or Fagushan led by Master

Shengyan; Huang 2008). Unlike the other two groups, however, Ciji was founded and is led by a nun, whose teachings promise that both lay persons and ordained Buddhists can achieve the status of bodhisattva (enlightened being or saint) through involvement in social welfare and other humanitarian actions. Ciji is a Mahayana Buddhist association (Mahayana is one of the three schools of the faith) devoted to the principle of cultivating self by giving. The founder Zhengyan's underlying principle is that Buddhism is not just for worship but the outworking of good works so that the "pure Land will not be in some faraway paradise but on this earth and in this world…." (Schak and Hsiao 2005: para 3). Therefore, Ciji is primarily a benevolent society although the founder is in charge of a monastic order. To help the reader understand Ciji's place as an international Buddhist charity, I now provide some background information on Buddhism.

Buddhism started with the Buddha, Siddhartha Gautama, who was born in Lumbini near the border of India and Nepal in 560 CE. Although 'Buddha' is a title, which means 'one who is enlightened or awakened', the first Buddha is acknowledged to be the founder of Buddhism. Siddhartha Gautama did not claim to be a god or a prophet in his lifetime. He was, according to his followers, a human being who became enlightened, understanding life and its realities in the deepest way possible.[2] In classical Buddhism, there are four central truths (for the noble or spiritually minded) that are generally accepted by all the schools of Buddhism:[3]

1. Suffering is a reality.
2. The cause of suffering is human desire and passion.
3. To be free from suffering, one has to be free of desire.
4. The way to be free of desire is to follow the 'eightfold path'.

Gautama Buddha called the eightfold path[4] the 'middle way'—the balanced path between the ascetic life of a monk and a life of plenty.[5]

After the death of Gautama Buddha, Buddhism was divided into three major schools, namely Theravada (the orthodox and conservative form), Mahayana (the reformed and somewhat syncretistic form), and Vajrayana (the tantric and mystical form).[6] For centuries, Theravada was the type of Buddhism observed in Sri Lanka, Thailand, Cambodia, Burma (Myanmar), and Laos. Mahayana has been practiced in China, Japan, Taiwan, Tibet, Nepal, Mongolia, Korea, and Vietnam.[7]

Mahayana Buddhism emerged in the first century as another school of Buddhism; it is referred as the 'Greater Vehicle' (literally, the 'Greater Oxcart'), because it is thought to open the door to people of all walks of life—not just monks and ascetics—in their search for enlightenment.[8] Mahayana Buddhism came into being because of the perception by certain Buddhist teachers that Theravada Buddhism, which they termed 'Hinayana', or 'Lesser Vehicle', had too narrow a conception of the Buddhist practice. Mahayana followers believe in a Buddhism that would liberate them from suffering so that they can attend to the well-being of others.

Mahayana Buddhism is practiced primarily in North Asia and the Far East, including China, Japan, Korea, Tibet, and Mongolia, and is thus sometimes known as Northern Buddhism. While Theravada Buddhism accepts only the Pali Canon as sacred scripture, Mahayana accepts other texts including the Sutras, which were written in Sanskrit.

Theravada and Mahayana Buddhists also differ in their perspective on the meaning of the ultimate purpose of life and the means of achieving it. Theravada Buddhists strive to become arhats, or perfected saints, who have attained nirvana or enlightenment (and therefore do not need to be reborn)—a hope reserved for monks and nuns. Mahayana Buddhists, on the other hand, hope to become bodhisattvas or living saints. These bodhisattvas

> unselfishly delay nirvana to help others attain it as well as the Buddha did. Mahayana Buddhists further teach that enlightenment can be attained in a single lifetime, and this can be accomplished even by a layperson.
>
> The various subdivisions within the Mahayana tradition, such as Zen, Nichiren, and Pure Land, promote different ways of attaining this goal, but all are agreed that it can be attained in a single lifetime by anyone who puts his or her mind (and sometimes body) to it.[9]

Mahayana is further divided into several subschools, such as Pure Land and Zen.[10] The founders of Pure Land Buddhism proclaimed that reaching nirvana through a life of monasticism is unrealistic. Pure Land also rejects the 'self-effort' of Buddhism. Instead, it proposes that the ideal way is for followers to be reborn in a Pure Land, where the worries of ordinary life do not interfere with the practices of the Buddha's teachings.[11] Pure Land Buddhism is based on faith in Amitabha Buddha, a former king in the remote period of time who gained enlightenment.[12] Amitabha Buddha presides over the Land of Ultimate Bliss (Clearly 2013). In the Pure Land, there is the absence of suffering, desire, and delusion that normally stands in the way of people's efforts to gain enlightenment in this world (Clearly 2013). A Buddhist follower gains entry into the Pure Land by simply invoking the name of Amitabha Buddha. This is followed by "contemplating the qualities of Amitabha, visualizing Amitabha, and taking vows to be born in the Pure Land" (Clearly 2013: para 6). Whilst it is unclear where the Pure Land is in reality—whether it is a state of mind cultivated through practice, or an actual place—what is clear is that within a Pure Land, the dharma is freely proclaimed and enlightenment is easily achieved.

Ciji's History

The Buddhism practiced by Ciji is a form of Pure Land Buddhism but, as indicated earlier and reflected in Figure 4.1, Ciji is creating its own version of Pure Land Buddhism. The founder of Ciji was influenced by her mentor Yinshun (1906–2005) who, in turn, was mentored by the Venerable Taixu (1890–1947). Taixu felt that traditional Buddhism was too focused on ritual and ceremony (Pitmann 2001) and tried to make Buddhism more in touch with the needs of society by encouraging its adherents to contribute to society and create a Buddhist community. His goal was to establish Mahayana Buddhism as a spiritual force in Taiwan and all around the world.

Taixu's student, Yinshun, a well-respected scholar, was also highly controversial in Buddhist circles. Venerable Yinshun questioned some of the fundamental practices such as the legitimacy of 'the eight heavy rules' for nuns, also known as *Garudhammas*, by pointing out that they were inconsistent with the Buddhist scriptures (Chen 2011: 16–17). The first of the eight rules says: "A nun who has been ordained even for a hundred years must greet respectfully, rise up from her seat, salute with joined palms, do proper homage to a monk ordained that day" (Snyder 2006: 447).

Furthermore, Yinshun developed an inclusive and humanistic form of Buddhism by opening the door for monks, nuns, and lay people to be part of Buddhism (Chen 2011). His goal was to reduce the rigid

Figure 4.1:

The schools of Buddhism and Ciji's place

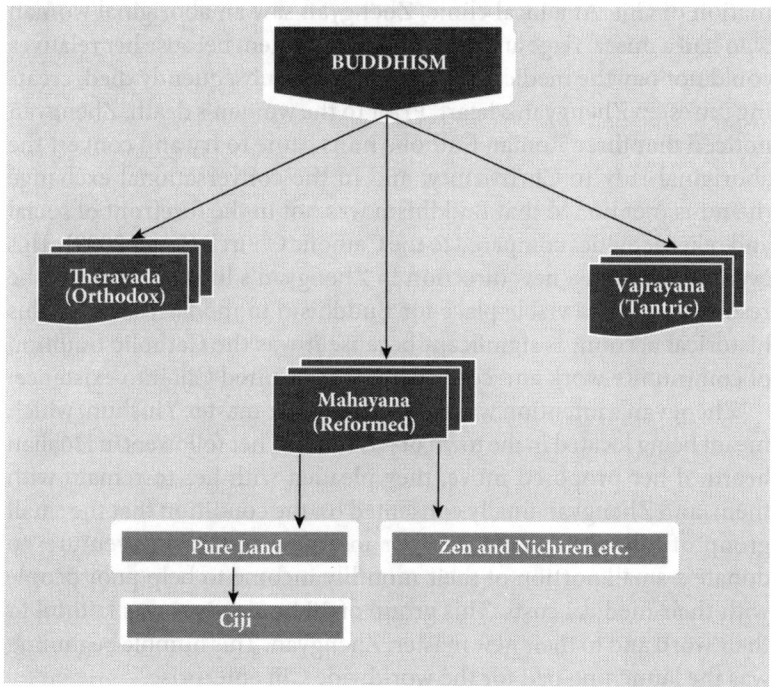

Source: James (2016).

requirements of the faith so that all citizens could partake of Buddhism and that the barriers between ordinary people and monks would be removed. Yinshun's pro-feminine stance and his belief in Buddhism for the masses resonated well with Zhengyan.

Ciji's amazing growth and current fame must also be understood in the context of the period when Taiwan was transitioning into a wealthy, industrialized, and materialistic nation in the early 1970s. Hence, Ciji was founded at the right time to give the Taiwanese people an understanding of the meaningful use of their wealth to benefit society in the Buddhist way.

Zhengyan, the founder, left home on two occasions,[13] and when she returned to her hometown in Hualian the second time, she chose to live a frugal and monastic life in a wooden cabin behind the Puming Temple "eating one meal a day, burning incense scars, and refusing alms for her own upkeep" (Jones 2009: 293). In 1966, an incident took place that precipitated a chain of events that eventually led to the formation of Ciji. At a local clinic, Zhengyan saw an aboriginal woman who had a miscarriage and was refused treatment because her relatives could not pay the medical fees. The woman subsequently died, creating unrest in Zhengyan's heart. Prior to the woman's death, Zhengyan noticed that three Roman Catholic nuns came to try and convert the aboriginal lady to Christianity, and in the conversational exchange the nuns mentioned that Buddhism was not in the forefront of social and relief activities compared to the Catholic Church (Jones 2009). This event ushered in a new direction in Zhengyan's life and work: as she resolved to find a viable place for Buddhism in modern society. This historical account is significant because it was the Catholic tradition of community work and conversion that inspired Ciji into existence.

Zhengyan's intention was to be close to her master Yinshun, which meant being located in the town of Jiayi. When her followers in Hualian heard of her proposed move, they pleaded with her to remain with them, and Zhengyan finally consented on the condition that the small group of followers would join her in a new and daring venture: to donate a small portion of their monthly income to help poor people with their medical costs. This group of 30 housewives was faithful to their word and to their new master, Zhengyan. This humble beginning was the launching pad for the worldwide Ciji enterprise.

Growth and Global Outreach

As indicated previously, Ciji was founded in 1966 in the founder's town in the eastern coast of Taiwan—Hualian. From a modest annual income of US$350, the organization now receives an annual income of US$150 million and possesses assets valued as high as US$9 billion (Goossaert and Palmer 2011: 300). It owns a TV station, a university, schools, medical centers, and two well-equipped, 900-bed hospitals.

The logo of the organization is a ship surrounded by lotus flowers and leaves, which implies the need for good karmic deeds to make this world a better place. In the logo, the ship stands for Ciji—steering this worldwide venture, and the eight petals represent the eightfold path of Buddhism.[14] Hence, there is a Buddhist underpinning to Ciji but as I point out in the forthcoming sections of the chapter, Ciji has reinterpreted Mahayana Buddhism and in the process produced a new form of the faith.

Ciji's aid focus for many years has been ethnic Chinese and Taiwanese diaspora people. However, exceptions have been made and the organization is now also involved in distributing aid and support to people of other races—such as the Nepali people during the earthquake disaster in 2015. It has also assisted in relief efforts in more than 30 countries including Rwanda, Chechnya, Venezuela, Turkey, and Papua New Guinea. However, cultural specificity is still the norm and the 'Pure Land' seems to be primarily for ethnic Chinese people.[15]

Under Zhengyan, the Ciji organization has three divisions—the foundation proper (with more than 100 staff members), the volunteer system with over 20,000 volunteers (some who donate a certain amount of money automatically reach the status as commissioners), and the monastery. Of the 10 million members, 4 million are in Taiwan and the rest in the Chinese diaspora (Huang 2014: 192).[16]

Ciji is the first Buddhist organization in Chinese society to carry out worldwide outreach. To do this, it has adapted traditional Mahayana Buddhist teaching, namely the Pure Land Buddhist rhetoric to transform the charity from the traditional 'begging bowl' idea of Buddhist almsgiving to a global, state-of-the-art, faith-based nonprofit organization. Zhengyan has cleverly adapted the concept of 'this worldly' Buddhism into her mission of compassion to the world. However, unlike Pure Land Buddhism that teaches the possibility of people becoming bodhisattvas and entering heavenly bliss, Zhengyan has transformed the Pure Land doctrine to mean that her followers can now actually create a utopian world by their acts of compassion, in obedience to her own version of the Buddhist dharma (teachings).

Ciji operates as a transnational body, with offices in 46 countries. The Ciji Taiwan headquarters act as the spoke in the wheel of the worldwide empire (Huang 2002).[17] Ciji almost has a need for expansion because their belief system is based on the fact that only through the worldwide propagation of Ciji teachings can the Pure Land be created and sustained.

Goods, relief, money, teachings, and bone marrow donations travel from one Ciji center to another, linking a network of Chinese followers and supporters globally. In traditional aid program, aid moves from the United States and the other first world countries to developing and underdeveloped countries. In this instance, the aid programs are managed from the Taiwan headquarters, with the aid flowing in all directions where the need is greatest. The largest overseas branch of the organization is in the United States, which has nine regional branches with a total of 60 offices throughout the nation comprising a total of 50,000 members and 400 commissioners.[18] Ciji uses a variety of languages in the media to communicate, recruit, and raise finances. In the main, it has a fourfold focus: charity, medical relief, education, and culture. Spirituality underpins these four streams of the organization.

Charity

Ciji's outward focus and benevolence came at a time when Taiwan was becoming a vibrant economic giant in East Asia—part of the well-known '4 Asian tigers'. Taiwan's growth was due to many factors, such as high food production with the assistance of US foreign aid, good infrastructure, and a highly educated population.[19] Zhengyan used her humanistic ideas of Buddhism to capitalize on the growing middle class in Taiwan. Ciji's website under 'Mission of Charity' captures this benevolent goal: "Educating the rich to help the poor; inspiring the poor to realize their riches." Ciji claims that as the rich give to the poor they will be "enriching themselves through contribution … bringing out the good in everyone."[20] As Ciji grew, it increased its scope of delivering support to society and assistance to the poor which includes distributing relief goods to the poor, on a monthly basis; branches have lists of the poor in their areas who come each month to receive medical treatment, haircuts, and cash donations.

Medical Relief

Recognizing that the poor may miss out on proper medical care, Zhengyan started the Tzu Chi Free Clinic for the poor in 1972. In 1986, the Hualien Tzu Chi General Hospital opened, and its guiding principle is 'respecting life and patient-centered treatment'.[21] The medical mission later led to additional hospitals in Yuli, Guanshan,

Dalin, Taipei, and Taichung where the medical staff and volunteers are guided by four values called the 'Four Entireties' of patient care: the entire treatment process, the patient's entire body, the patient's entire family, and the well-being of the entire medical team.[22]

Of special interest is the bone marrow donation program, which is now a global phenomenon. Ciji's bone marrow registry, established in 1993, has a huge database of information on volunteer donors to match the needs of those who are in need of marrow transplants, making this the largest data bank in Asia and the third largest in the world.[23]

Education

Hualien, where Ciji's headquarters is located, is a poor area with few public medical and education facilities and a high percentage of aboriginal and marginalized people. To address these concerns, in 1989, the Tzu Chi Nursing College was formed. In July 2000, Ciji completed the establishment of its well-rounded education program which offers a curriculum from kindergarten, elementary school and middle school to high school, college, and graduate studies. The guiding principles are 'kindness, compassion, joy, and selfless giving'.[24] Respect for life and faith in human nature is the foundation, and 'education of virtue, education of life, and education of the entire person' is the goal.[25]

Culture

Ciji's mission of culture has as its aim: "to purify the human mind, to pacify our society, to help those who suffer, and to rectify frenzied and chaotic acts."[26] Ciji not only records culture but creates culture for future generations.

At Tzu Chi University, based in Hualien, secular education is offered (including an international program offering the PhD degree in biomedical sciences), but students have to take religion as a minor subject.[27]

The Youth Corps is an integral part of Ciji's religious training in which students from institutions not connected with Ciji have access to the teachings of Zhengyan. Some of the Ciji Youth Corps chapters in the United States have regular activities, a separate web link, and activities apart from the Ciji branch. Most of the local volunteers come from the Youth Corps. Besides, Ciji leaders look to the Youth Corps as the means of crossing cultures in this predominantly Chinese organization.

> Ciji youth are our future because they study abroad and have cross-ethnic social connections. When they are out of school and start working, they may draw in their classmates, colleagues and friends. (Cited in Huang 2002: 8)

Some scholars, like Laliberté (1999), have argued that Ciji's cultural outreach seems to be directed more toward proselytizing than education because this is the primary means of attracting volunteers, who form the backbone of the organization. DeVido (2010) raised concerns about Ciji's use of power in promoting its Buddhist agenda during vulnerable times, such as with Project Hope after the 1999 Taiwan earthquake when schools were rebuilt according to Buddhist architecture and copies of Zhengyan's book *Still Thoughts* were donated to the affected schools. Notwithstanding these criticisms, it is clear that Ciji has greatly improved Taiwan's social and medical facilities, especially in the poorer areas.

Reinterpreting Buddhism

What Ciji has achieved is to amass the help of grassroots supporters and volunteers to impose a Buddhist framework in many societies. It brings Buddhism into the lives of people and gives them a chance to make a difference in the world. In the process, Ciji has removed the barriers between monks and nuns who were previously seen merely as holy people who perform rituals as 'shut ins' in monasteries. Ciji has introduced Buddhism into everyday life involving the laity. This creates a sense of identity and purpose within Taiwanese society and amongst the Chinese diaspora, helping to propagate Buddhism in a different way.

Gautama Buddha, the founder of Buddhism, was concerned about the reality of suffering. Zhengyan and Ciji do not question the fact of suffering, rather they are actively working to resolve suffering though concrete ways.

As mentioned previously, Ciji's Buddhism takes after the Mahayana school and is part of Pure Land Buddhism, which believes that devotees can attain enlightenment and enter the Pure Land. However, Ciji has gone beyond the teaching of humanistic Buddhism (*Renjian Fojiao*) of Zhengyan's mentors (Pacey 2012). Unlike Pure Land Buddhism, Ciji takes the attention away from a concern with rebirth in the Pure Land to the creation of a Pure Land here and now (*Renjian Jingtu*) (Chen 2007; Pacey 2012).

Zhengyan is revered by her followers and this high regard is likened culturally to that of the founder of a Japanese new religious movement rather than a leader of a traditional Chinese–Buddhist association. Historical evidence supports this sentiment because during the Japanese occupation of Taiwan (1895–1945), many Taiwanese Buddhist monks and nuns were sent to Japan to be educated in Japanese Buddhism (Li 1996).

Although Zhengyan studied Buddhist doctrines and scriptures in the early days, the traditional literature became less and less important as she went on to acquire other teachings and blended them into her new form of religion. From her youth, Zhengyan was attached to the Bodhisattva Guanyin (also known amongst the Chinese as Kwan Yin) and portions of the Lotus Sutra (the most cherished scriptures of Mahayana Buddhism). Guanyin is the Buddhist Goddess of Mercy, although from time immemorial she has been worshipped as a folk deity and known by different names. When Zhengyan's mother was ill, Zhengyan appealed to Guanyin who reportedly appeared to Zhengyan. The mother was healed and Zhengyan, in turn, devoted her life to Buddhism and took the vow to become a vegetarian. Zhengyan is now closely identified with Guanyin and, according to Zhengyan's followers, Zhengyan exhibits Guanyin's divinity through her deeds of healing and nurturing—albeit through medical science, technology, and modern techniques unlike Guanyin's purely 'miraculous' interventions.

All the statues and pictures dedicated to Zhengyan by her followers, which are displayed at Ciji's premises including the hospitals and the convent, are exclusively in the form of the female image of Guanyin (Li 2005).

When thanking her followers, Zhengyan made a reference to the members of Ciji as being the arms and eyes of Bodhisattva Gyanyin (Li 2005). This reference is far from being coincidental because Ciji scholars have observed that "over the years Zhengyan has become an incarnation of the bodhisattva Guanyin for her followers" (DeVido 2010: 63–78; Jones 2009: 299).

As pointed out, Guanyin has a long history with the Chinese people dating back to folk religion in the premodern times. Zhengyan's link with Guanyin is a means to tap into the religious consciousness of the people and reinforce her spiritual leadership.

> The model provided by the Thousand-armed and Thousand-eyed Guanyin has long affected the religious life of Taiwanese Buddhist women by persuading them that recognition in a patrilineal society is possible. But, the younger generation of scholar nuns possesses a new set of social resources, such as higher education and a commitment to the modernization of Buddhism—they have put the image of Guanyin to a new use…. (Li 2005: para 41)

Huang and Weller (1998) also pointed out another feature of Ciji Buddhism: Zhengyan's books are very popular and have become 'quasi-scriptural' for Ciji members; in fact, they are given a far superior place in the organization than any other Buddhist scriptures (Huang and Weller 1998: 383). Zhengyan's lack of emphasis on higher Buddhist studies may seem odd for a nun who was taught and ordained by Yinshun, the most revered Chinese–Buddhist scholar of the early twentieth century (Jones 2009). Laliberté (1999: 110) has noted that despite the coveted place of education in its four main missions, Ciji's publications on Buddhist teachings are relatively few compared to the other Buddhist missions in Taiwan such as the Fagushan or Dharma Drum Mountain.

Forty years after Ciji was established, Zhengyan officially announced the formation of Ciji's dharma path.[28] Dharma, a term that refers to the teachings of Buddha, was used by the historical Buddha to point people to the path that leads to enlightenment. Therefore, Zhengyan has created her own Dharma based on the Lotus Sutra, which is the collection of teachings and principles that her followers, known as Jing Si disciples, take part in.[29]

One of the strong criticisms of Zhengyan is that she is setting herself up as another Buddha because Ciji's Jing Si cafes are selling crystal glass ornaments of Buddha that resemble Zhengyan rather than the traditional Buddha image. These crystals range in price from NT$330,000 (approximately US$10,000) upwards.[30] However, it can be argued that in Mahayana Buddhism, the bodhisattva will not enter nirvana until all living beings are able to enter nirvana. These bodhisattvas are understood to be de facto gods to be venerated and petitioned.[31]

Certain remarks made by Zhengyan give the impression that she has also adopted Confucian and traditional Chinese worldviews because she advocates that natural disasters are directly related to human behavior, and that they will continue to inflict mankind as long as there is disunity and unrest in human society: "The only way to mitigate this is for all human beings to repent and reflect on our wrong actions and change our ways. So, we should remind one another of this all the time and work together and help each other."[32] Because natural catastrophes are the reason for Ciji's activism, Zhengyan's humanistic Buddhism therefore consists of transforming both human and physical nature.

Zhengyan has also borrowed techniques from Christianity because Ciji is now holding Sunday schools (a Church-based format of imparting Christian knowledge to young children) at Ciji centers in the United States and also placing the book of teachings of Zhengyan in hotels and motels, similar to the Gideon's ministry, a Christian-based entity that places Bibles in hotels and motels throughout the world.[33]

Therefore, Ciji's Pure Land Buddhism is syncretistic, based on the following: Mahayana Buddhist concepts, Japanese Buddhism, Confucianistic ideas, and Christian techniques—all focused on creating a utopian society here on earth with Zhengyan being given the status of a living Buddha.

Feminization

Traditional Chinese culture is considered to be patriarchal, and generally nuns are not well respected for they are believed to represent women who are abandoned or have difficultly fitting into Chinese society (Chan 1953; Li 2005). Seen in this light, the approximately 8 million lay women who make up 80 percent of Ciji's membership and are conscientiously engaged in the fourfold mission of the organization, is a new paradigm in Taiwanese society. This is one of the few Buddhist organizations with a female head and a monastic order of nuns underpinning the whole philanthropic organization. Pacey's (2012) study reveals that at Ciji, it is the norm for women to be above men in leadership and authority; furthermore, men need to acquire feminine traits like compassion to fulfil the goals of the organization. An interesting case in point is revealed in Huang's analysis (2003), which showed the intrinsic place of tears and weeping in the movement.

> Sometimes they weep together, and many members trace their conversion to an inexplicable flood of tears. Uncontrolled crying is especially common among the female followers, who often sob, yet never wail. They remember having cried, and never try to stop any tearful fellow participant from crying, even during the most tranquil ceremonies. (Huang 2003: 78)

The relationship between religion and feelings as a nonverbal characteristic is commonly observed in many faiths (Mitchell 1997). Anthropologists of religion have studied emotion as a phenomenologically based experience in certain ritual contexts, such as healing and spirit possession (Boddy 1989; Csordas 1997). However, the weeping that takes place in Ciji is unique in that it occurs in multiple contexts and often, quite uncontrollably. Huang (2003) believes that the emotion is related to the charisma of the founder (with her almost cultlike personality) and the predominantly female composition of the group.

Testimonies of male converts to Ciji's form of practical Buddhism show a tendency for the men to develop feminine-like traits upon conversion. Huang, a successful businessman who had no sense of the finer things in life, upon his conversion, became more balanced in temperament and compassionate in heart (Yuan and Ruan, cited in Jones 2009: 301). Lin, who was entrenched by evil vices, was thrown out of his home and later tricked by his family members into attending a Ciji meeting where he heard a sermon by Zhengyan. The conversion story describes the dramatic change in Lin.

> At first he [Lin] was so angry at the trick that he ran away and spent the night in the forest around the Vihara, but went back the next day and heard the master preach. She touched his heart and he repented in tears and became a stalwart Ciji member. His family took him back, he found new meaning for his life, and has led many others to join Ciji. (Huang 1996: 245–47)

According to Lindholm (2013), other scholars have discovered an androgynous element[34] in the Ciji practices: "... over time the male and female templates are becoming more alike in their uniforms and behaviours. Women can do heavy labor. Men are allowed to proselytize" (Lindholm 2013: 19).

Paradoxically, Zhengyan's teaching also seems to encourage women to be faithful to their husbands even if the husbands have mistresses. In her sermons and discourses on marriage, Zhengyan seems to overlook the responsibility of unfaithful husbands, teaching instead that women need to look within themselves to make sense of their husbands' behaviors. Zhengyan is convinced that if women display love, tenderness, and compassion, their wayfaring husbands will reciprocate with acts of love and faithfulness: "Love the person he loves, so everybody will be happy" (cited in Chen 2011: 18).

So, in reality, Ciji's core belief is fundamentally based on traditional and Confucian values of respect and social harmony. The women in Ciji may seem to appear liberated because of their leadership roles in calling the shots in the organization, but they cannot 'rock the boat' and must maintain harmony and balance even when their marriages are threatened by mistresses (Chen 2011).

Spiritual Capital

Zhengyan's inspiration and deep personal charisma have drawn many people to the movement. The personal appeal of the founder comes to the followers through her sermons either listened to live or though videotapes. One of the followers recounts how she became a follower.

> One day I got some tapes of the Rev Zhengyan's speeches. I was so touched by listening to her compassionate voice that I found myself crying in the kitchen. I finally found the master with whom I really wanted to work. (Cited in Huang 2002: 11)

Zhengyan's sermons and 'pearls of wisdom' are an important feature in the Ciji organization. For example, in one of her sermons she argues the case for 'this world' Buddhism.

> If in this life, we are giving of ourselves and making positive contributions that benefit others, then in our next life we will certainly have a life of blessings and wisdom. So let us walk the Bodhisattva Path now, in this life, and cultivate blessings and wisdom. Don't wait until

a future life to do it. If we don't plant the seeds now, how can we reap the conditions to do so in our next life?[35]

Her sermons are the means of conversion to the Ciji form of faith where new volunteers are brought in and followers reinforced in their beliefs. Her book of aphorisms and teachings *Still Thoughts* is her signature publication and is essential reading for all followers (Huang and Weller 1998). Devotees often enter the movement through an encounter with Zhengyan either directly or indirectly through her tapes or sermons.

Zhengyan's charismatic appeal is noted by many scholars as the factor that integrates and unifies the Ciji movement, and various reasons have been suggested for her strong hold on her followers. The Taiwanese scholar-cum-Ciji member Lu Huixin (1994) argued that it is Zhengyan's ability to exercise the dual role of 'strict father and gentle mother simultaneously' (a trait that resonates with Chinese culture) that explains her charisma (Lu 1994: 11). Jiang Canteng (cited in Jones 2009) observed that it is Zhengyan's eloquence in communicating in the *Minnan* dialect, also known as *Taiyu*, the native tongue of the majority of Taiwan's population, that enables her to address the issues within peoples' hearts, thereby winning them over. Another reason that is suggested is her disciplined approach to life owing to the hardships she encountered in her early life and the training under her two masters "which included fasting, scripture chanting, burning of incense scars, hand-copying sutras," and the observance of difficult vows (Jones 2009: 298). All these factors, including the stories that circulate about her 'Godlike' qualities plus the references in Ciji literature to her title, *Shangren*, or 'supreme leader', have contributed to Zhengyan's enormous charismatic appeal.

Summing up, Zhengyan's appeal is a 'total package' consisting of her extraordinary life and work and her carefully crafted form of real-world Buddhism that makes sense to the modern Chinese, especially the womenfolk. A snapshot of a how one Ciji official conducted a meeting of 700 volunteers gives an indication of this.

[A]t the beginning of the year-end meeting of volunteers at the Taipei branch of the Tzu Chi Foundation [Ciji], the young emcee, dressed in her Tzu Chi uniform, asked the crowd of seven hundred, mainly middle-aged women: 'Why do you volunteer for Tzu Chi'? A brief silence was followed by the timid responses of several female voices from all parts of the auditorium: "[Because we] love the Supreme Person (ai shangren)." Blushing, the master of ceremonies smiled and, somewhat pedantically, replied: "Oh, Of course, we all love the Supreme Master. But we volunteer for Tzu Chi because we are ourselves shanxin dashi (benevolent persons). We are here because of da'ai (great love, universal love)." Huang (2008: 30)

Zhengyan's charismatic personality has been both a "magnet and motivator bringing people not so much to join Ciji as to convert to it" (Jones 2009: 298). This has helped steer the organization to become more of a "hub-and-spoke form of corporation rather than a bureaucratic one" (Jones 2009: 298). Zhengyan, as the acknowledged leader of Ciji, takes responsibility for all decisions and directives in spiritual and organizational matters. Many scholars have predicted that Zhengyan's decision not to name her successor (in keeping with the founding Buddha who refused to elect his successor) "will make for a difficult, but probably not fatal, period of transition" (Laliberté 1999: 117).

The Politics of Soft Power

Ciji's involvement in Mainland China is an interesting study in the role of 'soft power' in international relations. Nye (1990, 2004) introduced the concept of soft power (as opposed to coercion, sanctions and inducements) as "getting others to want the outcomes that you want"—to shape what others want by being attractive (Nye 2004: 5). He argued that a country's culture, politics, and values may have inherent qualities of attraction (Nye 2004). To convey the dynamics of Ciji in Mainland China, I provide some historical background.

> In 1885, the Qing Empire of China sanctioned Taiwan as the twenty second province of China. After the war with Japan, Taiwan was ceded to Japan as a colony and the Japanese occupied Taiwan from 1895 to 1945.[36]

Following Japan's defeat in World War II, Japan relinquished control of Taiwan, and Chiang Kai-shek of the Chinese Nationalist Party, also known as Kuomintang (KMT), reestablished control over the island. Soon after the Chinese Communists defeated the KMT forces in the four-year civil war which commenced in 1945, the KMT-led regime moved to Taiwan and established their base of operations there to fight back the communists in the Chinese mainland (Mack 2014).[37]

The People's Republic of China (PRC) government in mainland China, led by Mao Zedong, commenced plans to 'liberate' Taiwan by military force. This ushered in Taiwan's de facto status as an independent nation from the Chinese mainland, a situation which continues till today (Mack 2014).

China–Taiwan relations have been strained since the Kuomintang seized power and declared Taiwan an independent nation separate from China, while China still upholds the One China policy. Therefore, it is interesting that Ciji, a Taiwan-based Buddhist charity, entered China in 1991.

Ciji's involvement in the PRC began when it undertook aid operations after severe floods affected Central and East China. Since then, Ciji has embarked on a massive and comprehensive program of constructing schools; by 2010, Ciji had rebuilt 13 schools in Sichuan plus nursing homes and upgrading and developing infrastructure in undeveloped inland areas, such as the Guizhou province.[38] Other ongoing activities include: distribution of rice and goods to the poor; providing scholarships for marginalized students; free medical clinics; and environmental and recycling programs. In all these activities, Ciji has been careful to uphold its secularized policy on aid work and so public religious gatherings have not been encouraged although some religious observances have gone on in the homes of followers. Even though Ciji is a religious organization, it has learned how to downplay its faith-based nature in carrying out its operations in China (Laliberté 2013).

Since the initial flood relief work, Ciji has extended its social and cultural reach into 28 provinces, municipalities, and autonomous regions in China. In March 2008, Ciji became the first organization represented by a non-Mainland resident to be registered with the Chinese government.[39] During the Sichuan earthquake, Ciji was also one of the few organizations that the Chinese government granted privileges to bring in overseas aid workers for relief activities (Howard and Wong 2008).

In August 2010, Ciji became the first overseas NGO to be approved by the Ministry of Civil Affairs to set up a nationwide charity foundation. In China, the usual procedure has been for overseas organizations to register with the Ministry of Commerce as business entities.[40]

Part of the attraction of Ciji in China is its nonpartisan and apolitical nature. In fact, Ciji's emphasis on benevolence, education, and culture has garnered much praise from Chinese authorities. Furthermore, the Ciji foundation received the coveted China Charity Award in 2006 and again in 2008 from the Ministry of Civil Affairs for its social work in Chinese society, an unprecedented move on the part of the Chinese authorities.[41] Foreign bodies working in China are seldom recognized, but Ciji's work has changed the perception of the politburo. Apparently, provincial authorities give more leeway to organizations, so Ciji has a lot of projects located in the provinces (Laliberté 2013). The form of Ciji Buddhism—which contains Confucianistic and traditional Chinese elements—seems to be another attraction for China. Laliberté (2013) suggested that the Chinese authorities may be more open to Ciji extending its spiritual teachings into China in an effort to check the spread of Christianity because the authorities prefer Buddhism to thrive in China rather than Christianity. I would add that China's softening toward Ciji may be an attempt to counter the widespread criticism against the government's strong stand against the outlawed Falun Gong cult (founded by Li Hongzhi in 1992, based on teachings from Buddhism, Daoism, Confucianism, and Chinese folklore).

Through all these overtures by Ciji, the Chinese government seems to have experienced a change of heart about certain religious entities. China is beginning to see that there is a place for faith-based organizations in making significant contributions to nation building in concert with Chinese authorities.

Conclusion

Traditional Buddhism has been understood as a faith of personal meditation and salvation through the devotee's involvement in an assortment of deeds that usher in the state of nirvana (blissful nothingness) or the state of Buddhahood, if one is successful. Pure Land, Mahayana Buddhism, which focuses on good deeds for society rather than personal introspection, is a new paradigm in the Mahayana sect of Buddhism. The Pure Land is a reference to entering the bliss though good works. However, Ciji's Pure Land Buddhism consists of creating the Pure Land here and now through charity and compassion. Hence, Zhengyan has created a new form of 'this world' Buddhism.

The main spiritual capital in Ciji is the founder, Zhengyan, and her highly charismatic personality. In fact, as the reincarnation of the goddess of compassion, Guanyin, Zhengyan is thought to have become a Buddha—having reached the status of enlightenment. Thus, Zhengyan is revered and worshipped. By drawing upon Guanyin's influence, Zhengyan has extended Guanyin's healing power through modern medical technology and therefore widened the reach of Guanyin to a transnational audience.

Her sermons are a dharma of a new kind. She has developed a comprehensive worldview that intersects with every aspect of postmodern life, including marriage, environment, and natural disasters.

Although shrouded in controversy (notably that the founder has divinized herself, Ciji proselytizes after disasters and the belief that the Pure Land is still largely for a select ethnic group), Zhengyan has successfully transformed Buddhism into a transnational phenomenon combining it with Confucianism, traditional Chinese folk religion, Christian techniques, modern medical science, global networking, and organizational technologies. Ciji's entry into Mainland China and the nation's changing perception of faith-based organizations has opened the door for more study into contemporary, international relations.

The key question that remains is this: With all Ciji's accomplishments and the pervasive and tenacious spirit of the founder, who controls the group as its supreme master, what will the future hold for Ciji when the founder exits from the scene?

Notes

1. See http://content.time.com/time/specials/packages/article/0,28804,2066367_2066369_2066393,00.html
2. See https://thebuddhistcentre.com/text/who-was-buddha
3. See http://www.britannica.com/topic/Four-Noble-Truths
4. The eightfold path flows out of the fourth noble truth taught by Gautama Buddha and each of the eight teachings begin with the word 'Sama' which refers to 'proper', 'whole', or 'perfect' aspects of living—speech, thoughts, wisdom etc.

5. See http://www.britannica.com/topic/Four-Noble-Truths
6. Vajrayana celebrates the mystical and meditative form of Buddhism and deeply associated with it is the sacred mandala, a representation of the universe used as an aid for meditation.
7. See http://buddhism.about.com/od/basicbuddhistteachings/a/basicshub.htm
8. See http://www.religionfacts.com/mahayana
9. Ibid.
10. See https://www.thoughtco.com/introduction-to-buddhism-449715
11. See http://buddhism.about.com/od/purelandbuddhism/a/pureland.htm
12. Amitabha is a Sanskrit rendition of the term 'Infinite Light'. The actual time period is not recorded but it is believed that a monk named Dharmakara made a number of vows, and one of them was that once he attained Buddhahood—all people who have faith in him will be granted the privilege of being reborn into his paradise called *Sukhavati*, the Pure Land.
13. Zhengyan is believed to have run away from home when she was young owing to her search for spiritual truth and fulfilment.
14. See http://tw.tzuchi.org/en/index.php?option=com_content&view=article&id=87&Itemid`=288&lang=en
15. Although Ciji is located in many parts of the world and of late the four missions have impacted people of various ethnic groups, it seems that its focus is still on the ethnic Chinese people (or nations with Buddhist inclinations).
16. See http://content.time.com/time/specials/packages/article/0,28804,2066367_2066369_2066393,00.html
17. See http://tw.tzuchi.org/en/index.php?option=com_content&view=article&id=1207%3Aguidance-to-newly-certified-tzu-chi-volunteers-&catid=116%3Atzu-chi-path&Itemid=324&lang=en
18. See http://www.tzuchi.us/
19. See http://www.povertyeducation.org/the-rise-of-asia.html
20. See http://www.tzuchi.org.au/en/index.php?option=com_content&view=article&id=293%3Atzu-chi-missions&catid=58%3Atzuchi&Itemid=283&lang
21. Ibid.
22. Ibid.
23. Ibid.
24. See http://www.tzuchi.org.tw/en/index.php?option=com_content&view=article&id=293&Itemid=283&lang=es
25. Ibid.
26. Ibid.
27. See http://eng.tcu.edu.tw/
28. See http://tw.tzuchi.org/en/index.php?option=com_content&view=article&id=309%3Atzu-chi-dharma-teachings-sutra-of-immeasurable-meanings&catid=101%3Aphilosphy&Itemid=265&lang=en
29. Ibid.
30. See http://jingsi.com.tw/main_index/products_show/b/251/4/7
31. See http://buddhism.about.com/od/purelandbuddhism/a/pureland.htm
32. See http://neptuner.666forum.tw/t2232-topic
33. See http://www.tzuchi.us/

34. It is interesting that Zhengyan has the title of Master and of late, she is referred to in Ciji writings as 'he' which opens itself to different conclusions.
35. See http://tw.tzuchi.org/en/index.php?option=com_content&view=article&id= 1207%3Aguidance-to-newly-certified-tzu-chi-volunteers-&catid=116%3Atzu-chi-path&Itemid=324&lang=en
36. See http://www.populararticles.xyz/Article/NewsIssues/chineseculture/201512/ 394084.html
37. Ibid.
38. See http://tw.tzuchi.org/en/index.php?option=com_content&view=article&id=64 7%3Atzu-chi-opens-chinas-dirst-overseas-ngo-office&catid=77%3Amissionofch arity&Itemid=177&lang=en and http://blogs.reuters.com/faithworld/2010/08/20/ taiwan-buddhist-charity-tzu-chi-sets-up-shop-in-atheist-china/
39. Ibid.
40. Ibid.
41. See http://chinadevelopmentbrief.cn/directory/tzu-chi-buddhist-compassion-relief-foundation/

References

Boddy, J. 1989. *Wombs and Alien Spirits: Women, Men and the Zar Cult in Northern Sudan*. Madison, WI: University of Wisconsin Press.

Chan, Wing-tsit. 1953. *Religious Trends in Modern China*. New York, NY: Columbia University Press.

Chen, C. H. 2007. "Building The Pure Land on Earth: Ciji's Media Cultural Discourse." *The Journal of Media and Religion* 6(3): 185–99.

———. 2011. "Feminist Debate in Taiwan's Buddhism: The Issue of the Eight Garudhammas." *The Journal of Feminist Scholarship* 1(Fall): 16–32.

Clearly, J. C. 2013. *Introduction to Pure Land Buddhism*. Accessed on 24 September 2015 from http://www.ymba.org/books/taming-monkey-mind-guide-pure-land-practice/introduction-pure-land-buddhism

Csordas, T. J. 1997. *Language, Charisma and Creativity: The Ritual Life of a Religious Movement*. Berkeley, CA: University of California Press.

DeVido, E. A. 2010. *Taiwan's Buddhist Nuns*. Albany, NY: State University of New York Press.

Goossaert, V. and D. A. Palmer. 2011. *The Religious Question in Modern China*. Chicago, IL: University of Chicago Press.

Howard, F. and E. Wong. 2008, 16 May. "In Departure China Invites Outside Help." *The New York Times*. Accessed on 20 December 2015 from http://www.nytimes. com/2008/05/16/world/asia/16china.html?_r=0

Huang, C. J. 1996. *Dharma Master Zhengan: One Hundred Stories*. Taipei: Jiya Wenhua Publications.

———. 2002. "What Travels? Notes on a Globalizing Buddhist Movement from Taiwan." In *Questionable Returns* Vol. 12, edited by A. Bove, 1–14. Vienna: IWM Junior Visiting Fellows Conferences.

Huang, C. J. 2003. "Weeping in a Taiwanese Buddhist Charismatic Movement." *Ethnology* 42(1): 73–86.

———. 2008. "Gendered Charisma in the Buddhist Tzu Chi (Ciji) Movement." *Nova Religio: The Journal of Alternative and Emergent Religions* 12(2): 29–47. DOI: 10.1525/m.2008.2.2.29.

———. 2014. "From Diasporic to Ecumenical: The Buddhist Tzu Chi (Ciji) Movement in Malaysia." In *Proselytizing and the Limits of Religious Pluralism in Contemporary Asia*, edited by J. Finucane and R. M. Feener, 191–209. New York, NY: Springer.

Huang, C. J. and R. P. Weller. 1998. "Merit and Mothering: Women and Social Welfare in Taiwanese Buddhism." *Journal of Asian Studies* 57(2): 379–96.

Jones, C. B. 2009. "Modernization and Traditionalism in Buddhist Almsgiving: The Case of the Buddhist Compassion Relief Tzu-chi Association in Taiwan." *Journal of Global Buddhism* 10(S.I.): 291–319.

Laliberté, A. 1999. *The Politics of Buddhist Organizations in Taiwan, 1989–1997*. Ph.D. Dissertation. Department of Political Science, University of British Columbia, Vancouver BC.

———. 2013. "The Growth of a Taiwanese Buddhist Association in China: Soft Power and Institutional Learning." *China Information* 27(1): 1–25. DOI: 10.1177/0920203X12466206.

Li, D. T. 1996. "Religion and Colonial Discourse: The Historical Transformation of Buddhism in Taiwan, 1895–1995." *Bulletin of the Institute of Ethnology Academia Sinica* 81(Spring): 19–52.

Li, Yu-chen. 2005. "Guanyin and the Buddhist Scholar Nuns: The Changing Meaning of Nun-Hood." *Selected Materials on Modern Taiwanese Buddhism*. Accessed on 20 December 2015 from http://buddhistinformatics.ddbc.edu.tw/taiwanbuddhism/tb/md/md11-04.htm

Lindholm, C. 2013. "Introduction." In *The Anthropology of Religious Charisma: Ecstasies and Institutions*, edited by Charles Lindholm, 1–32. New York, NY: Palgrave Macmillan.

Mack, L. 2014. *Taiwan History: A Brief History of Taiwan*. Accessed on 2 December 2015 from http://chineseculture.about.com/od/historyofchina/a/Taiwan-History.htm

Mitchell, J. P. 1997. "A Moment with Christ: The Importance of Feelings in the Analyses of Belief." *The Journal of the Royal Anthropological Institute* 3(1): 79–94.

Nye, J. 1990. *Bound to Lead: The Changing Nature of American Power*. New York, NY: Basic Books.

———. 2004. *Soft Power: The Means to Success in World Politics*. New York, NY: Public Affairs.

Pacey, S. 2012. "A Buddhism for the Human World: Interpretation of *Renjian Fojiao*." *Anthropology in China*. Accessed on 16 September 2015 from http://www.cnanthropology.com/article-911-1.html

Pitmann, D. A. 2001. *Toward a Modern Chinese Buddhism: Taixu's Reforms*. Honolulu: The University of Hawaii Press.

Schak, D. and H. M. Hsiao. 2005, May–June. "Taiwan's Socially Engaged Buddhist Groups." *China Perspectives*. Accessed on 20 December 2015 from http://chinaperspectives.revues.org/2803?lang=en

Snyder, D. N. 2006. *The Complete Book of Buddha's Lists—Explained*. Las Vegas, NV: Vipassana Foundation.

5

The New Face of Islam in the West:
The Case of Islamic Relief

Introduction

The purpose of this chapter is to discuss the new image Islam is fermenting in the West, especially in the United Kingdom and the United States. I do this primarily through a case study of Islamic Relief (IR)—one of the most influential transnational aid agencies built on an Islamic foundation but cleverly being transformed so as to be seen as a purely secular entity. I begin the chapter by considering some key perspectives on how readers can come to an understanding and appreciation of Islam. I then give an overview of the various types of Islamic transnational aid agencies, paving the way for the case study of Islamic Relief. I conclude the chapter with a brief analysis of the findings and a few reflective questions on the opportunities and threats facing IR.

How Should We Understand Islam?

Bulliet (2013) has built a strong case that the period 1300–1900 was the 'golden age' of Islam, yet this highly civilized time frame is not adequately discussed in academic circles. Bulliet's (2013) assertion points to the varied and complex nature of Islam especially when we see it in its many dimensions: historical, theological, cultural, and political. For the purpose of this chapter, we will look at three main standpoints that shape Islam.

First, there are the two theological schools of which categorize Islam. The world's Muslims are predominantly Sunni, with a significant minority of about 15 percent who are Shiites. Shiites are the dominant group in Iran, as they were in Iraq until the fall of Saddam Hussein in 2003. The United States and other Western nations have always considered Shiite Islam the more radical version of Islam until the birth of ISIS—a radicalized form of Sunni Islam that surpasses Al-Qaeda. ISIS is therefore a 'game changer' in several Western countries and in countries such as Indonesia, Malaysia, and Singapore where the Muslims are of the Sunni tradition and Shiite Islam is not encouraged (see Chapter 7).

The second standpoint is the political and nonpolitical aspects of the faith reflected in the terms 'Muslim' and 'Islam'. The terms Muslim and Islamic are often used interchangeably in the public sphere, the media, and even in academic writing. However, according to Denoeux (2002), in sociopolitical studies, 'Muslim' refers to a religious and cultural reality, whereas 'Islamic' has the connotation of political intent. For example, when we refer to a Muslim nation, we are alluding to a country where the majority of the people are followers of the Muslim faith. However, to label a nation as an Islamic state is to assert that this country bases its authority and constitutional basis on Islam. Furthermore, such nations subscribe to a form of Islamic fundamentalism, which implies a return to the literal foundations of the faith, and more than likely, this is a reference to an extreme or radicalized element within the Islamic faith. Because the term 'Islamic' may also refer to those who subscribe to the fundamental tenets of their faith, some scholars prefer to use the term 'Islamic revivalists' for fundamentalists who hold a highly politicized view of Islam (Rabasa et al. 2004).

It is important to recognize the diversity within Islam even in Fundamentalist Islam. Discerning scholars have observed a multiplicity of Muslim views on religious matters, politics, social issues, human rights, governmental roles, and educational content depending on the particular school or theology of Islam. The Rand Corporation (Rabasa et al. 2004) has studied the Muslim world and the varieties of Islam and Muslims' proneness to violent activities and has come up with a comparative typology (Table 5.1). On the left side of this continuum are the radical elements and on the right are the more liberal secularists.

The third major standpoint arises from the different perceptions within the Arab and the non-Arab Muslim worlds. Even though only 20 percent of the Muslim world are Arabs, Arabian perspectives and interpretations of Islam seem to dominate worldwide Muslim thinking and practice. Salafism (from the word 'Salaf', which means 'predecessor' to the prophet Mohammed), a movement from Saudi Arabia, calls for a return to the traditional ways of Islam. This, coupled with the fact that the holy sites of Islam[1] are situated in the Middle East and that the Quran's

Table 5.1:
A comparative typology of Islam

Radical Fundamentalists	Scriptural Fundamentalists	Traditionalists	Liberal Secularists	Modernists	Authoritarian Secularists
Mostly political, e.g., ISIS	e.g., Jama'a al Tabligh	e.g., Mainstream Shiites	e.g., Secular parties in Turkey and Indonesia	e.g., Muhammadiyah	e.g., The Ba'ath Party

Source: Adapted by the author Jonathan James (2016) from the Rand Corporation (2014: 7–14). Used with permission from the Rand Corporation.

Arabic nature cannot be violated, is the reason to explain this prevailing perception of Arabian supremacy. Another reason for the importance given to Arabian Islam could be the fact that the Muslim Brotherhood (a group that bemoans the loss of Islamic identity and fervently calls for Islam's return to a traditional and singular faith community) is located in the Middle East. There is controversy over the relationship between the Muslim Brotherhood and Salafism. The Brotherhood certainly accepts the teaching of Salafism[2] but it differs in its strategy for implementing the objectives of Salafism. Whereas Salafism wants the traditional and literalist version of Islam to be implemented immediately, the Brotherhood prefers to use the techniques of Western democracy and policies that engage with modernity in every dimension of life to ultimately bring about its reform objectives.[3] Incidentally, the Arab nations also happen to be the crucible for some of the world's most serious economic, social, and political disorders as evidenced by the fact that the world saw one of the largest movements of refugees from the Middle East (primarily Syria and Iraq) to Europe in August 2015.[4]

The Growth of Muslim Aid Agencies

Islamic traditions have always encouraged charitable giving through the obligatory zakat[5] (the 2.5 percent of income for the needy, given as an offering) as well as the waqf[6] (the religious endowment for Muslim causes given through financial institutions). The Hadith,[7] which is considered a revered, holy book—second only to the Quran—speaks of the importance of giving; the Islamic works system has to be carefully observed by Muslims for entry into heaven: "Heaven has 8 doors. He who prayed will be called from the door of prayer. He who paid zakat will be called from the door of zakat. He who fought will be called from the door of Jihad" (Al-Ghazali 1989: 427). Therefore, Western governments who come up with counterterrorism laws, such as imposing regulatory measures for money transfers, are overlooking the fact that *hawala*—an informal system through which the zakat and waqf are given—predates the modern banking system and continues till today. International financial systems estimate that the annual flow of funds through the hawala system is anywhere from US$70 billion to US$2 trillion (Pasas 2005).

A spate of human disasters has been largely responsible for the birth of the modern Islamic transnational aid organizations. This, coupled with the perceived hegemony of Western and Christian-based agencies, prompted the launch of Muslim aid agencies. Petersen (2012) has constructed a typology of transnational Muslim NGOs that operate as aid agencies. She has concluded that these organizations came into being through four significant events which she has termed as 'defining moments': the famine in the North of Africa (the 1980s); the conflicts in Afghanistan (1980–90); the war in Bosnia (1992–95); and the 9/11 terrorist attacks in the United States (2001; Petersen 2012: 764). An elaboration of each follows.

The famine in the Horn of Africa in the 1980s precipitated the establishment of several Muslim NGOs, principally the International Islamic Relief Organization of Saudi Arabia (IIROSA). Benthall and Bellion-Jourdan (2003) argued that IIROSA and other Gulf-based NGOs came into being to directly counteract and challenge Western hegemony in the field of aid to Muslim nations. This led to the establishment of many Muslim aid agencies which Petersen (2012) labelled the 'Da'watist' type of NGO. Da'watist, from the Arabic term Dawa, stands for an invitation and, specifically, it refers to an invitation for Muslims to submit to Allah and his mission.[8] These agencies were formed primarily to alleviate the suffering of fellow Muslims as a 'missionary' duty through aid and other means.

The conflict in Afghanistan (1980–90) saw the emergence of a second type of Muslim aid agency—the 'Jihadist' NGO (Petersen 2012: 768), which were not just to provide aid but to support "... more directly in the fight against the enemy.... In other words [it] simultaneously involved ... relief and Jihad (struggle)." Examples of Jihadist organizations include the Egypt-based Arab Doctors who established the Human Relief Agency in 1985; the Islamic Call Committee established by the Kuwait-based Society for Social Relief in 1986 (the branch of the Muslim Brotherhood); and the US-based Mercy Relief established in 1986 (Benthall and Bellion-Jourdan 2003: 73).

The war in Bosnia (1992–95), which was reported in much of the world's media, drew the attention of many Muslims to the plight of Muslims in this war-torn territory. This brought about the birth of a new wave of NGOs that were Western based but led by the immigrant Muslim population. These agencies include the Muslim Hands (1993) from Britain and the North American Global Relief Foundation (1990).

These organizations are called 'solidarity-based NGOs' as opposed to the Da'watist and the Jihadist types of NGOs, because their stance is one of neutrality rather than involvement in the politics of the conflict.

The final defining event, according to Petersen (2012), was the 9/11 attack in the United States in 2001. As suspicions arose that the American attacks were funded by Muslim NGOs, fueled in part by the media and US intelligence, this event spawned the birth of another cluster of Muslim NGOs—the 'secularized' type. Muslim NGOs, such as Islamic Relief and Muslim Aid, which were already in existence, started to quickly reposition themselves on a more secularized platform. They moved away from building mosques and strengthening the *Umma* (the community of Muslims worldwide) to involvement in "poverty reduction, sustainable development and capacity building … reflecting mainstream Western conceptions of aid…." (Petersen 2012: 773).

Islamic Relief

Islamic Relief is a transnational aid organization set up in the United Kingdom, with offices in 40 countries and it fits into the secularized category of Muslim NGOs as conceived by Petersen (2012). Known as IRW, this is one of the largest international Islamic charities in the world, with a $240 million operating budget and nearly 300 employees. IRW was founded in 1984 in the United Kingdom by a group of concerned postgraduate students; "[it] is an international relief and development charity which envisages a caring world where people unite to respond to the suffering of others, empowering them to fulfil their potential."[9] In this study, we refer to both the UK parent organization: IRW and the US branch, that is, IRUSA. The mission of IRUSA, based in Alexandria, Virginia, is to provide "relief and development in a dignified manner regardless of gender, race, or religion, and … empower individuals in their communities and give them a voice in the world."[10] It is a nonprofit humanitarian organization (approved by the Internal Revenue System in the United States),[11] with an aim to "provide rapid relief in the event of human and natural disasters and to establish sustainable local development projects, allowing communities to better help themselves."[12] IRUSA is an affiliate of IRW.[13] Toward the end of 2011, IRUSA had a collaborative partnership with the U.S. Department of Agriculture's (USDA) Center for Faith-based and Neighborhood Partnerships, as part of the Michelle Obama initiative[14] (Toplansky 2012).

A Muslim Charity

IR has carefully reinvented and positioned itself as an aid organization on par with its Western counterparts such as Christian Aid, Red Cross, and World Vision. This involved partly desacralizing its Islamic ideology so that it is seen as a secular humanitarian entity.[15] IRW is fully aligned with international standards of development. It has signed the Red Cross/Red Crescent code of conduct for NGOs, which prohibits proselytism and discrimination.[16] Furthermore, it has won the respect of international aid agencies and works actively with UN agencies such as UNICEF and WHO, to name two. This does not mean its Islamic values are annihilated. On the contrary, these values are still there as the IR website points out so clearly:

> These traits express the belief and define the culture of the organization. We remain guided by the timeless values and teachings provided by the revelations contained within the Qur'an and prophetic example.[17]

IRUSA specializes in refugee assistance and has had long-term experience working with the UN and specifically the United Nations Relief and Works Agency (UNRWA), the aid agency for Palestinian refugees.

And during the fasting month of Ramadan, special donations are sought for by IRUSA.

> It is up to Islamic Relief donors to give Ramadan food packages for Ramadan, and how many packages available to distribute this year and every year in Mogadishu is dependent on donor generosity…. With limited food packages donated to Somalia year, Islamic Relief had to make the difficult decision to prioritize those with special needs so that they will have food to eat by the first day of Ramadan. IRUSA donors helped with this effort and were part of the pool of 300 food packages distributed to disabled residents and their families in Mogadishu behind enclosed courtyard doors where they and their families could safely collect the food items.[18]

IRW and its affiliates operate on the Islamic moral economy, because its operations are guided and informed by Islamic principles from the Quran and the Hadith. This moral economy works well because Sharia-compliant banking institutions are chosen to partner with IR drawing on the principle of mutuality as it endeavors to establish close-knit communities, where Islamic principles are maintained. As Kroessin (cited in in Igoe 2015) reported:

> In my opinion there are clear areas in which the mission of aid and development organizations and the values of Islamic financial institutions overlap.
> In Kenya, Islamic Relief is working closely with a leading Kenyan Sharia-compliant bank, in a project funded by the U.K. development agency [Department for International Development]. This project aims to deliver easily accessible financial services to poor, marginalized pastoral communities in northeastern Kenya. This is a good example of the Islamic moral economy in action: the bank's involvement will impact its bottom line by building future customers, while Islamic Relief is providing vital financial services to people who can't get ordinary bank loans, bank accounts and so on. (Kroessin, cited in Igoe 2015)

IR caters to the Islamic practice of Zakat[19] and in their website, ample space is devoted to this.

> Offering zakah [zakat] is a religious obligation of all Muslims, and is the third of the five pillars of Islam (right after prayer). In Arabic, zakah means purification, growth and blessing. Paying zakah is meant to remind Muslims to be appreciative of the blessings that Allah (swt) has bestowed upon them, and to help empower those who have less.
> Islamic Relief collects and distributes zakah to those who are most in need, in accordance with Islamic guidelines. Giving your zakah through IRUSA means you can help provide emergency food, shelter for refugees, job training, medication and so much more.
> No matter who you send your zakah to, there's one thing in common: The people who receive it are truly grateful. It's more than a percentage, and more than a check—it's a link between hearts.[20]

The IR website even provides Zakat calculators[21] to help Muslims work out the percentage of their income that constitute their religious dues for the cause of Islam (Khan 2012: 100).

The underlying motivation for Muslim donors who give to IR is to adhere to the Muslim faith. The chief executive officer of IRW mentions that the name and the logo of IR (a mosque and two minarets) are the main motivators for securing Muslim donors (Khan 2012: 100). IR frequently refers to the Quran and the Hadith in their websites, printed literature, advertisements, and Islamic TV channels (Khan 2012: 100). Clearly, IR is a Muslim charity that caters primarily to Muslims—both donors and recipients of support.

Cultural Proximity and Networks

Aid efforts and development work have always been promoted in the Western media as a monopoly of the West, but there are more than 400 aid agencies associated with the Muslim faith (Clarke and Titensor 2014). Besides, the 2.5 percent giving that every Muslim gives for the poor usually goes through unofficial channels, such as the hawala, and therefore is not captured by Western media.

IR's Muslim ethos and staff are thought to have a positive effect in Muslim countries. In fact, organizations like IR were propelled into being because of the long-held monopoly of Western and Christian-led aid organizations. What Al Jazeera is to the news media, IR is to the aid agencies; Al Jazeera, the Muslim version of Cable News Network (CNN) was launched in part because of Western hegemony on media news coverage, especially the news coming out of the Middle East. Western aid workers may lack the cultural understanding and religious sensitivity in dealing with Muslims in the fields where disaster and dislocation of people take place (Kirmani and Khan 2008). In fact, studies have shown that Western aid workers bring with them the attachments and baggage of the West. "These actors serve as vectors for spreading and promoting values, norms and forms of social organization that are often perceived as alien to local beneficiaries" (De Cordier 2008: 9). Anecdotal evidence suggests that aid workers and volunteers who do short-term work are often ill-equipped to deal with Muslims, and some Western female aid workers dress too casually causing offence to the traditional mores of Islamic society.[22] Then there have been accusations levelled at certain Christian aid entities who combine relief and development with religious activities and even conversion (Ghandour 2003). De Cordier (2008) also found that some Western aid agencies were aligned with groups associated with armed conflict in some war-torn regions, thereby exacerbating the climate of polarization. In light of these factors concerning Western dominance, studies have shown that there is a place for Muslim aid agencies. For example, in the relief work undertaken in Aceh, Indonesia, after the Tsunami, it was the Muslim aid agencies that helped make access possible in this previously impenetrable region and "to some extent in smoothing the way for good working relationships" (Benthall 2008).

IRW's work in a war-torn and ravaged district in Mali, West Africa (which takes an inclusive approach to Muslim organizations on the ground) could be the model for future development work in Muslim countries undertaken by Muslim agencies.

> The project ... involves ... cereal banks, artisans' and food marketing cooperatives, school rehabilitation projects and literary centres. A special feature of this programme is that the local partners are Islamic associations. This contrasts with the history of external aid to Mali which has ... sought to marginalize Muslim networks.... (Benthall and Bellion-Jourdan 2003: 92)

Secularized

IR's mission statement shows how it has stripped back its Islamic heritage to appear as a secular humanitarian organization.

> Islamic Relief USA is a community of humanitarians—staff, volunteers, affiliates, supporters, partners, donors—who have been working together for a better world for more than 20 years.... Islamic Relief USA operates seven regional offices in the United States.... These IRUSA offices have been serving to educate, inform, and raise awareness about our various relief and development projects for years. Additionally, IRUSA holds seminars, banquets, concerts, and other public awareness programs across the country to help fund domestic and international projects.[23]

It is also possible to see IR's efforts to tame its Islamic persona (to what Westerners are comfortable with) in terms of economic rationalization—

using Western models of aid management for development in the Muslim world. The process of desacralizing IR was done with the assistance of a media savvy PR team and the elite community of Muslims living in the West. The politics of compromise used there was 'give and take'—and the result was a new *da'wah*: the religious mission of Islam stripped of conventional religious ideology and replaced with the trimmings of Western enterprise, development ethics, and imaging. So the aims of the Islamic community are still advanced in the fields (the Muslim nations and countries with large Muslim populations) but in the donor countries of the West, IR is just another humanitarian aid agency. IR is a signatory to the Copenhagen initiative—the Core Humanitarian Standard (CHS), an international quality and accountability framework that sets out nine commitments for member organizations involved in humanitarian and crisis response.[24]

IRUSA meets all of the standards for charity accountability of the Better Business Bureau (BBB) Wise Giving Alliance, a national charity monitoring group affiliated with the BBB system and is on the US government's Combined Federal Campaign (CFC) charity list, whilst also being a signatory to the code of conduct of the International Federation of Red Cross and Red Crescent Societies.

IRW is a member of the following international organizations: UK Aid, Aston Business School, Bond for International Development, and UNICEF, and its appeal is that it takes an integrated approach to alleviating poverty and promoting sustainable development outcomes.

IRW has taken the initiative in international advocacy on issues related to the Muslim world. According to its website, IRW "regularly visits the UN Headquarters in New York to speak with member States … offering them our expertise on humanitarian issues and faith sensitive approaches to complex topics" and "organizes side events with UN agencies and Governments at global forums such as the Commission for the Status of Women, the High Level Political Forum, and the UN General Assembly."[25] High-level politicians and aid organization leaders have endorsed IR and its multifaceted activities largely because of its compliance with Western standards of governance and aid culture.

The model of Islamic aid organizations like IR is based on operating a relief organization as a business, with a media savvy outlook and being careful to conform within the specific regulatory frameworks of Western aid agencies. IR does this well within the economic and political settings of the West, particularly in the United Kingdom and the United States. Surprisingly, studies have also shown that secularizing Islamic aid organizations affects Muslims in the fields (the aid-receiving countries) because some Muslims expected more from agencies like IR and were disappointed with the secular Islamic aid approach. For example, Palmer (2011), in his study of IR's efforts in Pakistan, reported the following comments from an aid recipient on the ground:

> We want Islamic Relief to establish a mosque inside the camp as we think they are Muslim and they should understand our needs. We can live without food but we can't live without our religion. (Cited in Palmer 2011: 103)

Although this is only one study, and IR was not at fault for implementing its broad policy in the field, it reflects the irony—IR's raison d'être was to be an alternative to Western hegemonic agencies; but in the end, IR's broad structures, institutional processes, and organizational procedures have ended up making it look just like the Western aid agencies—at least to some aid recipients. So this creates ambivalence; on the one hand, IR represents a form of moderate Islam to the Western public but on the other hand, it is too secular and non-Islamic in the eyes of some of the beneficiaries of IR's support on the ground.

Political Links

In spite of many controversies about IR (as mentioned in the following section), there has not been much scrutiny of IRW and its branches by Western governments. This could be due to the legitimacy conferred on IR by politicians around the world, who are impressed by the breadth and scope of IR's aid efforts as reflected in its carefully crafted communications.

IRW receives funding from the British government, and several cabinet ministers and even Prince Charles, heir to the throne, have participated in Islamic Relief fund-raising events and endorsed its work (Westrop 2013). In 2009, the British Foreign Office sponsored the IRW's 25th Gala dinner and in 2011, the Conservative Party in Britain screened an IRW video at its annual conference (Westrop 2013).

Westrop's (2013) investigations revealed that IR's political economy is such that there are links to UK Government officials.

> In 2011, the Scottish Government provided £398,000 as part of its £9 million International Development Fund. Humza Yousaf, a Scottish National Party member of the Scottish Parliament ... presently the Minister for External Affairs and International Development ... [was] formerly the media spokesperson for Islamic Relief. (Westrop 2013: para 1)

The current US administration is particularly cordial toward Islamic Relief as they appointed the former CEO of IRUSA into a prestigious office in the US State administration:[26]

> In April 2010, Mr. Ayoub was appointed to the U.S. Agency for International Development (USAID) Advisory Committee on Voluntary Foreign Aid (ACVFA). Along with other leaders in the international development field, Mr. Ayoub provides advice, analysis and recommendations to USAID on the most pressing development issues in the world today. Most recent, Mr. Ayoub was appointed to the U.S. State Department's Religion and Foreign Policy Working Group, where he will be advising on humanitarian issues.[27]

Reinventing Islam in the West: A New *Umma*?

A new Islamic space is being created in the West—one that coheres with Western ideology and resonates well with the educated and the elites of Western society, the governments, and their related agencies and other transnational humanitarian organizations. This new landscape is both physical and virtual. It is physical because a community with religious significance now exists and it is virtual because this community is not bound by geography and territory alone—for example, Muslims in the United Kingdom and the United States can help refugees in Syria via Internet donations. The flows of funds, personnel, and spiritual capital are connecting and assisting Muslim communities around the world.

Allievi (2003) explained that Islam for centuries was perceived by the West as the 'other'—an external player but "nowadays Islam is an internal social actor of the West" (Allievi 2003: 6). IR has carefully redesigned Islam through a collective presence with new cultural and religious meanings attached to Islam. This new landscape is constructed by a multiplicity of means but primarily through the media and is poised to change the whole perception and image of Islam. In some ways, this new public sphere can be seen as the construction of a new *Umma*—this is an Arabic word meaning 'community' or 'nation'.[28] In the context of Islam, the word *Umma* is used to mean the diaspora or 'community of the believers' (*ummat al-mu'minin*), and thus the whole Muslim world.[29] Muslim *Umma* also refers to the unity of Muslims all over the world, thereby privileging it with a transnational meaning.

> The Islamic *Umma* can be considered one of these social transnational spaces … we find the simultaneous presence of capital of an economic type (i.e.) financial resources), but also of human capital (skills and know-how), and lastly of that fundamental resource which is social capital made up of social links (a continuous series of translations, both face to face and indirect, to which the participants contribute and in which they find shared meanings, memories, future expectations and symbols…. (Allievi 2003: 8)

IR donors have referred to IR and its aid programs as being part of the worldwide Muslim community; quoting the Hadith, "the believers … are like one single body" (Khan 2012: 100).

IRUSA has special programs and projects to assist refugees to resettle in the United States, especially in Detroit, Kentucky, and Baltimore (where the Muslim population is higher than other cities) where hundreds of Syrian refugees have been resettled because of 'the rich Muslim community there'.[30] So IRUSA networks have aided in the enlarging of Islamic communities in the United States and at the same time, they are strengthening the *Umma* abroad. This has been described variously by scholars as 'new global sacred geographies' (Werbner 1996), 'transnational solidarities' (Soysal 2000), and 'geo-religion' (Allievi 1998).

IR also regularly supports projects in sensitive countries where Muslims have been ostracized by the Western media and govern-ments. It is reported that IR donors give priority to situations where they 'consider Muslims [are] victims', such as when the West projects these Muslims in the media as the criminals or the unjust ones (Khan 2012: 101). Donors prefer to support IR because of its 'strong Muslim identity' (Khan 2012: 101). The disadvantaged Muslims around the world are highlighted and they become the means of eliciting support for IR's aid programs from donors—who are the lifeblood of IR's operations.

As mentioned previously, IR's use of media is critical in forming the new public sphere. It intentionally counters the Western media stereotypes of Muslims as Jihadists, terrorists, and the like. IR uses newspapers, TV (as well as Muslim satellite television channels), the Internet and social media, political meetings, fundraisers, seminars, and campaigns to increase its new profile in the West. For example, the Google promotional website (Think with Google) has shared the success story of how IR informs donors and the significance of its use of the most advanced strategies in digital marketing.

> The charity's goal is to be present in the moments that matter to donors, so a comprehensive digital marketing program is essential to engage donors....
>
> "Search advertising enables us to be on Google around the clock when donors are looking for causes to donate to. In the moments that matter, search ads help us to be there," explains AIDA Digital Director Hassan Imtiazi. "During emergencies and disasters we can launch campaigns within hours. We don't think there is any other media outlet available which can be as powerful as search ads."
>
> To effectively grab the attention of the audience during key times, the ability to add sitelinks to search ads provides a key advantage.... During one of our major appeals last year, metrics show that we achieved over 10,000 conversions specific to the appeal's sitelinks. Overall click-through rate for sitelinks in our brand campaign during the period was 16%. The stats show around a 50% uplift in conversions from the previous year during the same appeal type.[31]

IR's use of media has encouraged multidirectional relations between donors in the United States and the United Kingdom and the disadvantaged Muslims abroad. For example, IR launched a July 2014 urgent appeal, claiming that the "Palestinian people now face the prospect of another devastating conflict, and the worst humanitarian crisis since the eight-day war of 2012."[32] According to IRW's Facebook page, the financial appeal raised £250,000 and was broadcasted live on the Islam Channel.[33] Another similar campaign raised the public consciousness about the plight of victims in Palestine.

[IRW] initiated a November 2006 campaign, 'Counting Orphans in Beit Hanoun', presenting profiles of orphans whose parents were allegedly killed in the Gaza 'massacre' and claiming that restrictions on movement and the crippling financial embargo are creating a humanitarian crisis in Palestine.[34]

Lewis (1998) found that 90 percent of the funds collected in the United Kingdom for charity went to the countries of migrant origin. Other studies showed that 'Islamodollars', a term referring to money for Islamic purposes, flowed in both directions (Allievi 2003). Therefore, IR's aid culture has empowered Muslims both in the donor countries and in the fields where aid is administered.

The media has been used to legitimize Islam in the West, especially in changing the negative image in the Western collective memory and vocabulary of people in the United Kingdom and the United States from terrorism, suicide bombers, and mass killings to saving, enabling, and empowering people in need. Allievi (2003) also alluded to the significant media development by IR, together with other aid agencies of the same genre, in 'written Islam'—because Islamic tenets were previously passed on orally and with the upsurge in the use of Western media, the teachings, practices, and ideas of Islam have now taken on permanency because as texts, they can now be quoted in a 'footnote or put in a bibliography' (Allievi 2003: 15). IR also undertakes research on gender issues and publishes academic working papers on topics specific to Muslims. According to the IRW website: "the Policy & Research team at Islamic Relief works to provide sound research, up-to-date analysis, and clear guidance on a range of issues, such as poverty reduction, human rights, gender justice, climate change and conflict transformation."[35] In one such paper by McDonald (2013), three controversial issues were mentioned in a scholarly manner: women's lack of access to mosques, polygamy, and female circumcision.[36] Sadly, whereas these issues were raised in a promising manner, the underlying motivations and the rampant practices referred to were not adequately addressed leaving the reader with more questions than answers. Umbrage is taken in the Quran, with the use of many quotations to support equality between men and women, but no clear solutions and ethical pointers are given about these three practices that are obviously troubling issues in the Muslim world.

Controversies

Controversies loom widely about IR because of allegations by three governments (Israel, UAE, and Russia) that IR has links with terrorist groups. On 19 June 2014, Israel's defense minister made a pronounce-ment that IRW was illegal, based on its alleged role in funneling money to Hamas and banned it from operating in Israel and the West Bank (Hamas has been designated a terror organization by Israel, the United States, EU, and Canada). According to news reports, the decision was made "after the Israel Security Agency (Shin Bet), the coordinator for government activities in the territories, and legal authorities provided incriminating information against IRW."[37] IRW announced that it would suspend the alleged operations and conduct an internal inves-tigation to look into the matter, but no clear answers have been given to the public since then.

> The Birmingham-based charity, which is widely respected, stre-nuously denied that it had any links with Hamas and said it was 'extremely surprised and concerned' by the [Israeli] minister's claims. But [IRW] said it was investigating the allegations and had chosen to effectively suspend its involvement in DEC until the process was completed.[38]

Soon after this incident, IRUSA distanced itself from IRW and made a point in their website that IRUSA is an independent and legal entity. Yet money raised by IRUSA still flows to IRW, and IRUSA still looks to IRW for visionary leadership and some board members are members of both entities.

Allegations of connections between IR and terrorism raise concerns, especially when IR is also advocating and enabling the resettlement of Middle East refugees in the West.

Another controversy is that a few of the board members of IRW have been known to have vested interests and some may have links with the Muslim Brotherhood[39] (Westrop 2013).

The financial reporting of funds is another contentious issue because in 2013, IRUSA's income was deliberately propped up to appear that it received more funding than it did for the explicit purpose of influencing a high-powered donor to give to IRUSA. The former CEO of IRUSA,

Abed Ayoub, was reported to have overstated the annual returns of IRUSA (the current IRUS CEO is Anwar Khan).

> While he was CEO of IR-USA, Ayoub presided over a period of falsely inflated growth for the well-known Islamic charity. By grossly misstating the value of deworming drugs, IR-USA gave the appearance of having over received over $160 million in donations in 2010. When it used corrected valuation techniques in 2011, IR-USA reported contributions of only $60 million. The fraudulent bookkeeping of 2001–2010 enabled IR-USA to attract larger institutional donors than it otherwise would have, along with political endorsements from top Democrats and partnerships with federal agencies. Smaller Islamic charities were some of the victims of this fraud, because federal officials have often encouraged Muslim donors to give their zakat to larger, more 'trustworthy', charities like IR-USA.[40]

IRUSA's financial management problems prompted an independent, nonprofit watchdog organization to downgrade IRUSA's privileged position among US aid agencies.

> In May of 2013, the financial rating of Islamic Relief USA, the nation's largest Islamic charity, was downgraded from four stars to two stars by the non-profit watchdog Charity Navigator. By October of 2013, it was announced that IR-USA's chief executive officer, Abed Ayoub, was leaving IR-USA to take over a northern Virginia charity now known as United Muslim Relief (UMR), that had dropped its old name, 'Muslims Without Borders' one day earlier. (GMB Website 2014)

Analysis

The Western hegemony of aid agencies has brought about Islamic aid agencies like IR, and Islamic aid organizations now enjoy a privileged position for relief efforts in Muslim majority lands.

Using Petersen's (2012) typology of the four types of Islamic aid agencies—Da'watist, Jihadist, Solidarity based, and Secularized—IR definitely fits neatly into the last typology, the secularized aid agency. However, a close examination of IR shows that residual elements of the other typologies may also be present in some form.

This study reveals that a Muslim presence in the public sphere was created soon after IR was established in the United Kingdom and the United States. Media (both old media and new media), networking, and advocacy have been used to construct a new Islamic identify and community in the West. The Muslim community, and what it stands for, has moved from the periphery to the center and flourished. This presence is important because it is the means by which the Western public now perceives Islam with a new set of lenses. IR's use of media is set in the context of ideological, political, and economic imperatives and its Western approach appeals to many people in the West. The idea of 'soft determinism' (Levinson 1997), which involves the interplay between the information presented and human action and planning that shaped its use and impact, can also help us understand the reception of IR's media messages in the West. IR's understanding of current social forces and trends has helped it to contour its message and promote ideas and ideologies of modern Islam appropriately. In this respect, IR's strategy appears to resemble that of the Muslim Brotherhood in so far as using Western, modern, and democratic means to achieve its long-term Islamic goals.

IR has created a new *Umma* within the United States and the United Kingdom. Furthermore, this transnational *Umma* is strengthened as aid, development, funds, and relief reach the Muslim countries. There is a reciprocal action between Muslims in the West and Muslims in Islamic nations as both can relate to each other. The dynamics of Islam is changing as the concept of a singular center of Islam is being challenged—there are multiple centers and the United States and the United Kingdom are fast becoming part of this interlocking web of Islamic networks.

The image of Islam is changing as Islam is being redefined and a different comprehension of Islam is taking place in the eyes of the West. This will undoubtedly affect not only Islam but also the image and value system of the West itself. However, that change is not that comprehensive because there are ambiguities within IR—because it is perceived differently in some Western and Muslim nations.

Whilst IR's public relations materials are heavy on rhetoric, they often do not contain clear and definitive answers especially on controversial issues and practices.

Petersen's typology (2011: 1) 'developmentalizing Islamic aid', and 'Islamizing development aid' may be applicable to my study of IR.

By the phrase, developmentalizing Islamic aid, Petersen (2015) referred to NGOs who seek to adjust their ideologies to the culture of development aid, hoping to curry favor with the Western aid organizations. And by Islamizing development aid, Petersen (2011) depicts the strategy of NGOs who create ideologies that appeal and satisfy conservative Muslim nations and people. There is little doubt that in an effort to bridge widely differing expectations from their audiences, IR has adjusted its ideologies. However, IR's approach in trying to appease the West and satisfy the Muslim world simultaneously is ambiguous and confusing. IR seems to aspire to operate in two constellations—the Western aid culture and the Islamic *Umma*. But can IR achieve a coherent ideology by coalescing the culture of aid and the religious *Umma*?

I have referred to controversies surrounding IR's flows, transparency, and political economy. The critical concern for Western authorities will be whether these controversies are well founded, thereby undermining the state sovereignty and security of Western nations.

Conclusion

Islamic Relief is a Muslim aid organization that came into being in the West to counteract the dominance of Western aid organizations and their propensity to politicize aid. My case study of IR suggests that the cultural and ideological dimensions of IR are generally acceptable in the Muslim contexts and in the West, IR has contributed to Islam being redefined: once thought as 'the other', Islam is slowly moving from the periphery to the center. But there are ambiguities within IR, and it is perceived variously in the West and amongst some of the Muslim nations.

Controversies surrounding IR have been examined and, although no incontrovertible evidence has been produced to prove that IR is directly linked with terrorism, there is some unease with IR even in the wake of its fairly good image and track record.

In the language of Petersen, IR has been developmentalizing Islamic aid and Islamizing development aid. How much longer can IR juggle these two strategies? Will other more radicalized Islamic aid organizations come into being in the meantime? Will Western state sovereignties be compromised, putting IR's activities in jeopardy? These questions about IR's opportunities, challenges, and threats will no doubt continue to consume researchers as we await the future direction of IR and other like-minded organizations. However, one issue is clear: Islam's perception is changing in the West. And, the West is changing because of IR's involvement with Western nations. In the future, scholars may continue to dichotomize Islam and the West; however, they must also acknowledge and attend to Islam in the West.

Notes

1. The Al-Masjid Al-Haram Mosque, Mecca; the Al-Masjid an-Nabawi Mosque, Medina, and the Al-Aqsa in Jerusalem are a few of the holy Islamic sites situated in the Middle East.
2. Salafism is not so much an organization, as a movement based on a worldview of religious issues. Salafi Muslims may not be opposed to cooperation with other Muslims but they are very set about their identity and their preference to follow the Islam of the first generation. They reject 'innovations' (*bid'ah*) introduced by modern-day Muslims. The Muslim Brotherhood has indicated that it follows the Salafi movement. Although most Salafis may not accept this, the Brotherhood is also a reform movement, which promotes adherence to the example and teachings of Muhammad. See: https://www.worldwatchmonitor. org/research/2594227
3. The Brotherhood is influenced by the teachings of Sayyid Qutb, whereby a strategy for reform, which engages strategically with the modern world, is used.
4. The BBC reported that according to UNICEF, the Middle Eastern wars are depriving some 13.7 million children out of education. See http://assistnews.net/index. php/component/k2/item/950
5. Zakat is an obligatory donation for the cause of Islam.
6. Waqf is a charitable trust (Islamic endowment) that is formed for some divine causes such as worship, building of mosques, education (schools/universities), relief (shelters/refugees camps), public or community services, etc. The waqf originator invests a property in perpetuity so that it remains in service. It cannot be sold, donated, or bequeathed.
7. The Hadith, in Islam, is second in authority only to the Quran. The Hadith is a record of the Prophet Mohammed's life, actions, and deeds. A saying in the Hadith is called a *Sunnah*. These Sunnah were transmitted by word of mouth down through the centuries having been memorized (hence pointing to the oral nature of Islamic culture) first by Muhammad's companions and other Muslims. Therefore, the Hadith is the written record of the oral traditions.
8. See http://www.islamtomorrow.com/dawah/event_planning.asp
9. See http://www.islamic-relief.org/
10. See http://irusa.org/

11. IRUSA is a 501c (3) organization in accordance with the IRS agency in the United States. All donations for these organizations are tax deductible.
12. See http://irusa.org/
13. IR refers to Islamic Relief in a generic way whilst IRW is a reference to Islamic Relief Worldwide and IRUSA, Islamic Relief USA.
14. USDA is a cabinet-level agency that oversees the American farming industry.
15. The term 'desacralizing' was first used by Petersen in 2010 in reference to Muslim aid agencies.
16. Originally known as the International Federation of Red Cross, in 1983 this organization's name was changed to the League of Red Cross and Red Crescent Societies. The word 'cross' caused offence to Muslim nations and hence the change in name for the Muslim nations.
17. See http://irusa.org/
18. Ibid.
19. The meanings are the same. In Arabic, zakah is the proper pronunciation, because the last letter of the word is a round 'taa' sound. People from the Indian/Pakistani backgrounds, because of the Urdu influence, mostly use Zakat. Other Arabic words that have different spellings and pronunciations include: Jannah/Jannat; Sunnah/Sunnat; Jama'ah/Jamaat; Ummah/Ummat. Ummah is also spelt without the letter 'h' at the end.
20. See http://irusa.org/
21. Zakat donations can be seen as controversial in some sectors because under Sharia law, Zakat donations can be used for several Islamic causes including Jihad for the sake of Allah.
22. See http://muslimmatters.org/2014/11/17/the-hypocrisy-of-feminist-outrage/
23. See http://irusa.org/
24. See: http://www.corehumanitarianstandard.org/
25. See http://www.islamic-relief.org/
26. The US State Department or the Department of State (DoS) is the federal executive department responsible for international relations of the United States, comparable to the foreign ministry in some countries.
27. See http://irusa.org/
28. *Umma*, sometimes spelt Ummah, is an Arabic word meaning 'community' or 'nation'. In the Quran, the word has spiritual connotation where Allah has sent his messengers to each *Umma*.
29. See http://islamic-dictionary.tumblr.com/post/4353858659/ummah-arabic-%D8%A3%D9%85%D8%A9-is-an-arabic-word-meaning
30. See http://irusa.org/
31. See https://www.thinkwithgoogle.com/intl/en-ae/case-study/islamic-relief-reaches-out-through-digital-to-immediately-and-efficiently-connect-with-donors/
32. See http://www.islamic-relief.org/
33. See http://www.ngo-monitor.org/article.php?operation=print&id=4279
34. Ibid.
35. See http://www.islamic-relief.org/
36. These three examples represent a sampling of the most repressive forms of gender persecution of women especially in Islamic fundamentalist societies.

37. See http://www.jpost.com/Operation-Brothers-Keeper/Israel-bans-Islamic-Relief-Worldwide-from-West-Bank-due-to-Hamas-ties-359934
38. See http://www.telegraph.co.uk/news/worldnews/11073602/Islamic-Relief-turns-down-Gaza-funds-after-Israeli-ban.html
39. The Muslim Brotherhood is a radicalized organization that uses democratic principles and modern strategies but has the goal of a return to traditional Sharia law. The words of former President Morsi of Egypt reflect this intention: "The Koran is our constitution, the Prophet Muhammad is our leader, jihad is our path, and death for the sake of Allah is our most lofty aspiration ... sharia, sharia, and then finally sharia. This nation will enjoy blessing and revival only through the Islamic sharia." (See http://www.nationalreview.com/corner/304243/meet-egypts-new-president-obama-endorsed-largely-secular-muslim-brotherhood-andrew-c) Western leaders may mistake the pragmatism of the Brotherhood leaders for ideological flexibility. However, whilst the flexibility is strategic, their end seems to be the same with the Salafi movement and other fundamental groups.
40. See https://moneyjihad.wordpress.com/2014/11/09/leadership-shuffle-at-u-s-islamic-charities/

References

Al-Ghazali Abu Hamid. 1989. *The Remembrance of Death and the Afterlife*. Translated by T. J. Winter. Cambridge: Islamic Texts Society.

Allievi, S. 1998. *Les conventis a Islam: Les nouvaeux musubmans d'Europe (The Conventions in Islam: The New Muslims of Europe)*. Paris: L'Harmattan.

———. 2003. "Islam in the Public Space: Social Networks, Media and Neo-Communities." In *Muslim Networks and Transnational Communities in and Across Europe*, edited by S. Allievi and J. S. Neilsen, 1–27. Leiden: Brill.

Benthall, J. and J. Bellion-Jourdan. 2003. *The Charitable Crescent: The Politics of Aid in the Muslim World*. London: I. B. Tauris.

Benthall, J. 2008, 26 June. "Have Islamic Aid Agencies a Privileged Relationship in Majority Muslim Areas? The Case of Post-Tsunami Reconstruction in Aceh." *The Journal of Humanitarian Assistance*. Accessed on 19 August 2015 from https://sites.tufts.edu/jha/archives/153

Bulliet, R. 2013. "Islam: The 'Open Civilization'." Accessed on 19 August 2015 from https://www.youtube.com/watch?v=tUmgtmvLaJw

Clarke, M. and D. Titensor, eds. 2014. *Islam and Development: Explaining the Invisible Aid Economy*. Surrey: Ashgate.

De Cordier, B. 2008. "The Humanitarian Frontline, Development and Relief and Religion: What Context Which Threats and Which Opportunities?" *Conflict Research Group*, Working Paper No. 10. Accessed on 7 September 2015 from http://www.psw.ugent.be/crg/Publications/working%20papers/workingpaper_decordier.pdf

Denoeux, G. 2002, June. "The Forgotten Swamp: Navigating Political Islam." *Middle East Policy* 9(2): 56–81.

Ghandour, A. 2003, 24 December. "Humanitarian Aid, Islam and the West: Contest or Cooperation." *Humanitarian Exchange Magazine.* Accessed on 9 September 2015 from http://www.odihpn.org/humanitarian-exchange-magazine/issue-25/humanitarianism-islam-and-the-west-contest-or-cooperation

GMB website. 2014, 11 November. "Islamic Relief USA Replaces CEO; Charity Once Part of a Michelle Obama Initiative." *The Global Muslim Brotherhood Daily Watch.* Accessed on 20 August 2015 from http://www.globalmbwatch.com/2014/11/11/islamic-relief-usa-replaces-ceo-charity-part-michelle-obama-initiative/

Igoe, M. 2015, 31 July. "What You Need to Know About Islamic Finance." *Devex Website.* Accessed on 7 September 2015 from https://www.devex.com/news/what-you-need-to-know-about-islamic-finance-86635

Khan, A. A. 2012. "Religious Obligation or Altruistic Giving? Muslims and Charitable Donations." In *Sacred Aid: Faith and Humanitarianism*, edited by M. N. Barnett and J. G. Stein, 90–114. New York, NY: Oxford University Press.

Kirmani, N. and A. A. Khan. 2008. "Does Faith Matter: An Examination of Islamic Relief's Work with Refugees and Internally Displaced Persons." *Refugee Survey Quarterly* 27(2): 41–50.

Levinson, P. 1997. *The Soft Edge: A Natural History and Future of the Information Revolution.* Oxon: Routledge.

Lewis, P. 1998. "Muslim Communities in Britain: Towards an 'Arab' Contribution to Religious and Cultural Understanding." In *Arabs and the West: Mutual Images*, edited by J. S. Neilsen and S. A. Khasawnih, pages 43–58. Amman: University of Jordan.

McDonald, L. Z. 2013. "Women, Faith and Justice: Framing an Islamic Approach to Gender and Development." Working Paper Series No. 03. *Islamic Relief Worldwide.* Accessed on 20 August 2015 from http://policy.islamic-relief.com/wp-content/uploads/2014/05/Islam-Gender-and-Development-Working-Paper.pdf

Palmer, V. 2011. "Analyzing Cultural Proximity: Islamic Relief Worldwide and Rohingya Refugees in Bangladesh." *Development in Practice* 21(1): 96–108.

Pasas, N. 2005. "Informal Value Transfer Systems, Terrorism and Money Laundering." *US Department of Justice.* Accessed on 20 August 2015 from https://www.ncjrs.gov/pdffiles1/nij/grants/208301.pdf

Petersen, M. J. 2011. *Summary: The Thesis for Humanity or for the Umma?* Accessed on 20 July 2015 from http://hum.ku.dk/kalender/2011/oktober/umma/summary_resume_marie_juul_petersen.pdf

——. 2012, August. "Trajectories of transnational Muslim NGOs." *Development in Practice* 22(5–6): 763–77.

Petersen. M. J. 2015. *For Humanity or for the Umma? Aid and Islam in Transnational Muslim NGOs.* London: C. Hurst & Company.

Rabasa, Angel M., C. Bernard, P. Chalk, C. Christine Fair, T. Karasik, R. Lal, I. Lesser and D. Thaler. 2004. "The Muslim World After 9/11." *The Rand Corporation.* Accessed on 10 July 2015 from http://www.rand.org/content/dam/rand/pubs/monographs/2004/RAND_MG246.pdf

Soysal, Y. N. 2000. "Citizenship and Identity: Living in Diasporas in Post War Europe." *Ethnic and Racial Studies* 1(23): 1–15.

Toplansky, E. F. 2012, 25 September. "Moslem Brotherhood in Terrorist White House." *Terror News*. Accessed on 15 August 2015 from http://terrornewsbriefs.blogspot. com.au/2011_09_01_archive.html

Werbner, P. 1996. "Stamping the Earth in the Name of Allah: Zikr and the Sacralizing of Space Among British Muslims." *Cultural Anthropology* 11(3): 309–38.

Westrop, S. 2013, 13 July. "UK Funds Terror Connections: Islamic Relief Worldwide." *Gatesone Institute International Policy Council*. Accessed on 31 August 2015 from http://www.gatestoneinstitute.org/3792/islamic-relief-worldwide-terrorism

6

The Gülen-Hizmet Movement: Reformed Islam or Revitalized Caliphate?

Introduction

In 2008, two international magazines (*Foreign Policy* and *Prospect*) conducted a poll to determine the world's most influential public intellectual. Surprisingly, a relatively unknown Turkish individual, Fethullah Gülen, won by a wide margin of 500,000 votes, prompting an article in the following edition of *Prospect* magazine in which Schwartz (2008), the author, answered the question that was obviously nagging many readers: Who is the real Fethullah Gülen?

Fethullah Gülen is a Turkish Islamic cleric (of the Sunni tradition) who is now in self-imposed exile in the United States. He was the founder of the Gülen-Hizmet Movement (GHM), a transnational organization based in Turkey with a net worth estimated to be at least US$25 billion.[1] GHM has a membership of anywhere between 4 and 6 million followers worldwide, some 1,000 schools, several universities, cultural groups, hospitals, media outlets, businesses, and a bank.[2] GHM is known as a counter entity to radical forms of Islam and presents a circumspect and moderate conception of Islam rather than the sharia-type version of the faith portrayed by Al-Qaeda and ISIS.

Gülen, who believes Islam is compatible with the West and Western science, deserves to be credited for his efforts in modernizing Turkish education, extending it to the underdeveloped frontiers, and consequently improving the nation's overall economic development. Gülen's goal is the empowering of a 'golden generation' of young people educated in science and maths with Muslim ethics as a foundation (Yildirim and Kirmizialtin 2004). The founder's goal is not limited to Turkey but extends throughout Central Asia and large sections of the world with a growing focus in the United States and other Western nations. The GHM gained much notoriety over the last few years and especially in mid-2016 after the attempted coup in Turkey, which, according to the President of Turkey Recep Tayyip Erdogan, was allegedly masterminded by Gülen followers.

Scholars like Balci and Miller (2012) have found that researching the GHM is not an easy task because the group is disingenuous. GHM disavows relationships between member organizations and has a tendency toward secrecy in many respects; for example, there are no membership records.

> There are many challenges in conducting research on the GHM. Certainly, one of the chief ones is the organization's cautionary approach, which has few footprints for researchers to follow. (Balci and Miller 2012: 14)

Where GHM has received both strong criticism and widespread adulation in Turkey and across the world, I take a nuanced approach in this chapter, with four main arguments, which are as follows:

1. Even though GHM is a product of the complex politico-social, religious, and historical circumstances of Turkey and Central Asia, its growth and current profile is mainly due to the charismatic and pragmatic nature of the founder and the symbiotic relationship forged between Fethullah Gülen and the AKP-led government (AKP is also called the Justice and Development Party). Unfortunately, in recent years, there has been a major fallout between these two allies.
2. GHM is a good example of the fusion of Islam and modernity and the positive effects of such a marriage especially in the realms of education and civic engagement.
3. GHM is actively presenting its version of Islam as a counter narrative to the radicalized understanding of Islam framed in particular by the Western media.
4. Although GHM is a 'breath of fresh air' among worldwide Muslim movements because of its perceived moderate version of Islam, its secretive, amorphous, and sprawling nature invites critical concern. Time will tell whether the Gülen agenda is merely the promotion of a religiosity based on inner piety (ethical Islam) and civic engagement, or whether it consists of veiled hopes for the revival of the Ottoman caliphate as part of a complex 'cultural jihad' strategy.

I begin with a brief overview of the life and charisma of the founder, Fethullah Gülen. I then present the theological underpinnings of GHM and go on to explore the following: the significant political influences that gave birth to the movement, GMH's operations, its promotion of a contextualized form of Islam, its controversies, and its future.

The Charisma of the Founder

Fethullah Gülen was born in 1941 in a village near eastern Turkey. The son of a teacher, Gülen learned Arabic and, at the young age of 16, he was exposed to the writings of Turkish Sunni reformer Nursi. In 1958, he was authorized by the state to become an Imam (Muslim preacher); after a stint of military service, he moved to Izmir to continue his religious activities. In 1962, he was accused of making seditious comments in his sermons, although the charges were later dropped (Seufert 2014). In 1969, his preaching took on a different turn as he modified the teachings of Nursi (see in the sequel) and Bahauddin Naqshband and came up with his own version of contemporary Islam for the masses. With the help of businessmen who believed in his vision, Gülen built dormitories (or lighthouses, *ışıkevi*) in Izmir because he had concerns that the new generation of Muslims would be swept away by the cares and snares of worldly living. His action of building dormitories for students dovetailed with Turkey's rapid urbanization and growth in its major industries. These dormitories/lighthouses provided a sense of community and purpose for young people.

From these humble beginnings, Gülen's mission began to grow and expand, first in Turkey, then all across the world. Gülen is the spiritual leader of the worldwide movement, GHM. His sermons and writings constitute the main discussions at his followers' meetings which are called 'conversations', and at the after-school mentoring sessions called *sohbet*.

Gülen currently lives in the United States, but he is regularly briefed on the issues facing the movement. His 'suggestions' are apparently interpreted as near commands according to one of his closest men and president of the Pennsylvania Camp, Askoy, who also said for Gülen that 'He knows everything' (cited in Hansen 2010). Gülen is referred by followers as *Hocaefendi* or 'the revered teacher'. Gülen has earned the right to be revered having built a vast empire of businesses and schools and amassed power in shaping modern Turkey. Today, thousands of Gülen's disciples hold influential positions in Turkey. Gülen's charisma and vision enabled him to be ahead of his time. During the 1960s in Turkey, leftist and rightist students constantly clashed in the streets. Universities were frequently closed. Gülen believed the new generation had lost its moral compass and could only regain it through education (Mercan, cited in Bilgincan 2016). As a charismatic leader, Gülen seized the moment and articulated to his people that there was a crisis—that humanity had strayed from Islamic morality and the solution was to bring people back to the fold through the building of lighthouses: "The lighthouses are places where deficiencies of people ... are closed up" (Gülen cited in Sen 2001: 111–12). Gülen saw the vision of empowering the young of Turkey through education and religion, and today, he is reaping the harvest of his investment and foresight.

Theological Underpinnings of GHM

Sufism

Besides the two main branches of Islam—Sunni and Shia (see Chapters 4 and 6)—Islam also has a mystical branch, Sufism, with its various Sunni and Shia subsets. Some scholars consider Sufism a sect within Islam, while others consider it an alternative way of approaching Islam through mysticism. Sufism is defined as "mystical Islamic belief and practice in which Muslims seek to find the truth of divine love and knowledge through direct personal experience of God" (Adherents of mystical Islam are known as Sufis and their religious life is known as Sufism; Schimmel 2012: para 1). Adherents of mystical Islam are known as Sufis and their religious life is known as Sufism (Schimmel 2012).

Sufism, like its counterpart Christian monasticism, originated as an early ascetic movement within Islam, with the goal of counteracting worldly temptations experienced by followers living in modern times. The earliest form of Sufism came into being during the Umayyad Dynasty (661–749)[3] less than a century after the founding of Islam

(Khanam 2006). During this period, teachers and followers who were prone to mystical Islam, meditated on selective passages in the Quran that focused on judgment and woe; therefore, these followers were referred to as 'those who always weep' (Yamin 2008: 205). Through intense devotion, Sufis hope to attain *ikhlas*, absolute purity (Lobel 2007). In their efforts to obtain purity, Sufis are dedicated to absolute trust in God (*tawakkul*), another defining concept in Sufism (Khanam 2006; Lobel 2007). The love of God for man and the love of man for God are two recurring themes in Sufi poetry and hymns.

Sufism later developed organizationally into fraternal orders, in which disciples followed the teachings of a leader–founder. The thirteenth century ushered in the golden age of Sufism, because it was the era of prolific writings and the flourishing of Islamic poetry. Significant leaders in this period included: Ibn Arabi of Spain, Ibn al-Farid of Egypt, Jalal ad-Din ar-Rumi of Persia, and Najmuddin Kubra of Central Asia (Khanam 2006). By this time, Sufi writings and thought had influenced the rest of the Islamic world and helped shape Islamic society.

The Sufism that is practiced by the GHM is based on Sunni Islam from the Hanafi School (one of the four subsets of Sunni Islam).[4] Gülen, the founder of GHM, defines Sufism in the following manner:

> Sufism is the path followed by an individual who, having been able to free himself or herself from human vices and weaknesses in order to acquire angelic qualities and conduct pleasing to God, lives in accordance with the requirements of God's knowledge and love, and in the resulting spiritual delight that ensues. (Gülen 1999: xiv)

The Influence of Said Nursi

GHM was also greatly influenced by the Sufi Islamic reformer Said Nursi (1878–1960) and his Nur movement (also known as the Nurcu Movement or Nurçuluk) in Turkey. GHM is one of the eight Islamic groups that are believed to have evolved as extensions of the teachings and work of Said Nursi who advocated a reinterpretation of Islam according to the needs of modern society. He taught that change should come through the formation of a new mindset in individuals, rather than through institutional transformation. Nursi authored several volumes of Quranic exegesis known as *Risale-i Nur* and is well known for his debates and other dialogue with Turkish people about religion, nationalism, and secularization (Yavuz 1999).

Interestingly, Nursi's life bears a striking resemblance to that of his protégé Fethullah Gülen. Though moderate in his views on Islam, Nursi was often misunderstood by the authorities and spent time in prison. Nursi was initially a supporter of Atatürk (the founder of modern Turkey); however, in 1925, he was arrested and accused of participating in activities that encouraged reviving the caliphate. While in prison, Nursi began to write what would later become one of Islam's most influential texts: the *Risale-i Nur* (Epistles of Light), a multivolume commentary on the Quran (Yavuz 1999).

Nursi's *Risale-i Nur* had a mixed reception in Turkey. For a time, it was deemed seditious and therefore banned by the authorities yet other segments of Turkey embraced the new teachings. This work eventually created the foundation for 'reading circles', Islamic communities that gathered to read, discuss, and practice the text, thereby establishing the fledgling Nur movement. The reading circle movement grew widely throughout Turkey. Hakan Yavuz (1999: 585) described the Nur movement as "a resistance movement to the ongoing Kemalist modernization process, [but also] 'forward-looking'." The Nur movement took Muslims to another level—from being Muslims in a confessional community to a civic-minded Muslim community in a secular society (Yavuz 1999).

In particular, Nursi brought four profound and revolutionary teachings, which helped to shape GHM which are as follows:

1. **Islam's compatibility with modernity:** Nursi adhered to a conservative and orthodox interpretation of Islam but one that made room for modernity. Nursi saw the potential for Islam to become a moralizing force capable of transforming Turkish society (Sukran 2012). He, therefore, sought to revive Islam in Turkey by blending it with the modern sciences, and, at times using mass communication as a means of propagation (Sukran 2012). Nursi also advocated many Western concepts such as nationalism, democracy, and human rights.

2. **A new form of jihad: greater jihad versus lesser jihad:** Nursi adopted the Sufi understanding of the 'other' in Islam—not as a reference to non-Muslims but rather to the self (Askoy 2015; Yavuz 1999). Likewise, Nursi took the term 'jihad' from the Arabic root

word 'to strive' to mean inner jihad. For Sufis, inner 'jihad' is a call to praise God and conquer the inner sins that cause problems in society: revenge, jealousy, envy, and treachery (Askoy 2015; Yavuz 1999). These are the sins that separate the believer from God and man; therefore, jihad is needed to separate oneself from these sins. Sufis identify this inner struggle to overcome inner desires as *jihad al-akbar* (the greater jihad) whereas war with the sword is termed *jihad al-asghar*, the lesser jihad (Askoy 2015; Yavuz 1999).

In doing so, Nursi adopted the understanding of jihad from the Meccan period (610–22),[5] when jihad was viewed as a non-violent activity of persuasion and conversation by contrast; in the Medina phase, jihad was interpreted by certain Muslims to mean war of conquest or conversion against unbelievers.

3. **The coexistence of religion and politics:** Religion, for Nursi, comprises a complex of continuities based on our subjective experience of everyday life. Even though he lived and fought through the atrocities of World War I and felt the pain of World War II, Nursi believed that politics is not the subject of the Quran. However, he made statements about politics in his formulation of the five principles, which are necessary to prevent a nation from anarchy: respect, compassion, refraining from what is prohibited (haram), security, and the giving up of lawlessness and being obedient to authority (Askoy 2015; Yavuz 1999). Nursi was careful though to add that these requirements are to be observed only if the leaders in control are free from self-interest. He described the politics of self-interest as savagery (Askoy 2015; Yavuz 1999). Nursi reconciled politics and religion by stating that the essence of democracy is derived from sharia and despotic regimes are opposed to sharia (Askoy 2015; Yavuz 1999).

Nur members were largely apolitical; however, that did not stop them from supporting the Islamist candidates, such as Neçmeddin Erbakan and the National Salvation Party in the 1970s. But following Nursi's death in 1960, disagreements among his members led to rifts within the movement (Yavuz 1999).

4. **The importance of dialogue:** Nursi encouraged his followers to think afresh on peacemaking as opposed to violence and warfare. In the 1950s, he preached that Muslims should join Christians

against atheism, and he made attempts to contact Pope Pius XII and Patriarch Athenagoras (Yavuz 1999).

Following in Nursi's footsteps, Fethullah Gülen began promoting interfaith dialogue in the 1990s in Turkey. Gülen developed ties with all Christian churches in Turkey including the Greek Orthodox and had meetings with Patriarch Bartholomew I and Armenian Patriarch Mesrob Mutafyan. He sought an audience with Pope John Paul II, which was held in Rome in 1998, and met the Sephardic Chief Rabbi of Jerusalem, Eliyahu Bakshi-Doron (Yavuz 1999).

Evolution of GHM

As I developed the narrative of GHM, it became apparent that Gülen is more interested in the creation of a 'cultural Islam' or 'civil faith' rather than a political Islam. For Gülen, Islam is a religion rooted in the soul—piety with the creator—God is the basis for piety in the world. Islam is a relational faith. And the purpose of faith is twofold: character formation, followed by good works.

The Gülen movement emerged from the Nur movement in the 1960s. Gülen's *cemaat* (or community of believers) came out of the Nur reading circle movement. However, there are additional characteristics that Gülen incorporated into GHM. Gülen was born in a village near Erzurum, the eastern border of what is now the Turkish Republic. This territory was contested by various nations, such as Russia, Persia, and the Ottoman Empire. The people around Erzurum therefore held diverse interpretations of Islam—some strongly embedded in Turkish nationalism. Consequently, this Turkish nationalistic understanding of Islam led Gülen to become more of a Turkish nationalist in his approach than Nursi. Also, Gülen was influenced by neoliberal economic policies. Thus, the Gülen movement took Nursi's orthodoxy (right theology) and turned it into orthopraxy (right practice). Praxis is important because, in GHM's view, Islam is not only about praying regularly and reading the sacred texts; it is about creating and working in real-world institutions. In this sense, GHM is 'this worldly' in its outlook: it wants to create a form of 'paradise' in this world—an educational system, hospitals, institutions, and related entities.

Hence, Gülen's activism does not consist of traditional 'mission-ary' endeavors: it permeates society through educational, business, professional, and civil sectors, that is, through a network of educated Muslims influencing society.

As indicated previously, to understand GHM and its current operations, one must be aware of the political and historical context of Turkey. Therefore, I now provide a brief sketch of the history of Turkey.

A Historical and Political Sketch of Turkey

In the first century, Christianity took root in Turkey through the Apostle Paul's missionary journeys there. Turkey was then part of the Roman Empire. A season of persecution against Christians came to an end in 313 AD when the Emperor Constantine became a Christian.[6]

In the middle ages, Turkey, under Byzantine rule,[7] saw the flourishing of the arts and architecture (New World Encyclopedia 2014). However, in the seventh century, the Arabs attempted to conquer Constantinople (the capital of the empire) but were held out for over 300 years. In the eleventh century, the Seljuk Turks from Central Asia moved South taking Baghdad in 1055 and soon afterwards, the Turks ruled most of Turkey introducing Islam and Turkish culture (Teall and Nicol 2015). After centuries of the establishment of Turkish culture, the Mongols defeated the Turks in 1243. The subsequent withdrawal of the Mongols left Turkey divided into a number of states (Teall and Nicol 2015).

Around 1288, a leader named Osman created a new state in Turkey, which later led to the Ottoman Empire. In the fourteenth century, the Ottomans gradually extended their territory and in 1453, Constantinople came under Turkish control. Subsequently the Turks made inroads into Europe capturing the Balkans and Egypt (Lamazoff and Ralby 2012). The sixteenth century was the golden age of the Ottoman Empire because it amassed power, territory, and riches especially under Sultan Suleiman I (1520–66). Known as Suleiman the magnificent, the Sultan (also known as Caliph) captured Hungary in 1526 (Quataert 2005). The Turks were defeated at sea by the Spanish and Venetians at the battle of Lepanto in 1571. Nevertheless, the Turks were a force to be reckoned with. In 1573, they captured Cyprus (Quataert 2005).

In the seventeenth century, the Turkish Empire declined, and the Turks surrendered Hungary by signing a treaty in 1699. In the eighteenth century, after a series of wars with Russia, the Turkish Empire had to face Russia's claim for more territory (Quataert 2005). The nineteenth century marked the slow decline of the Turkish Empire, despite the efforts of Sultan Abdul Hamid II (1876–1909) to modernize Turkey by constructing a comprehensive railway and telegraph system (Shaw and Yapp 2016). During this time, Romania and Serbia became independent (later Bulgaria followed suit in 1908). In 1908, a revolution took place in Turkey, which forced the Sultan to call for elections which shortly after led to the weakening of the caliphate and its eventual abolishment.

Turkey's decision to back Germany in World War I meant that Turkey was defeated in the World War I and therefore lost its empire. The Treaty of Sevres in 1920 divided and allocated the empire to Britain, France, and their allies (Lewis 1961). This prompted an Ottoman commander, Mustafa Kemal, to lead a war of independence against the 'foreign' forces, which ultimately led to the signing by the allies of the World War I of the historic Treaty of Lausanne, Switzerland. Turkey gave up all claims to the remainder of the Ottoman Empire and in return, the allies recognized Turkish sovereignty within its new borders (Lewis 1961, 1993). Kemal, who then became the first president of the republic of Turkey, later became known to his people as Atatürk, 'Father of the Turks'. Atatürk is also known for his strict implementation of modernization that emphasized economic development and secularization (Findley 2005). He fused Turkish culture with European laws, introduced the Latin script, outlawed the wearing of scarfs by women and the fez by men, and gave women the right to vote. More importantly, he was responsible for the separation of Islam from the state—following the Western model. He remained president of Turkey until his death in 1938 (Balfour 1979; Gunter 2012).

Turkey remained neutral in World War II but joined NATO in 1952. In 1960, the Turkish army staged a coup, but shortly afterwards new elections were held and democracy was restored. A series of coups have punctuated the chequered history of modern Turkey. Then in 1999, Turkey was formally accepted as a candidate for EU membership (Findley 2005).

After two Islamic parties were banned (the Welfare Party and the Virtue Party), in August 2001 a group led by Abdullah Gül and Recep

Tayyip Erdogan (a former mayor of Istanbul) formed the AKP (or AK Party, *ak* in Turkish means 'white' or 'clean'), as a democratic and conservative political party. Unlike its predecessors, the AKP did not focus on an Islamic agenda, although the political roots of the AKP and some of the party's political endeavors (including its proposed regulation of the display and advertisement of alcohol, and the head scarves worn by some AKP leaders' wives) meant that the AKP was viewed with suspicion by some segments of Turkey right from the outset.

In spite of the fact that the AKP was a relatively new party, it won enough seats in the November 2002 parliamentary elections to earn a decisive majority in the 550-seat parliament. The AKP-led government had espoused a foreign policy that intentionally cultivated friendships in the region, offering trade, visa-free travel, and economic aid. This policy has been termed 'Strategic Depth', and it basically involves Turkey rebuilding ties with the nations that once constituted the former Ottoman Empire (Coskun 2016).

It is important to note that a strong relationship was forged between GHM and AKP leaders even before the formation of the AKP party. Political observers such as Sunier (2014) have asserted that Gülen's backing was responsible for AKP's landslide victory in the 2002 general elections. GHM and the AKP enjoyed a symbiotic relationship over the years forging extensive political, economic, and legal reform in Turkey, some of which were felt even in the state and military elites: "It was thus under the AKP's authority [that GHM] accumulated influence in Turkey's police forces, the judiciary, the military and in the Ministries of Education, Foreign Affairs, Trade and elsewhere" (Hendrick 2016). The relationship between GHM and AKP developed and seemed to be strong until late 2011 when both groups tried to consolidate their power bases, which led to a breakdown in their partnership (Hendrick 2016).

Understanding GHM and Gülen

Contextualized Turkish Islam

Turkish nationalism is important for Gülen. As a student of history, he believed that Turkey had a lot to offer the world. So he envisaged a form of Turkish Islam that was influenced by Sufism and enriched with Turkey's historical, cultural, and political experiences with the West. Gülen's initial expansion plans for GHM was in Central Asia and the Baltic region because his sense of nationalism was steeped in the legacy of the Ottoman Empire. Gülen was known to have looked at the map of Turkey as he reminisced the glorious days of the past. According to Koyuncu-Lorasdaği (2010: 225): "Gülen directed businessmen who were sympathetic to his cause to invest in reconstruction of the Turkish republics."

At the basis of Gülen's teachings is the notion that state and religion should be reconnected as they were in Ottoman times and that Turkey should be the beacon for the Balkans and the republics in the Caucasus. Through Gülen, a 'neo-Nur' philosophy was integrated into Turkish and pan-Turkic nationalism, which explains his success among ethnic Turkic peoples in post-Soviet Central Asia. Through hundreds of private schools operating in the Central Asian republics, GHM has given Turkey a new strategically significant cultural and economic role to play. At the same time, GHM expanded to the former Soviet republics, where communism prevailed; the movement offered a sense of cultural and religious identity to communities after the fall of Communism.

> Starting with the collapse of the Soviet Union in 1991, Gülen dispatched his students to the former Soviet republics of Central Asia, where he rightly suspected that they might find some postcommunist youths in need of religion. (Hansen 2010)

It was very strategic that Gülen and the GHM began their efforts in the immediate region and not in the Arab world. The Arab world was not sympathetic toward this movement because they perceived that GHM did not have an accurate understanding of Islam.[8]

Gülen's approach seemed to reconstruct the actions and strategic policies of the previous Turkish governments and the current government of Erdogan up until the early part of 2000 when rifts began between AKP and GHM. For example, following Gülen's approach, Turksoy, an international organization for development of Turkic culture and art, was set up in Ankara in 1993 by the Turkish Ministry of Culture.[9] Its goal was to establish initiatives within the 'Turkic world' (Othman 2009).

It came into existence after the culture ministers of Turkey, Turkmenistan, Kazakhstan, Kyrgyzstan and Turkish Republic of Cyprus as well as the autonomous Russian republics of Tatarstan and Bašqortostan signed an agreement of cultural cooperation. According to the agreement, the new organisation was established in order to support the cultural restructuring in the Trans-Caucasus region and around the world.... Turksoy's goals are: to establish friendly relations among Turkish-speaking peoples and nations; explore, disclose, develop, and protect the common Turkic culture, language, history, art, customs, and traditions as well as pass them down to future generations. (Othman 2009: para 13–14)

Creation of Modern Turkey

There have been two different strategies for implementing modernity in Turkey since the nation became a republic. The first strategy of modernity was the one used by Mustafa Kemal, the founder of the Turkish Republic, referred to as 'top-down modernity', or Kemalism. Kemalism was based on two principles: nationalism and secularism (Ozgur 2012). In Turkey, secularism was equated with modernization and to some extent Westernization, but unlike its Western counterpart, Turkish secularism did not necessarily mean separation of religion and politics. However, the masses wanted more of religion and less of secularism and so a happy medium had to be negotiated.

The second strategy of implementing modernity in Turkey was a 'bottom-up modernity': this was done at the grassroots level and was based on the principle that changes had to become internalized by the masses rather than imposed by the state. The second form of modernity allowed room for religion in the public sphere. However, it did not want religion to become a tool of politics, in case people implicated religion if something went wrong in the political realm (Ozgur 2012).

The Nur movement wanted religion to remain above politics, because Nur was concerned that politics could corrupt religion. Gülen borrowed this ideology and the 'bottom-up strategy' and made GHM an agent of Turkey's transformation. He used educational institutions, business enterprises, and cultural organizations to bring transformation about.

Reaching Both Turks and Host Nations

GHM's global strategy is unique compared to other Turkish organizations, such as Alevi and some Kurdish associations. GHM's aim from the start was to go beyond expatriate Turks and focus on members of the host nation. GHM made its presence felt in a wide spectrum of influential entities—ranging from education to commerce to culture, where members of both host communities and Turkey were serviced (Turam 2004).

GHM does not build mosques and Islamic centers. Neither does it openly preach the Islamic message. GHM, as a rule, does not participate in overt religious activities even in Muslim countries in Central Asia and Africa. In Europe and the United States, its religious nature is almost veiled. Instead, GHM in the West actively forges strategic links with Christian and Jewish organizations, thus making it easier for GHM to establish itself in communities that have negative perceptions toward Islam (Balci 2014). This strategy also enables GHM to initiate special connections and networks with local political, religious, and cultural leaders and with institutions that offer financial, emotional, and political support for their various projects. Host nations have warmly welcomed GHM because its entities and services can be embraced by the locals with no religious strings attached (Balci 2014).

In this way, GHM has used soft power to enhance Turkey's image in new countries. Through GHM's educational initiatives, the Turkish language and culture have received a favorable reception. For example, each year GHM sponsors a Turkish-language Olympiad in Turkey where students from the worldwide network of Gülen schools gather and compete (Balci 2014). The event receives wide coverage from the media (most of the Turkish media is owned by GHM) and therefore results in a positive image of GHM and enhances Turkish culture. However, critics (Hendrick 2013; Ozipek 2009) have indicated, as I will elaborate in the following section, that religious activities do take place in GHM in informal settings and as extracurricular activities.

A Focus on Education

As intimated previously, GHM's primary emphasis is on education. This is arguably the spiritual and intellectual heart of the movement. Gülen's reading circles turned into dormitories, coaching centers for examinations, and ultimately into full-fledged schools. It is estimated that 75 percent of Turkey's 2 million elementary school students are enrolled at institutions operated by GHM (cited in Sharon-Krespin 2009). Beyond this, GHM oversees thousands of elite secondary schools, colleges, and student dormitories throughout Turkey, as well as private universities, the largest being Fatih University located in Istanbul.

Just before Turkey became a republic in 1923, only 10 percent of the males and 1 percent of females were literate in Anatolia, the Asian part of Turkey (Guvebnc 1998). Hence, the great need for the nation was to improve its literacy level and overhaul its entire educational system. In the 1960s, the youth of Turkey became the focus of a massive educational plan by the government. Gülen and GHM, inspired by Sufi teacher Nursi and the felt need of the hour, decided to make education their main focus. Theirs was an educational plan with a spiritual foundation and a nationalistic focus: "If we are able to implant in the young firm belief, pure and sound thoughts, a strong feeling of love for nation and country ... then the young will maintain their essential dignity against mental and spiritual corruption" (Gülen 2001: para 6). Gülen's aim seems altruistic, but it is also very pragmatic and strategic: His followers target youths in the eighth through twelfth grades, mentor them in the *ışıkevi* (lighthouses), educate them in GHM schools, and prepare them for future careers in legal, political, and educational professions.

Has GHM been successful in its educational goal? The alumni of Gülen schools have successfully enrolled at universities in Turkey and abroad. Graduates from GHM schools are among the new echelon of Turkey's leaders, and many others have "obtain[ed] influential positions at diplomatic or international institutions, [all this] suggests that the group's objectives are being met" (Balci 2014). Besides, GHM's sociocultural and spiritual objectives also seem to be fulfilled.

The success of Gülen movement schools stems both from the success of the students (and the satisfaction of the parents) and from the prestige and goodwill they enjoy among local and political authorities for promoting integration and acting as a social mediator. (Balci 2014: para 12)

GHM schools have created intense competition amongst students wanting to gain entry because the schools have gained a reputation for good results. The spirit of competition is also seen among the various companies offering private tutoring services, granting discounts for students who scored well (Tansel and Bircan 2003). Therefore, the GHM schools are highly sought after not just for the level of education offered but because the graduates from these private schools form a new 'socio-moral conservative elite' (Seufert 2014: 5). Graduates and would-be students are aware that joining GHM is the means for upward mobility in Turkish society (Hendrick 2013).

The movement's success and influence is not just in Turkey but beyond. GHM followers are steeped in Turkish nationalism as evidenced by the fact that they help to spread the country's language and culture around the world.

> But it is not just Central Asia that hosts Gülen schools. They are also in far-flung Muslim countries like Indonesia, Sudan and Pakistan as well as mostly non-Muslim countries like Mexico and Japan. (Hansen 2010)

In the United States, there are approximately 140 charter schools in 26 states with a total enrollment of more than 45,000 students (Humire 2016). This constitutes the largest charter school network in the United States—and in the United States, all charter schools are partially funded by American taxpayers.[10] Unfortunately, GHM has been under investigation since 2011 by the local and federal US authorities for a series of alleged corporate misdemeanors.[11]

The Community: Cemaat

Membership into GHM begins with students who are enrolled at the various centers of learning, lighthouses, schools, and universities.

> [S]tudents [recruited are] highly educated young people. Once a member, they follow a trajectory of intense learning and reflecting on a wide variety of sources of knowledge. Although they must study Islamic sources and perform religious duties as part of the training, they are always required to complete a successful educational career in society…. The genuine source of spirituality is not the sermon … but the collective building of schools and the encouragement of economic enterprises. (Sunier 2014: 2200)

Carefully assigned GHM mentors mentor each student after school. The emphasis is on the oral transmission of knowledge and experience of a senior disciple to the student. This transmission of knowledge is termed *sohbet* and the *sohbetler* are the venues for this 'discipling' activity. *Sohbet* sessions include reading Islamic texts, discussing fund-raising, networking, and relating knowledge to actual situations (Hendrick 2013). Ozipek (2009) revealed that 'indoctrination' took place amongst student followers over a period of time.

An interesting phenomenon at the *sohbet* is weeping. Gülen starts preaching and then he breaks out into intense weeping, which triggers the act of weeping amongst the followers as the lights are deliberately turned down. According to anthropologists Myer (2006) and Hirschkind (2006), this is a highly ritualized activity and it is part of religious training and disciplining that enhances the spiritual competence of the leader. Furthermore, it has the ability to form a strong sense of bonding between leader and follower.

> We argue that the specific features of the sessions and the ways in which followers are involved in them, demonstrate how religious knowledge production, authorisation and ritual practice are inextricably linked to one another and come together in the sermon. (Myer 2006 and Hirschkind 2006, cited in Sunier and Sahin 2015: 232)

Meyer termed the practice of weeping the 'aesthetics of persuasion' based on her work on Pentecostal churches in Ghana and the way leaders of these churches build up communities of followers through aesthetics as a persuasion mechanism: "[It] convinces religious believers of the truthfulness of the connection between them and God or the transcendental" (Myer 2010: 756). Hence, Gülen extends his sense of authority over the group in a spiritual manner, making use of sensory and emotional perceptions. It is at these sessions where Gülen's leadership as a moral guide and an Imam and his sway on the followers are evident.

Business Enterprises

Using education as its foundation, GHM produces an assortment of textbooks, materials, and audio cassettes of Gülen's sermons. There are some 110 stores that sell GHM products in Turkey and other countries (Hansen 2010). In 1983, GHM followers established Kaynak Holding, a conglomerate of some 15 companies involved in IT, retail, food, publishing, and other services. The publishing subdivision of Kaynak Holding has 28 publishing labels. Books on Gülen, Sufism, Ottoman history, and related topics are produced every year (Hansen 2010). Kaynak Publishing also houses Academi (the academic publisher for GHM) which is deemed to be GHM's 'central ideational node' where the intellectual inner circle of the movement congregates to think, strategize, publish, and translate the movement's seminal works into several languages (Hendrick 2013: 93).

In 1986, GHM members acquired Zaman, the newspaper publishing company that was owned by Feza Media. This virtually gave GHM control of the press and the TV broadcasting network in Turkey. Most of the companies 'owned' by GHM, which are referred to as Gülen-inspired companies, are owned by Gülen's inner circle but under different names. In the same way, men inspired by Gülen have established Bank Asya, which grew to be Turkey's largest Islamic bank. TUSKON, a businessmen's association with GHM, boasts 50,000 companies as members. Ebaugh (2010) reported that Gülen followers give between 5 and 20 percent of their income to the movement's projects.

Organizational Aspects

Fethullah Gülen is unequivocally the leader of GHM. However, his networks of Gülen-inspired organizations, Gülen schools, and businesses, are organized as separate entities or networks, all of which are motivated and energized by Gülen's inspirational teachings and tenets. Gülen is the spiritual and administrative link in this great web of Gülen entities. Hendrick (2016) came to the conclusion that 'strategic ambiguity' is the term that accurately describes GHM's organizational set up.

> [The Gülen movement] is not organized as a centralized bureaucracy, and its hierarchy is not organized under the direct leadership of Fethullah Gülen. Rather, the ... organizational strategy is 'flexible,' 'networked', and 'lean'.... Its ability to form alliances, to recruit

sympathizers, and to market its identity is both highly malleable and increasingly difficult to define. (Hendrick 2013: 26)

There are three main reasons for GHM's organizational structure. First, it allows the promotion of unified diversity so that distinct organizations can come together with some common core qualities (Hendrick 2013). For example, the US charter schools are registered under different company names in each state such as Harmony schools, Concord schools, and the like—disavowing any connection with GHM. Second, this model of organization is lean, flexible, and easily adaptable as GHM organizes and replicates itself in different countries (Hendrick 2013). Third, it allows deniability should one entity be the subject of inquiry by the authorities. GHM has mastered the art of giving formulaic answers to the media and other sources that 'there is no organic connection' between GHM and its vast array of mass media outlets, companies, schools, and cultural centers (Hendrick 2013: 228). Whereas there is no legal or institutional connection between the entities in question, it is also clear to scholars that intangible connections lead to Fethullah Gülen and his inner circle (Hendrick 2013).

Threefold Hierarchy

As described previously, GHM is a collective identity movement based on several layers of membership. At the heart of the movement is the group of deeply loyal followers who constitute the inner circle (Figure 6.1). This upper echelon consists of Gülen and his chief advisors and loyalists who have the utmost respect for the founder. The second echelon takes the form of business contacts and friends who support Gülen and the movement with finances, emotional support, and influence. The third tier is composed of sympathizers who, although removed from the halls of power, are nevertheless critical in shaping public opinion on the movement. Academics, media personnel, politicians, and civic leaders would be part of this group. There is also a powerful further layer (not depicted in Figure 6.1)—the consumers of GHM's services. These would typically be students, the news and TV audiences, and the purchasers of the GHM products.

Figure 6.1:

The hierarchy of GHM

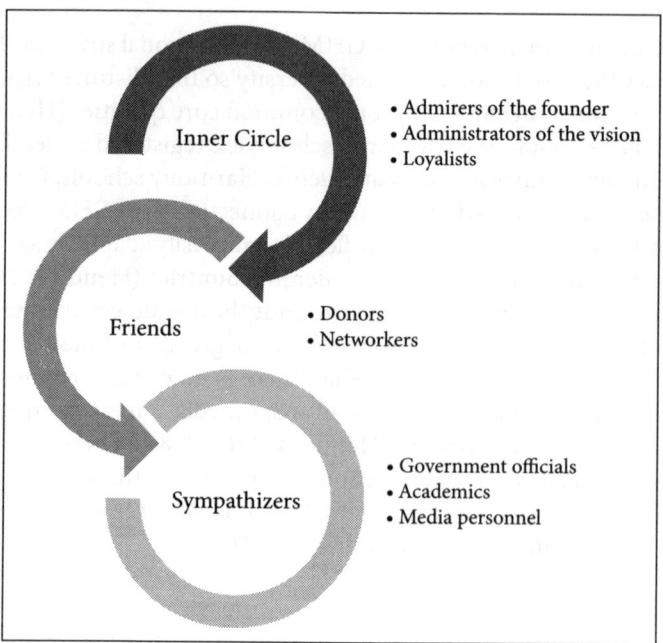

Inner Circle
- Admirers of the founder
- Administrators of the vision
- Loyalists

Friends
- Donors
- Networkers

Sympathizers
- Government officials
- Academics
- Media personnel

Source: James (2016).

GHM's PR Strategies

GHM takes pains to portray a positive public image. In Turkey, it owns and operates media agencies that continually frame its image as a moderate Islamic organization with a cultural and dialogical agenda. In the United States and other Western nations, GHM is one of the few Muslim organizations that does not focus on the 'politics of representation in regard to Islam', rather, it engages in active dialogue earning acceptance from public and media officials (Seufert 2014: 6).

As mentioned in the introduction, Gülen won the *Foreign Policy* and *Prospect* title of the most influential public intellectual in 2008. However, it was discovered that soon after the poll started, Gülen's candidacy was announced on the front pages of GHM's newspaper and all its media corporations including television and radio, multiple publications, and the GHM's 25 official websites. Apparently, mass e-mails were sent by his followers encouraging people to vote for Gülen (Hendrick 2013).

A former columnist and editor of a GHM publication admitted: "All these activities show that a very powerful Turkish lobby is being established in the US" (Gulerce 2007, cited in Hendrick 2013: 209). One can conclude that GHM unashamedly lobbies in the corridors of power at Washington DC, USA and organizes trips and vacation itineraries for political, civic, media, and academic leaders from around the world to visit Turkey, see the GHM philosophy and operations, and then become apologists for the movement.

Controversies and Future

GHM may control the media in Turkey, but it has been observed that some of these media organizations pursue an agenda at odds with the movement's publicly stated ideals. For example, the English version of *Zaman*, the widely circulated newspaper is often quite different from the Turkish one.

> Remarks about enemies of Islam, perfidious Armenians, and Mossad plots are edited out of the English version, as are other comments that sound incompatible with the message of intercultural tolerance. For example, *Today's Zaman* last year published Gülen's criticism of the [Turkish] government for failing to solve long-standing issues over the rights of Kurds, but omitted [Gülen's] ambiguous prayer: "Knock their [Kurds'] homes upside down, destroy their unity, reduce their homes to ashes, may their homes be filled with weeping and sup-plications, burn and cut off their roots, and bring their affairs to an end." Gülen's supporters will insist that he was referring only to the Kurdistan Workers' Party, or PKK, which the United States quite properly considers a terrorist group. But many ethnically Kurdish citizens of Turkey heard this as a call for genocide and were terrified by it. (Berlinski 2012: para 23)

GHM's operations in the United States and other Western nations may create a backlash because of GHM's policy of strategic ambiguity and consequently its lack of transparency.

The schools, in 25 states, have anodyne names: Horizon Science Academy, Pioneer Charter School of Science, Beehive Science and Technology Academy. Thousands of Turkish nationals, almost all of them male, have come to America on H-1B visas specifically to teach in them. The schools focus on math and science, and their students often do well enough on standardized tests. The administrators say that they have no official ties to Gülen, and Gülen denies any connection to the schools. But federal forms required of nonprofits show that virtually all the schools have opened or operate with the aid of Gülen-inspired groups—local nonprofits that promote Turkish culture. (Berlinski 2012: para 25)

The recent stalemate in relations between the AKP-led Turkish government and GHM has added another spanner in the works for GHM because GHM's initial success and growth came as a result of the strong union between these two key players. If President Erdogan succeeds in decimating GHM, he stands to lose his moderate and democratic credentials that were carefully built over the years. If GHM is proven guilty of perpetuating the coup in Turkey, this will add weight to the proposition that GHM, although apolitical in its presentation, has indeed political power within Turkey, which will harm its reputation of being a moderate expression of 'cultural Islam'. If GHM is vindicated, it will be a major boost to the movement, but its standing in Turkey will be significantly weakened after the recent 'cleansing' of Gülenists from Turkish civil society. Beyond this, the current rift between GHM and the Turkish government will greatly affect Turkey's political and economic stability after years of amazing growth and development. Furthermore, the rift is bound to affect US–Turkey relations and the world's geopolitical balance because Turkey (a member of NATO), has been an important ally to the United States in the fight against ISIS.

To sum up, GHM presents itself as a reformed and revitalized Islamic movement which underscores its belief in cultural and 'market' Islam. Furthermore, its liberal approach has opened the door for Islam to be perceived differently in Western multireligious societies. On the other hand, there are accusations that GHM is concealing its true identity and ultimate goal.[12] It is disputed whether Gülen 'inspires' or 'commands', and whether GHM schools in the United States have abused both state and federal US laws.

GHM has admirers within Turkey and throughout the world. Criticisms about their operations, motivations, and practices abound (see Ozipek 2009; Sharon-Krespin 2009), but on balance, one fact cannot be dismissed: GHM has played a significant role in the modernization of Turkey and its rise to global prominence. What remains to be seen is whether GHM continues to promote its version of cultural and 'market' Islam or, if it has a larger, hidden agenda.

Notes

1. This is a conservative estimate made by Joseph M. Humire (2016), *the executive director of the Washington DC-based, global think tank, the Center for a Secure Free Society (SFS).* GHM's strategy of strategic ambiguity prevents researchers from anything more definitive. See: http://thehill.com/blogs/congress-blog/education/272424-charter-schools-vulnerable-to-controversial-turkish-movement
2. As mentioned in note 1, these figures are also not definitive.
3. The early Umayyad dynasty was focused on expansion. The army consisted of Arab and largely Syrian soldiers who extended the borders of Islam. War was waged against Byzantium. War spread into Asia Minor and Constantinople was besieged; eastward, the army penetrated into Khorasan, Turkistan, and northwestern India, spreading along the northern coast of Africa, to take hold of parts of Spain. This vast empire gradually acquired an Arab Muslim persona.
4. The Hanafi School is one of the four major schools of Sunni Islamic legal reasoning and jurisprudence. It was based on the teachings of Abu Hanifa (d. 767), a merchant who lived and taught in Kufa, Iraq. The other three schools are: Shafi'i, Hanbali, and Maliki.
5. Most scholars view the Quran's verses revealed by Muhammad in two distinct divisions: "in Mecca when his community of followers was weak and more inclined to compromise, and those revealed in Medina, where Muhammad's strength grew" (Bukay 2007: 3–11).
6. See http://www.newworldencyclopedia.org/entry/History_of_Christianity
7. The western part of the Roman Empire was under Byzantine rule.
8. Olsen asserts:

   The Hizmet movement in Turkey, a non-Arab country, largely Hanafi, is yet another indicator of the stagnation of Sunni religious establishments. This has also been the case in many largely Arab countries and even … in non-Arab countries as well. The expansion and tenacity of the Islamic State in Iraq and Syria (ISIL) and now elsewhere, and its predecessors from 2004 onwards, is yet another indication of the challenges awaiting the Sunni religious establishments and the regimes they support, not just in the Middle East but in other parts of the world as well. In the case of the Shia, they believe that the above-discussed situation now presents a propitious time to end the sectarian, political, bias, discrimination and brutality they have suffered at the hands of Sunnis for 1,400 years and that God is now on their side and their struggle is righteous. This is a wakeup call for Sunnism and largely Sunni countries. Baghdad, Damascus and Beirut are now dominated by the Shia. Jerusalem, the third most significant city in Islam, is governed by Jews. Dissident Shia are beginning to challenge the Sunni Saudi dynasty. (See http://hizmetmovement.blogspot.com. au/2016/01/sunnis-shia-differences.html)

9. Whilst I cannot prove a direct link between the formation of Turksoy and GHM's regional policies as advocated by Gülen, it is a known fact that GHM and the AKP share a common ideology and have worked hand in glove before the current rift.

10. Approximately 61 percent of funds for charter schools come from American tax-payers according to the Center for Education Reform (See https://www.edreform. com/issues/choice-charter-schools/research/).

11. GHM is the subject of at least five federal and some state-level investigations according to Joshua Hendrick (2013) in *Gülen: The Ambiguous Politics of Market Islam in Turkey and the World*.

12. In 1999, Turkish television aired footage of Gülen delivering an infamous sermon which many Gülen loyalists claim was redacted by Gülen's critics. However, because the 'genuine' footage was not released by GHM, the controversy continues.

> You must move in the arteries of the system without anyone noticing your existence until you reach all the power centers ... until the conditions are ripe, they [the followers] must continue like this. If they do something prematurely, the world will crush our heads, and Muslims will suffer everywhere, like in the tragedies in Algeria, like in 1982 [in] Syria ... like in the yearly disasters and tragedies in Egypt. The time is not yet right. You must wait for the time when you are complete and conditions are ripe, until we can shoulder the entire world and carry it.... You must wait until such time as you have gotten all the state power, until you have brought to your side all the power of the constitutional institutions in Turkey.... Until that time, any step taken would be too early—like breaking an egg without waiting the full forty days for it to hatch. It would be like killing the chick inside. The work to be done is [in] confronting the world. Now, I have expressed my feelings and thoughts to you all—in confidence ... trusting your loyalty and secrecy. I know that when you leave here—[just] as you discard your empty juice boxes, you must discard the thoughts and the feelings that I expressed here....
>
> When everything was closed and all doors were locked, our houses of *isik* [light] assumed a mission greater than that of older times. In the past, some of the duties of these houses were carried out by *madrasas* [Islamic schools], some by schools, some by *tekkes* [Islamist lodges].... These *isik* homes had to be the schools, had to be *madrasas*, [had to be] *tekkes* all at the same time. The permission did not come from the state, or the state's laws, or the people who govern us. The permission was given by God ... who wanted His name learned and talked about, studied, and discussed in those houses, as it used to be in the mosques. (Gülen, cited in Sharon-Krespin 2009)

References

Askoy, N. 2015. "Meeting the Challenges of Modernity as Experienced by Said Nursi, Iqbal and Abduh." *MA Thesis.* Accessed on 10 August 2016 from https://rucore. libraries.rutgers.edu/rutgers-lib/47246/PDF/1/

Balci, B. 2014. "What Future for the Fethullah Gülen Movement in Central Asia and the Caucasus?" *The Central Asia-Caucasus ANALYST.* Accessed on 1 August from http://www.cacianalyst.org/publications/analytical-articles/item/13006-what-future-for-the-fethullah-g%C3%BClen-movement-in-central-asia-and-the-caucasus?.html

Balci, T. and C. L. Miller. 2012. *The Gülen-Hizmet Movement: Circumspect Activism in Faith-Based Reform.* Newcastle upon Tyne: Cambridge Scholars Publishing.

Balfour, P. K. 1979. *The Ottaman Centuries: The Rise and Fall of the Turkish Empire.* New York, NY: Morrow.

Berlinski, C. 2012. "Who is Fethullah Gülen?" *City Journal.* Accessed on 15 August 2016 from http://www.city-journal.org/html/who-fethullah-g%C3%BClen-13504.html

Bilgincan, M. 2016. "Everything You're Ever Wanted to Know About Fethullah Gülen." *Gazeta Warzawska.* Accessed on 5 August 2016 from http://gazetawarzawska. com/politics/4165-pm-20160721

Bukay, D. 2007. "Jihad or Peace? Abrogation in Islam." *Middle East Quarterly* XIV(4 Fall): 3–11.

Coskun, B. B. 2016. "The Post-Davutoglu Era in Turkish Foreign Policy." *E-International Relations.* Accessed on 20 September 2016 from http://www.e-ir.info/2016/06/03/the-post-davutoglu-era-in-turkish-foreign-policy/

Ebaugh, H. R. 2010. *The Gülen Movement: A Sociological Analysis of a Civic Movement Rooted in Moderate Islam.* New York, NY: Springer.

Findley, C. V. 2005. *The Turks in World History.* Oxford: Oxford University Press.

Gülen, F. 1999. *Pearls of Wisdom.* Fairfax, VA: The Fountain.

Gunter, M. M. 2012. "Turkey: The Politics of a New Democratic Constitution." *Middle East Policy* 19(1): 119–25.

Guvebnc, B. 1998. *History of Turkish Education.* Ankara: Turkish Education Association.

Hansen, S. 2010. "The Global Imam." *New Republic.* Accessed on 8 August 2016 from https://newrepublic.com/article/79062/global-turkey-imam-fethullah-Gülen

Hendrick, J. D. 2013. *Gülen: The Ambiguous Politics of Market Islam in Turkey and the World.* New York, NY: New York University Press.

———. 2016. "Fethullah Gülen: Public Intellectual or Public Enemy?" *The Conversation.* Accessed on 15 August 2016 from http://theconversation.com/fethullah-Gülen-public-intellectual-or-public-enemy-62887

Hirschkind, C. 2006. *The Ethical Soundscape: Cassette Sermons and Islamic Counterpublics.* New York: Columbia University Press.

Humire, J. M. 2016. "Charter Schools Vulnerable to Controversial Turkish Movement." The Hill website. Accessed 12 August 2015 from http://thehill.com/blogs/congress-blog/education/272424-charter-schools-vulnerable-to-controversial-turkish-movement

Khanam, F. 2006. *A Simple Guide to Sufism*. Baltimore, MD: Goodword Books.

Koyuncu-Lorasdaği. B. 2010. "The Prospects and Pitfalls of the Religious Nationalist Movement in Turkey: The Case of the Gülen Movement." *Middle Eastern Studies* 46(2): 21–234.

Lamazoff, A. and A. Ralby. 2012. *The Atlas of Military History: An Around-the World Survey of Warfare Through the Ages*. San Diego, CA: Thunder Bay Press.

Lewis, B. 1961. *The Emergence of Modern Turkey*. New York, NY: Oxford University Press.

———. 1993. *Islam and the West*. New York, NY: Oxford University Press.

Lobel, D. 2007. *A Sufi–Jewish Dialogue: Philosophy and Mysticism in Bahya Ibn Paquda's 'Duties of the Heart'*. Philadelphia, PA: University of Pennsylvania Press.

Myer, B. 2006. "Religious Sensation: Why Media, Aesthetics and Power Matter in the Study of Contemporary Religion?" Amsterdam: University of Amsterdam. Inaugural speech, 6 October 2006: Faculty of Social Behavioural Sciences. Accessed on 2 October 2015 from https://www.researchgate.net/publication/241889837_ Religious_Sensations_Why_Media_Aesthetics_and_Power_Matter_in_the_ Study_of_Contemporary_Religion

———. 2010. "Aesthetics of Persuasion: Global Christianity and Pentecostalism's Sensational Forms." *South Atlantic Quarterly* 109(4): 741–63.

New World Encyclopedia. 2014. "Middle Ages". Accessed on 10 August 2015 from http://www.newworldencyclopedia.org/entry/Middle_Ages

Othman, E. 2009. "Fethullah Gülen: The Neo-Ottaman dream of Turkish Islam." *AsiaNews.it*. Accessed on 10 August 2016 from http://www.asianews.it/index. php?l=en&art=15165&size=A

Ozgur, I. 2012. *Islamic Schools in Modern Turkey: Faith, Politics and Education*. Cambridge: Cambridge University Press.

Ozipek, A. 2009. "Cultivating a Generation through Education: The Case of the Gülen Movement." Accessed on 2 August 2016 from www.etd.ceu.hu/2009/ ozipek_aydin.pdf

Quataert, D. 2005. *The Ottaman Empire: 1700–1922*. Cambridge: Cambridge University Press.

Sen, M. 2001. *Turkish Entrepreneurs in Central Asia: The Case of Kazakhstan and Kyrgystan*. Dissertation. Ankara: Turkey: Middle East Technical University.

Seufert, G. 2014. "Is the Fethullah Gülen Movement Overstretching Itself?" *SWP Research Paper*. Accessed on 10 August 2016 from http://europesworld.org/wp-content/uploads/sites/3/2014/01/2014_RP02_srt.pdf

Schimmel, A. 2012. "Sufism." *Encyclopaedia Britannica*. Accessed on 1 August 2016 from https://www.britannica.com/topic/Sufism

Schwartz, S. 2008. "The Real Fethullah Gülen." *Prospect*. Accessed on 1 August 2016 from http://www.prospectmagazine.co.uk/magazine/therealfethullahglen

Sharon-Krespin, R. 2009. "Fethullah Gülen's Grand Ambition." *The Middle East Quarterly* 16(1): 55–66.

Shaw, S. J. and M. E. Yapp. 2016. "Ottoman Empire." *Encyclopaedia Britannica*. Accessed on 12 August 2016 from https://www.britannica.com/place/Ottoman-Empire

Sukran, V. 2012. *Islam in Modern Turkey: An Intellectual Biography of Said Nursi.* New York, NY: SUNY Press.

Sunier, T. and M. Sahin. 2015. "The Weeping Sermon: Persuasion, Binding and Authority Within the Gülen-Movement." *Journal of Religion and Culture* 16(2): 228–41.

Sunier, T. 2014. "Cosmopolitan Theology: Fethullah Gülen and the Making of a 'Golden Generation'." *Journal of Ethnic and Racial Studies* 37(12): 2193–208.

Tansel, A. and F. Bircan. 2003. "Private Tutoring Expenditures in Turkey." *ERF Working Papers Series* 0333. Ankara: Middle Eastern Technical University.

Teall, J. and D. M. Nicol. 2015. "Byzantine Empire." *Encyclopaedia Britannica.* Accessed on 15 August from https://www.britannica.com/place/Byzantine-Empire

Turam, B. 2004. "A Bargain between the Secular State and Turkish Islam: Politics of Ethnicity in Central Asia." *Nations and Nationalism* 10(3): 353–74.

Yamin, M. 2008. "Sufism: A Syncretic Path for Peace." *Transcendent Philosophy Journal* 9: 205–24.

Yavuz, M. H. 1999. "Towards an Islamic Liberalism? The Nursi Movement and Fethullah Gülen." *The Middle East Journal* 10(1): 584–604.

Yildirim, Y. and S. Kirmizialtin. 2004. "Fethullah Gülen's Golden Generation: Integration of Muslim Identity with the World Through Education." Accessed on 15 August 2016 from http://www.Gülenmovement.us/fethullah-Gülens-golden-generation-integration-of-muslim-identity-with-the-world-through-education.html

7

ISIS: Epistemology, Eschatology, and Empire of a Revolutionary Movement

Wars and persecutions are, at bottom, expressions of rivalry between contending claims to immortality and ultimate spiritual power.
                                                        —Robert Jay Lifton (1979)

Introduction

On 6 June 2006, the then President of the United States George W. Bush made this triumphant announcement:

> Last night in Iraq, United States military forces killed the terrorist al Zarqawi. At 6:15 p.m. Baghdad time, special operation forces, acting on tips and intelligence from Iraqis, confirmed Zarqawi's location, and delivered justice to the most wanted terrorist in Iraq.... Now Zarqawi has met his end, and this violent man will never murder again....[1]

Bush's statement was partly justified: Zarqawi was the most wanted terrorist at that time; however, Bush's sense of optimism about the killing of Zarqawi was short-lived. Zarqawi's new terror group, ISIS, soon emerged to test and taunt the world with unprecedented savagery as its primary strategy. ISIS is more than a terrorist organization: it is a revolutionary movement intent on reinstating an Islamic caliphate that was conceived in the seventh century.[2] Now led by self-imposed Caliph, Abu Bakr al-Baghdadi, ISIS resorts to using the Quran and the Hadith[3] as its textual authority and an 'end times' prophetic message of religious cleansing for the world of apostates, which is inhabited by everyone who does not adhere to the radical Islamic teachings of the Caliph.

In this chapter, I argue that the historical, theological, and sectarian divisions within Islam have left uncertainties about the final authority for the faith. This has set the scene for groups such as ISIS to take advantage of the situation and use Islam's sacred texts and teachings to create a form of apocalyptic Islam that offers people an answer to the ultimate questions of significance and purpose both in this life and the life to come.

I begin by giving an overview of the origin of the Islamic faith, including the Sunni–Shia divide and related issues. I then give an overview of the genesis of ISIS and explain how this movement authenticates itself, its apocalyptic narrative, and its quest for empire in the launch of a caliphate. I conclude by discussing the future of ISIS in light of the war against terror by the United States and its coalition partners around the world.

Islam's Beginnings and Its Contested Place in the Middle East

The Beginning of Islam

Mohammed, revered by Muslims as the last and foremost Prophet, transformed nomadic, tribal people into a world civilization and faith when he founded Islam (which means submission to Allah) in the early part of the seventh century (Mussalli, Newby, and Mussalli n.d.). This new monotheistic faith addressed every conceivable aspect of society, including rules for banking, behavior, worship, charitable giving, family, and politics. The main source or text for this worldview is the Holy (or Noble) Quran written in the Arabic language. It is a document consisting of 114 chapters called surah (also sura, or *surat*) with a number of verses per chapter (Harleem 2004).

When Mohammed died in 632 AD, Islam was firmly established in major population centers of the Middle East and Arabian Peninsula and was poised to expand. However, succession of leadership proved to be a sore point amongst his followers. One group elected Abu Bakr, one of Mohammed's close friends and advisors. They anointed him as the first Caliph, that is, the leader of the faith (Hitti 1970). The group who elected Bakr were called Sunni, which is from the Arabic word sunna for 'way'. In choosing Bakr, the Sunni believed that fidelity to 'the way' was more critical than selecting a relative of Mohammad, who may or may not be faithful to the sacred teachings (Hitti 1970; Lewis 1993).

The other group insisted that leadership succession must come through a blood relative of Mohammed. They put forward the name of Ali ibn Abi, the cousin of Mohammad but he failed to be elected. This group was called Shia, which is a conglomeration of the Arabic words for followers/supporters of Ali, or *shi'atu Ali*, because of their support for Ali. Ali was passed over twice before being successfully selected as Caliph in 656 AD, but his term lasted only 5 years because he was murdered in 661 AD (Hitti 1970).

Husayn ibn Ali, grandson of Mohammed (and son of Ali ibn Abi Talib), a Shiite Muslim hero, was the next Caliph (and known as the 'third Imam')[4] following the ways of his grandfather. Unfortunately, he was deemed a threat by the Sunni Muslims, leading to his untimely death in 680 AD (Hitti 1970; Lewis 1993). Hence, this 'bad blood' between the Sunni and Shia groups has lasted for more than 1,400 years. Conservative Sunnis view Shias as heretics and apostates and this ill will is reciprocated by the Shias. Strictly speaking, the penalty for apostasy in the Quran is death. So again, we face the perennial question: Who is the legitimate interpreter and executor of Islam after Mohammad?

The Sunni–Shia Divide

It is impossible to understand Islam, ISIS, and the dynamics of the Middle East without an overview of the Sunni–Shia divide because the main dialectic in Islam is within its own camp.[5] Islam is divided into two schools—Sunni and Shiite from the seventh century onwards after the death of the prophet Mohammad because two groups emerged with two different names as to who the rightful heir was.

Table 7.1 shows the various dimensions of differences between the Sunni and Shia schools with both groups agreeing that Mohammad is the final prophet and that the five pillars of Islam are significant. Both groups also believe that the Quran is the Holy Book and revere the Sunnahs[6] of Mohammed. The Shiites, however, have taken the position that the teachings of the Imams (religious teachers or clerics in Shia) are equally authoritative.

It is important to note that Sunnis represent 70–80 percent of the population of Muslims worldwide. Over the 1,400 years, a conflict of identity and theology has surrounded these two Islamic groupings, although there has been uneasy peace during most of this time and a few trigger points that have instigated problems.

Saudi Arabia and Iran are two decisive countries that need to be watched in the Middle East as they both have the potential to influence the geopolitics of the region. These two oil-rich countries are in many ways responsible for the escalation of tensions in the region. Saudi Arabia is in competition with Iran over the leadership of the Arab Muslim world. The Kingdom of Saudi is anti-Shia and has influenced the formation of many Sunni extremist groups. By the same token, Iran backs the Assad regime in Syria and has an anti-Sunni focus. A major trigger that caused widespread problems between Sunni and Shia followers was after the Iranian revolution in 1979 when Ayatollah Khomeini made Iran a Shia-dominated Islamist nation. This caused an immediate Sunni backlash. After the fall of Saddam Hussein in Iraq in 2003, brought about with the help of the United States, the Shiites took over the government in Iraq for the very first time. This has brought about much unrest and spawned terrorist Sunni groups to become active. The formation of ISIS can be traced back to this historical incident.

In the period between the years 2011 and 2013, the Arab uprisings, known popularly as 'Arab Spring',[7] virtually got rid of many totalitarian regimes which in a strange way upheld a state of uneasy peace over the years. Without these draconian structures, sectarian and religious violence between Sunni and Shia forces could escalate.

Iraq, Syria, and Lebanon are inhabited mainly by Sunnis, and the more radical Shiites are located in Iran. It has been the plan of various radical Shiite Muslims to overthrow the governments of Iraq, Syria, and Lebanon to form a kingdom representing a crescent of Shiite control (Taheri 2016).

The current civil war that is raging in Syria (85 percent Sunni and 15 percent Shia) involves thousands of militants from all over the Muslim world embroiled in sectarian violence.[8] Saudi Arabia, Qatar, and Turkey are funneling funds and arms against the Shiite President Assad while the government of Iraq and the terrorist group Hezbollah are supporting the Assad regime.

Mozaffari (2007) argued that although the Quran is the holy book it is very hard even for Muslims to reach agreement on certain teachings especially the concept of war and Jihad. This is not dissimilar to other

Table 7.1:

Sunni and Shia compared

Aspects of Comparison	Sunni	Shia
Date of origin of two schools	Approximately 664 AD	Approximately 664 AD
Original recognized leader(s)	The first four Caliphs: Abu Bakr, Umar, Uthman bin Affan, and Ali ibn Abi Talib	Ali ibn Abi Talib only (Mohammad's cousin)
Percentage of Muslims today	80–90	10–20
Countries with majority	Turkey, Jordan, Saudi Arabia, Indonesia, Iraq	Iran, Lebanon, Bahrain, Iraq
Radical groups	Hamas, Al-Qaeda, ISIS, Taliban	Hezbollah, Amal
Other groups	The Brotherhood	
Other sects	Salafi, Wahabi	Ithnā ʿAshariyyah, Ismāʿīliyyah,
Sources of authority	Quran, Sunnah (and Hadith) of Mohammad	Quran, Sunnah (and Hadith) of Mohammad and teachings of Imams
Who can rule?	Any Muslim leader who follows Mohammad	Only a descendent of Mohammad and Ali
Theological agreement	Mohammad is the final prophet, the five pillars of Islam	Mohammad is the final prophet, the five pillars of Islam
Views on the Mahdi (the Messiah)	Not here yet—will emerge soon	Already here—in hiding and will reveal himself soon

Source: James (2016).

religions such as Christianity where the Bible is interpreted differently; however, in the Quran there is more ambiguity.[9]

> Roughly speaking, it [the Quran] is divided into two very different and somewhat contradictory sets of statements, principles and commandments. The *surats* [chapters] are divided into the Mecca period of 12 years' length (from 610 to 622), and the Medina period of ten years' length (from 622 to 632). The first and initial period is characterised by relative moderation, toleration and pluralism. You find this aspect

of Islam in some verses in the Qur'an ...: *"You shall have your religion and I shall have my religion"*. (surat 109, verse 6)

We may call the Mecca period the moderate phase of Islam. In contrast, the Medina period is essentially characterized by politics, power, and war. Moderate and open-minded language and behavior give place to a power language. The following verse shows the change in the Qur'an's language when it states:

> And slay them wherever ye find them, and drive them out of the places whence they drove you out, for persecution is worse than slaughter. And fight not with them at the Inviolable Place of Worship until they first attack you there, but if they attack you (there) then slay them. Such is the reward of disbelievers. (s. 2, v. 191; Mozaffari 2007: 21–22)

Thus, the Medina period is considered the radical phase of Islam. The Quran appropriately reflects this phase of Islam. The reality is that some Muslims (known as cultural Muslims) refer to the Mecca period alone, and others (Islamists in particular) focus on the Medina period because this reflects the achievement and glory of Islam in its final shape. Then there is a third group (the overwhelming majority of Muslims) who acknowledge both periods (Mozaffari 2007).

Therefore, according to Mozaffari (2007: 18), the real message of Islam may not be easily articulated.

> [I]t is practically impossible to identify the 'real message' of Islam. Therefore, the world is facing various manifestations of Islam at a time when no consensus exists among Muslims on fundamental aspects of their faith, except for two cardinal, and thus very general points: the acceptance of the unity of God (Allah), and the reliability of the prophecy of Muhammad as the last Prophet.

Yet, while 'Islam' may appear generally elusive and ambiguous as a phenomenon, 'Islamism' as an ideology represents a more coherent, specific, and identifiable construction (Mozaffari 2007).

Islam and Islamism

In simple terms, Islam is a major world religion practiced by over a billion people and Islamism is a political ideology embraced by a subgroup of the broader Islamic community (Helfont 2015). This distinction has strong implications for both Muslims and non-Muslims. In the West, generally there exists a separation between Church and state where secular governance and religious freedom coexist. Islamism would be a threat to the West because the West would tend to impose its own standard of the separation of state and faith on Islamic nations (Helfont 2015). Therefore, whilst Islam as a religion would seem to have greater acceptance in the diverse context of several Western nations, Islamism, as a political ideology, would invite stronger critiques and even questions about its place alongside contemporary Western political systems (Helfont 2015).

It was in the twentieth century that rumblings over religion and politics began to take shape following years of silence after the ending of the Ottoman Empire in 1923 (Commins 1994). Regimes that were family driven were constrained to consider the need to rule for all the people. For example, in Egypt, debates took place where Islamists argued that their Islamic identity should form the foundation of the political order. In 1928, Hassan al-Banna drew on these modern ideas to form the first Islamist party, the Muslim Brotherhood, in Egypt. Banna and his Islamist followers kept looking back to the golden age of Islam, which they sought to reinstate. They were no doubt also troubled by the spread of Western colonialism and liberal secularism. Banna argued that just as the Prophet Muhammad was both a political and spiritual leader, their religion was inherently political (Mitchell 1993; Commins 1994). Not all Muslims agreed with al-Banna's Islamist claims about their faith. Some Muslim scholars argued that Islam and politics should remain separate, and others even called for secular liberalism in the practice of Islam[10] (Ali 2009). Despite this opposition, Banna's ideas progressed (Esposito 1991; Commins 1994).

Helfont (2015) explained the spread of political Islam from Banna to Sayyid Qutb, a controversial scholar.

As the 20th century progressed, Islamist intellectuals expanded upon Banna's ideas. Most famously, Sayyid Qutb argued that non-Islamist political systems, such as monarchy, democracy, and dictatorship, were inherently un-Islamic.... Qutb saw 'those who possess authority' in the Quran as referring to the temporal rulers, just as other scholars had done in the pre-modern period, but he made this status contingent on the righteousness of the ruler.... Esteemed Sunni Islamic scholars in the medieval period often rejected that interpretation in favor of seeing the rulers as possessors of authority.... Qutb's ideas spread widely in the Islamic World. Some groups took them in radical directions, claiming that Muslims who did not rebel against, or separate themselves from, un-Islamic political systems were not really Muslims—they were apostates and their blood was licit.... Eventually, Sunni Islamists fractured into groups with political ideologies ranging from the democratically elected Islamist party which currently rules the NATO member state of Turkey, to the extremists in the Islamic State and al-Qaida. (Helfont 2015: para 19)

The most significant Shiite leader to embrace this thinking was Ayatollah Ruhollah Khomeini, who led the Islamic Revolution of Iran in 1979. Khomeini proposed that authority was in the hands of the executive of a legitimate Islamic state (Raza 2014). In an unprecedented shift from Shiia tradition, he argued that while the last Imam (Al-Mahdi) remained in hiding, spiritual authority was now in the hands of the religious lawmakers (Raza 2014). In doing so, Khomeini indicated that he and Islamic scholars had authority—both spiritual and political (Abrahamian 1993).

Epistemology of a Movement: How ISIS Views Itself?

Epistemology is the branch of philosophy that examines the nature of knowledge, its sources, structure, and limits (Steup 2016). There is not a huge reservoir of knowledge about ISIS because it is a relatively new movement. Primarily ISIS itself provides what can be known about this movement. By examining its history, literature, symbols, and media usage, we can come to some conclusions about this group. Therefore, the focus of this section is to consider what ISIS thinks of itself. This will lead us to an understanding of the core issues of the movement and help us come to terms with its so-called 'appeal'. Our understanding of ISIS is also aided by our knowledge of Islam and its history over the last 1,400 years (and some background material has already been provided) because ISIS claims to be the true form of Islam and uses Islamic texts and symbols. Presumably, more will be revealed about ISIS as it pursues its 'battle plan' in the coming years.

Origin of ISIS

ISIS traces its origin in the mid-1990s to a Saudi entrepreneur, Abu Musab al-Zarqawi—a semiliterate but influential Jordanian youth who started his adult life in drugs and prostitution.

Zarqawi's desperate mother enrolled him in Islamic instruction at a local mosque where he converted to Salafism and was indoctrinated in militant Islamic ways. After serving a 5-year sentence in jail in Jordan, Zarqawi moved to Afghanistan in 1999 where the infamous Osama bin Laden invited him to make *bayat* (to pledge allegiance) to Al-Qaeda but Zarqawi turned him down, preferring to operate independently (Weaver 2006; Wood 2015).

After the American invasion of Iraq, Zarqawi moved to Iraq and was involved in insurgent attacks (aided by the outlawed Ba'ath Party),[11] including one in 2003 that killed a UN representative stationed in Iraq and several others people. Zarqawi's hatred of Shiism was deep (made worse by the installation of a Shite government in Iraq with the help of the United States), and he was dedicated to acts of provocation against the Shiites (Weaver 2006; Wood 2015).

In 2004, Zarqawi changed his mind and made *bayat* (gave allegiance) to bin Laden, renaming his organization Al-Qaeda in Iraq (AQI). After two years of service as an accomplished terrorist in Iraq, Zarqawi was killed by the US-led consolidated, interagency operation code named Task Force Black. But AQI's growth continued gathering momentum and funding to the tune of $200 million a year from a range of criminal activities. Zarqawi's successor as leader of AQI was Abu Ayyub al-Masri, who for reasons not known, changed the name of AQI to the Islamic State of Iraq (ISI). Jihadist activities continued under ISI until 2007 when hopes for a nonsectarian Iraq were anticipated. However, the Iraqi Prime Minister Nouri al-Maliki, a Shiite, lost the respect and support of the Sunnis and the US administration started the process of disengaging and handing over control to the locals. This resulted in a whirlpool of bitter sectarian violence. ISI was heavily involved in its share of violence. It was during this time that Ayyub al-Masri, the ISI leader, was killed in another US-led raid in April 2010, and soon after that ISI regrouped under Abu Bakr al-Baghdadi who made a further change to the name of the group— the ISIS (Wood 2015).

Baghdadi proved to be a strategic and visionary leader.

> He formed additional alliances with Ba'athist leaders while adding to ISIS's ranks through a series of deftly executed attacks on prisons in Iraq holding veteran jihadists. Mr Maliki was ISIS's first gift; the next was Bashar Assad, whose savage campaign to liquidate what began as a peaceful uprising turned Syria into a charnel house. ISIS infiltrated a small group across the border, and this cadre, in turn, founded the Nusra Front, the Syrian branch of al Qaeda. Nusra became part of the Syrian rebellion, while ISIS preferred to ignore Assad and focus on establishing a foothold in Syria. In short order, the two groups split, and a civil war broke out among Syrian insurgents. ISIS won that war, absorbing many of Nusra's foot soldiers and terrorizing any non-extremist rebels. ISIS has emerged stronger from every confrontation. (Traub 2015: para 12)

ISIS took over large sections of northeastern Syria and Iraq, capturing villages and some key cities in both nations.

Summing up, Zarqawi was a significant figure in the formation of ISIS. Starting from his semiliterate life of thuggery, most of the novel tactical and strategic plans associated with ISIS are traced back to him[12]—from the brutal slayings of Shiite victims to the video-taped beheadings of Western hostages in orange jumpsuits. Clearly, Zarqawi's life cannot be ignored as we endeavor to come to terms with this revolutionary movement. Zarqawi conceived of a radical form of Sunni Islamism which continues under the leadership of al-Baghdadi.

How ISIS Views Itself?

On 29 June 2014, the first day of Ramadan,[13] the ISIS declared the restoration of the caliphate with Abu Bakr al-Baghdadi as the new caliph. Thus, Baghdadi's announcement was well timed to show ISIS's link with Islam. At the time of the announcement, ISIS introduced its state flag via the Internet. Experts on Islamic terrorism say that "the color, the calligraphy, and the choice of words on the flag all serve as a key to reading the group's history as well as unfolding a road map of where it sees itself going" (Prusher 2014: para 3).

The flag's stark black color with the *shahada* in the Arabic script (in common calligraphy)[14] saying *La 'ilaha 'illa-llah* (There is no God but God) is very significant. The flag has rough edges, with a white circle in the middle with three words: "God Messenger Mohammed." The word order is a very critical because even though this also is taken from the *shahada*, ISIS has taken the liberty to change the order of the words. The second part of the *shahada* actually reads 'and Mohammed is God's messenger' (Prusher 2014).

The significance of ISIS changing the word order is open to many interpretations, but it would seem that by placing the word God first, ISIS leaders have made an attempt to legitimize their group as one anointed by God himself. According to Hayder al-Khoei, an associate fellow of the Middle East and North Africa Programme at Chatham House in London:

> The power of the flag comes from the fact that the word 'Allah' is on it. The word itself is seen as sacred by Muslims and hence it becomes sacrilegious to desecrate the flag.... (Prusher 2014: para 6)

Shortly after the release of the flag, anti-ISIS Islamic groups threatened to burn the ISIS flag starting a #BurnISIS campaign, but later the Lebanese Minister of Justice, Ashraf Rifi (who is not a supporter of ISIS) intervened and asked that the burning of the flag be banned and that violators be given the 'sternest punishment', because burning anything with the word Allah on it is deemed blasphemous (Prusher 2014: para 6). This incident speaks volumes about Islam and ISIS. Whereas ISIS *is not Islam* (in the strict sense), it *is Islamic*, because it is richly embedded in Islamic teachings and imagery. And in the legalistic world of Islam, to burn the ISIS flag is to blaspheme against the faith.

Magnus Ranstorp (2007), an expert on Islamic fundamentalist movements (and the Director of the Swedish National Defence College), explained the significance of the flag in the following words:

> The most important thing is the color ... the solid blank flag, was the Prophet Mohammed's war banner.... This flag compresses time and space—it harks back to where they came from and where they are going. It is not just the color of jihad and of the caliphate, but it represents the coming of what some believers see as the final battle and the day of resurrection ... there's a kind of Islamic end-of-days element in the flag, pitting the forces of Islam against the Christian West. (Cited in Prusher 2014: para 9)

Hence, the flag carries rich symbolic weight mainly because of the stark black color. Color is important in Middle Eastern culture. Other Islamists militant movements in the region have colors in the flags— the Hamas flag is green and the Hezbollah uses yellow. I make further comments on the significance of the ISIS flag in the following section titled ISIS eschatology.

Also significant in the flag is the white circle, which is meant to represent what is known as the Seal of Mohammed, which the prophet is believed to have used in his lifetime to authenticate his correspondence to foreign leaders. One of the six major Hadith collections, the Bukhari, mentions the seal of Mohammad in the following words:

> Anas Ibn Malik said: Rasulullah (pbuh) [the prophet Mohammad] had a ring made of silver and its (inlaid) gem was also of silver. When the Prophet (pbuh) wanted to write to the leaders of foreign states, he ordered a seal-ring to be made. Rasullullah (saas) therefore had a ring made, the whiteness of which is still before my eyes. The inscription engraved on the ring of Rasulullah (pbuh) was 'Muhammad Rasulullah', of which in the first line was engraved 'Muhammad', in the second line 'Rasul', and in the third line 'Allah'.[15]

A version of the seal supposedly belonging to Othman, one of Mohammad's companions, is now permanently on display at the Topkapi Palace in Istanbul (Prusher 2014). The use of the seal by ISIS is intended to add historical authenticity and even a sense of prophetic succession to the mission of ISIS. Therefore, the flag tells us how ISIS views itself, as having a sacred mission and the larger goal—an Islamic State or a caliphate.

Taken together, the two Arabic phrases, the black flag, the seal of Mohammad, and the ancient-looking font of the Arabic script, all work to evoke a strong link to Islam and the prophet, the historical Islamic caliphate, and the fact that ISIS is ushering in the Islamic end times' prophecy.

ISIS's view of itself brings us closer to an understanding of its recruiting strategy and its appeal to contemporary youth. ISIS, the most expansive, radical religious sect that we have seen in some time, offers its adherents both literal immortality in the next life and a purposeful meaning in this life. The Western world and its civilization, especially the United States, represent the powers of darkness, and ISIS appeals to young men and women to gain significance beyond their wildest dreams: it enables them to fight the powers of evil and wage the ultimate battle against the West's immorality, materialism, and consumerism. Victory is certain, according to ISIS, because it is prophesied in sacred scripture.

ISIS represents, in vivid detail, what psychologist Ernest Becker called an 'immortality project' (Becker 1993: 4). For Becker, to be human is to experience a continual anxiety about our mortality; therefore, human existence is a continual drama to repel both physical death and our awareness of it.

> The anxiety always underneath the surface has catapulted us toward all manner of endeavors—both individual and collective achievements (whether 'healthy' or 'unhealthy', 'constructive' or 'destructive').... For Becker, it is not just the fact of death itself, but a particular facet ... of death that deeply bothers us: *its capacity to render us permanently insignificant*. As he says, what human beings really fear, is not so much extinction, but extinction *with insignificance*. [Humanity] wants to know that his life has somehow counted, if not for himself, then at least in a larger scheme of things, that it has left a trace, a trace that has meaning. And in order for anything once alive to have meaning, its effects must remain alive in eternity in some way. (Cited in Lifton 1979: 315)

For most people, the 'immortality projects' they join or adopt are 'harmless', and some have positive benefits. Religion has traditionally been a buffer against this form of anxiety. But religion, based on a hardened and dogmatic system of belief "that has a primarily anxiety-denying and worldview-defending mechanism, can be a particularly insidious medium through which death anxiety is buffered" (Roberts 2015: para 9). ISIS claims to be such a buffer for many people today. But the danger of ISIS is that its prospective members are second and third generation Muslims and Western youth disenchanted with postmodern society— all of whom live in Western nations. This poses a threat to Western nations. These people are the perfect targets for ISIS's propaganda.

Wood (2015) suggests that the 'allure' of the Islamic state is that its adherents "believe that they are personally involved in struggles beyond their own lives, and that merely to be swept up in the drama, on the side of righteousness, is a privilege and a pleasure—especially when it is also a burden" (para 105). Thus, Wood has linked ISIS's psychological motivation with its religious ideology and the attraction to violence (Wood 2015).

The rationale that ISIS uses to communicate its media messages for recruiting volunteers and soldiers is framed in strong religious terms drawn from the Quran, the prophet, and the Islamic history. Arguably, the antidote to this recruitment would be counterarguments that are embedded in Islamic theology. But beyond theology, a common sensical interpretation of texts must prevail because if everyone were to interpret their sacred texts in a way that dehumanizes other people and justifies outright violence, then it must be clear to them that regardless of the cause, the texts are being used for evil purposes which cannot be tolerated.

The ISIS Eschatology

The term eschatology comes from an aspect of religious theology, which refers to conceptions of the end of time such as the resurrection, migration of the soul, and new heavens and the earth. There are three types of eschatology (sometimes overlapping with each other): messianism (the expectation of a figure to usher in a new world); millennialism (the establishment of a 1,000-year reign of peace); or apocalypticism (a sudden destruction before a new world is created; Landes n.d.). Christianity, Judaism, and Islam are religions with an eschatological framework. Islamic eschatology is based on messianism (the expectation of the messiah—Al-Mahdi) and apocalypticism (destruction of the sin-sick world before the reign of righteous Islam begins) rather than millennialism.[16] Some Western scholars and media have mistakenly associated ISIS with millennialism (Furnish 2005).

The opening section of the Quran (*surat al-fatiha*) refers to Allah as the commander or master of the day of judgment, '*malik yom al-din*':

> What will convey to you what the Day of Judgment is? Again! What will convey to you what the Day of Judgment is? It is the Day when a self will have no power to help any other self in any way. The command that Day will be Allah's alone.[17]

However, unlike the Bible and the somewhat systematic apocalyptic teachings contained in the books of Daniel and Revelation, the Quran does not offer a clear narrative of the end times; therefore, Muslim teachers and scholars resort to the various Hadiths, which supplement the Quran with the prophet's teachings. This lack of clarity (and the fact that Sunni and Shia Muslims have different interpretations on this matter) of the Islamic end times gives ISIS yet another loophole for using the texts for its own interpretation of terror. Fromson and Simon (2015) argued that it is important to understand the history of the Hadiths in relation to ISIS's use of them.

> [they were composed] in the early years of Islam, a time of fierce internecine fighting between the followers of the Prophet's family (Shi'at Ali: the Shi'ites) and the Umayyad dynasty. This has opened the way for ISIS's leaders to become the masters of their own apocalyptic narrative—to read and interpret Islam's vast alternative corpus of apocryphal prophesy to suit their agenda. (Fromson and Simon 2015: para 58)

As pointed out earlier, Al-Qaeda was superseded by ISIS in part because an ideological dispute arose between the two organizations over the issue of eschatology (end times). Al-Qaeda wanted to wait to ensure gaining critical mass before launching its caliphate, which would catapult the end times. However, ISIS wanted to fast track its eschatological timetable by installing the caliphate immediately (McCants 2015). So what distinguishes ISIS from Al-Qaeda is ISIS's flagrant use of eschatology and its audaciousness in situating itself in the end times' scenario to legitimize its cause. According to Rasheed (2015), the eschatology of the movement is so powerful that it now underpins ISIS's battlefield strategy.

> [I]n July 2014 ISIS released the first two issues of *Dabiq*, a digital magazine, which is named after a Syrian town believed to be the site of a future apocalyptic battle—Islamic Armageddon (*Al-Malhama Al-Kubra*)—to be fought between Muslims and Romans. (Rasheed 2015: 40)

ISIS is working on the battle plan based on the belief that the end times' apocalyptic battle will take place in Dabiq, a city which is believed by ISIS to be the location where 'the first American crusader' was buried[18] (BBC Website 2016). In preparation for this battle, ISIS has deliberately engaged in brutal and graphic killings of Westerners using social media to disseminate their savagery in the hope that Western powers would send soldiers and military personnel to Syria and Iraq and especially to Dabiq, in order that their apocalyptic prophesies may be fulfilled and more soldiers recruited to their cause.

The horrific and coordinated Paris terrorist attacks in November 2015 by ISIS could have been motivated by France's historic involvement with Syria after the end of the Ottoman Empire and its infamous policy of divide and rule which created 'semiautonomous local states' called 'mandates' within the region (Fildis 2011: para 4). This raises the strategic question: Was ISIS taunting France through this attack to send troops to Syria?

Furthermore, the self-proclaimed Caliph, al-Baghdadi has announced his intention of carrying out an attack in the city of Rome, which he considers the seat of Christianity: "You [ISIS] will conquer Rome and own the world, if Allah wills" (cited in Rasheed 2015: 111).

According to Wood (2015), ISIS is laying everything on the line in its eschatological path and intends to bring about this end time by:

> … following the prophecy and example of Muhammad, in punctilious detail…. It is ready to cheer its own near-obliteration, and to remain confident, even when surrounded, that it will receive divine succour if it stays true to the Prophetic model…. That the Islamic State holds the imminent fulfilment of prophecy as a matter of dogma at least tells us the mettle of our opponent. (Wood 2015: paras 12, 109)

Likewise, US General Martin Dempsey believes the eschatology of ISIS is both the motivator and belief system that keeps it going.

> They actually … at least the senior leaders—believe themselves to be the heir to the caliphate. So this is not a group that can go half way. It has to keep moving toward its ultimate end-of-days apocalyptic narrative or it loses religious legitimacy. (Dempsey 2014: para 15)

It seems there is no turning back for ISIS because it has clearly revealed its battle plan and, as Fromson and Simon explain, "having raised eschatological expectations, there is enormous pressure on ISIS from its supporters to live up to the rhetoric" (Fromson and Simon 2015: para 45).

Central to the Islamic end times' message is that the Al-Mahdi or the Messiah will come to bring the world back to Islam and fight Islam's adversaries, which includes Jews and Christians, and that Isa (Christ), the Muslim Christ, will assist Al-Mahdi in this operation. Al-Mahdi (the rightly guided one)[19] is not mentioned in the Quran but appears in several Hadiths, which are highly regarded Islamic texts because they represent the actions, sayings and traditions of the prophet as recorded by others.

In a particularly vilifying manner, Muhammad ibn Izzat and Muhammad Arif describe the aforementioned tradition in the following words:

> The Mahdi will be victorious and eradicate those pigs and dogs and the idols of this time so that there will once more be a caliphate based on prophethood as the hadith states ... *Jerusalem will be the location of the rightly guided caliphate and the center of Islamic rule, which will be headed by Imam al-Mahdi....* That will abolish the leadership of the Jews ... and put an end to the domination of the satans who spit evil into people and cause corruption in the earth, making them slaves of false idols and ruling the world by laws other than the Shari'a [Islamic Law] of the Lord of the worlds. (Cited in Mitchell 2013: 69–70)

The black flag that ISIS uses is part of their belief that in the end time, messiah, the Al-Mahdi, will fight the mother of all battles. An army from the east who will be carrying black flags or banners of war will precede the Mahdi's ascendancy to power. Sheikh Kabbani explains this idea.

> Hadith indicates that black flags coming from the area of Khorasan will signify the appearance of the Mahdi is nigh. Khorasan is in today's Iran, and some scholars have said that this Hadith means when the black flags appear from Central Asia, i.e. in the direction of Khorasan, then the appearance of the Mahdi is imminent. (Kabanni 2003: 228)

Rasulullah [Muhammad] prophesized the final destination of this end time army: "Armies carrying black flags will come from Khurasan. No power will be able to stop them and they will finally reach Eela (Baitul Maqdas in Jerusalem) where they will erect their flags" (cited in Khan 2008: 240).

Among the many duties the Mahdi will accomplish according to various Hadiths[20] are:

1. He will conquer Israel for Islam and lead the 'faithful Muslims' in a final slaughter/battle against the Jews.

2. He will establish the new Islamic world headquarters from Jerusalem.
3. He will rule for seven years (possibly as much as eight or nine).
4. He will cause Islam to be the only religion practiced on the earth.

In the history of Islam, many messianic pretenders[21] have surfaced, usually during the times of tremendous societal discontent. The current upheaval in Muslim societies, especially in the Middle East, has led many Muslims to expect the coming of the Al-Mahdi and ISIS is definitely capitalizing on this sentiment for its own ends. McCants (2015) argued that the thirst for political power in Egypt, Syria, Iran, and elsewhere is being used by ISIS as the backdrop of its end times' scenario.

Thus, according to Fromson and Simon (2015), ISIS has interwoven its eschatology to its military strategy and linked eschatology to its strategic priorities—establishing a caliphate and bringing justice to the Shiites.

> According to Islamic tradition, the refounding of the universal caliphate is a prerequisite for ushering in the end times. A hadith attributed to the Prophet is frequently cited in this vein:
> Prophethood will be among you as long as God intends, and then God will take it away if He so wills.... Then there will be a tyrannical monarchy. It will be among you as long as God intends, and then God will take it away if He so wills. Then there will be a caliphate in accordance with the prophetic method....
> This phrase—'a caliphate in accordance with the prophetic method'— has become both a kind of unofficial ISIS motto and a source of prestige.
> (Cited in Fromson and Simon 2015: para 52)

To sum up, ISIS uses the eschatology of Islam to authenticate itself. It also capitalizes this end times' message as a powerful recruiting tool. It promises the youth of today (especially those in Western countries who do not feel accepted) a chance to participate in the final destruction of Western evil and Shiite apostasy so that Islam can be renewed to its glory days of the past including the appearance of the messiah, Al-Mahdi. ISIS's fixation with this apocalyptic narrative continues to be one of the keys to its success and widespread appeal.

ISIS and Empire

The motto of ISIS is *Baqiyya wa Tamaddad* which means 'enduring and expanding' (cited in Rasheed 2015: 3). This introduces another key difference between ISIS and Al-Qaeda: ISIS controls territory and has declared itself an Islamic State or caliphate. The term caliphate comes from the word Caliph (which means 'successor' in Arabic *khalīfah*). The Caliph rules the political–religious state consisting of Muslims. The first Caliph ruled the Islamic caliphate after the death of the prophet Muhammad in 632 AD. The caliphate's territory increased rapidly through conquest during its first two centuries to include most of Southwest Asia, North Africa, and Spain. Internal struggles later brought about the caliphate's decline, and it ceased to exist with the Mongol destruction of Baghdad in 1258 (Landes n.d.).

What is being presented by ISIS to its citizens is the almost roman-tic notion of an idealized past when Islam was in its glory days. This recollection of history has been contested by some scholars (Mallon 2014: para 2): "if it ever existed, it did not exist for a very long time … its form, authority and success differed greatly from place to place and time to time."

ISIS views its caliphate as the only legitimate government for Muslims worldwide and has asked for pledges of allegiance (*bayah*) from the global *Umma* (community of Muslims). In a speech titled 'hadtha wa'd Allah' (this is the Promise of God), ISIS spokesman Abu Muhammad al-Adnani made this claim:

> [I]t is incumbent upon all Muslims to pledge allegiance to the Khalifa Ibrahim [that is, Baghdadi] and support him. The legality of all emirates, groups, states, and organizations, becomes null by the expansion of the khilafa's authority and arrival of its troops to their areas.[22]

The implications of this new state and the call for allegiance is proving problematic for the international community, other jihadist groups, such as Al-Qaeda, who look for followers from the same community, and the citizens of this new political entity. Admittedly, the state of ISIS conforms to the criteria of what constitutes statehood according to the Montevideo Convention[23]—it has a governmental system, people under its rule, and a legal system and so forth. However, the international community continues to condemn its actions and its very presence. ISIS could potentially be recognized as other countries with Sharia also enjoy that privilege but the fact that it continues to cause outrage (because of its human rights violation and quest for more territory by force) and violates international law means it will take a long time before the international community views it as a "just governance that is worthy of international recognition" (Belanger-McMurdo 2015: para 12).

ISIS has released its manifesto—the only theoretical work of its kind, a 268-page document ominously entitled the *The Management of Savagery*[24] (Naji 2006). In it, the writer defines this key phrase:

We said earlier that if one contemplates the previous centuries, even until the middle of the twentieth century, one finds that when the large states or empires fell—whether they were Islamic or non-Islamic—and a state did not come into being which was equal in power or comparable to the previous state in its ability to control the lands and regions of that state which collapsed, the regions and sectors of this state became, according to human nature, subservient to what is called 'administrations of savagery'. Therefore, the management of savagery is defined very succinctly as the management of savage chaos!!

As for a detailed definition, it differs according to the goals and nature of the individuals in the administration. If we picture its initial form, we find that it consists of the management of peoples' needs with regard to the provision of food and medical treatment, preservation of security and justice among the people who live in the regions of savagery, securing the borders by means of groups that deter anyone who tries to assault the regions of savagery, as well as setting up defensive fortifications. (Naji 2006: 26, section 11)

Thus, ISIS aims to conquer 'apostate' nations and peoples, by allowing them to enter into the depths of savagery and then building a new order through their Islamic governance. Presumably, strict Sharia law is to be enforced in its controlled territory.

A video released by ISIS during Ramadan in 2014 urged Muslims from foreign lands to come to 'the land of Kalifah' (a reference to the caliphate of the ISIS-held empire; Traub 2015: para 4). While the narrator persuades Muslims in the video, this chant can be heard in the background:

Our State was established upon Islam
And although it wages Jihad upon the enemies
It governs the affairs of people
It looks after its flock with love and patience. (Traub 2015: para 4)

In an effort to combine the hardline massacring of apostates and the 'tending of the flock' of ISIS citizens, the ISIS propaganda machinery produces videos that are interspersed with brutal beheading footage as well as images of road repairs, medical clinics, and even the testimonies of grateful citizens.

This two-pronged media strategy is complemented by a two-tiered economic system with the income gap between ISIS fighters and citizens widening in favor of the fighters (El-Ghobashy and Nabhan 2017). Besides higher income, ISIS fighters enjoy benefits such as electricity, food, and medical care, which are costly for the other residents of the caliphate.

> Some hospitals treat only ISIS members, and others reserve the best care for the militants.... The quality of life for ISIS fighters and their families is much better than it is for those who simply live under the terrorists' control in the group's self-declared 'caliphate'. (Engel 2016)

In early 2016, the city of Raqqa in Syria was the central headquarters or capital of this caliphate where strong governance is practiced—unlike ISIS's newly acquired territories (Caris and Reynolds 2014). Whether ISIS is able to sustain such governance while involved in a war is in question, but initial studies show there is some level of competence.

> Through the integration of military and political campaigns, particularly in ... the capital.... ISIS has built a holistic system of governance that includes religious, educational, judicial, security, humanitarian and infrastructure projects among others. (Caris and Reynolds 2014: 4)

According to Chulov (Lock 2014), ISIS is run like a Mafia organization and its takings (taxes, revenue, and protection money) range anywhere between US$2 and 4 million per day. The enormous wealth of ISIS, plus its capacity to attract and trade in cash, crude oil, and contraband allows it to operate outside of approved banking channels (Di Giovanni, Goodman and Sharkov 2014).

However, despite all its propaganda, wealth and military might, ISIS is not invincible (it lost some territory in the middle of 2015),[25] and it is reported that people are trying to flee the ISIS territories (Engel 2016). ISIS is aware of this tendency (as loss of people or territory could endanger its image) and has in place strategies to prevent this.

> The group has accordingly placed IEDs [Improvized Explosive Devices] around entrances to cities it controls, such as Fallujah and Ramadi, to prevent escape, which simultaneously serve the larger purpose of preventing the [Iraqi Security Forces] from advancing. (Cited in Engel 2016: para 14)

What is perhaps as troubling about ISIS's quest for territory in the Middle East is its influence and support from other Islamic terrorist groups around the world, such as Boko Haram in Africa and Abu Sayyaf in the Philippines. In November 2014, ISIS announced that it received pledges of *bayah* (allegiance) from Islamic terrorist groups in Algeria, Libya, and the Sinai Peninsula (Rosen 2015). Any increase in groups that have pledged support is bound to be of concern to those committed to the 'war against terror'. Also of concern are the inspired and emboldened 'lone wolf' operatives such as the terrorist in Sydney, Australia's Lindt café terror attack in December 2014 and the Parisian attacks of 2015. These developments reinforce ISIS's strategic and ideological ambition to be a growing movement with worldwide influence.

Conclusion

The history of Islam and the Sunni–Shia dialectic are starting points to explain the genesis of ISIS. Furthermore, we saw that ISIS arose out of the complex circumstances of Jihadist activities, which brought about the US-led invasion of Iraq and the subsequent fall of Saddam Hussein.

The key to understanding ISIS is to see how it views itself. Understanding the socioeconomic and geopolitical origins of ISIS is critical as the world comes face to face with the leading contender to Western civilization and culture in the twenty-first century. ISIS is the most virulent strain of previous Jihadi terror movements such as Al-Qaeda. The persuasion and rhetoric that draws second and third generation Muslims and Westerners into ISIS is situated in the realm of Islamic theology and eschatology, and ISIS has cleverly manipulated the situation for its own ends.

ISIS is certainly not Islam but it is Islamic. The fact that even anti-ISIS Islamic groups cannot burn the ISIS flags because of the word 'Allah' enshrined in it—reveals the painful dilemma of the movement. Islamic theologians and teachers therefore need to reclaim Islam from its fanatical strain by shedding light on what Islam stands for and apply a sane method of interpreting its texts.

ISIS is more than a terror group. It is made up of three components: a revolutionary, Jihadi sect with an apocalyptic message, a theocratic Islamic state that demands submission from the international Muslim community (*Umma*), and a potentially worldwide Islamist force.

Hence, defeating this movement requires a multipronged strategy that addresses the threefold nature of ISIS. Islamic religious bodies and teachers need to develop an alternative religious narrative to the Jihadist propaganda. Governments around the world must be equipped with a comprehensive antiterrorism strategy and a de-radicalization plan for its citizens who are involved or could be attracted to ISIS. Well-coordinated and strategic military operations by the United States and allied forces need to continue. Beyond that, the sending of ground troops to Syria is perhaps not in the best interests of all concerned as this is exactly what ISIS wants.[26]

In some ways, Al-Qaeda could meet the ISIS challenge—ISIS came out of the association with Al-Qaeda and Al-Qaeda is still active. If a leadership or ideological change takes place within Al-Qaeda, it could lead to a new contest between old adversaries (Fromson and Simon 2015).

There is also the possibility that ISIS may be that kind of creature that cannot be killed by outsiders but could eventually destroy itself. Its blood lust and ruthless enforcement of Sharia law necessitates the death sentence to all who defy its interpretation of Islam. Hence, self-implosion could be a possible scenario for ISIS.

Understanding ISIS is the key to its eradication. But while the debate continues, whether ISIS can be defeated or not, one thing is clear—since the dawn of ISIS, the rules of engagement in terms of war, statehood, international terrorism, and Islamic sectarianism have changed and are changing.

Notes

1. See http://www.nytimes.com/2006/06/08/world/middleeast/08cnd-zarqawi-text.
   html?pagewanted=print&_r=0
2. A political–religious state or empire comprising the Muslim community and the
   lands and peoples under its dominion in the early centuries following the death of
   the Prophet Muhammad. The Caliphate is headed by a Caliph (Arabic *khalīfah*,
   'successor'). Historically the empire of the Caliphate grew rapidly through
   conquest during its first two centuries through the Umayyad Caliphate and the
   Abbasid Caliphate to include most of Southwest Asia, North Africa, and Spain.
   The Abbasid Caliphate came to end after the Mongol destruction of Baghdad in
   1258. During the Ottoman Empire initially led by Osman (1258–1326), the role of
   Caliph was obscured although territory was gained including the famous capture
   of Constantinople in 1453. The Ottoman Empire declined and ceased when Turkey
   became a republic in 1923.
3. The Quran is the absolute word of Allah according to Muslims and the Hadiths
   are the historical accounts of the revered prophet Mohammad written by members
   of the inner circle of Mohammad.
4. His name is also spelt as Husain, Hussain, and Hussein.
5. See http://www.cfr.org/peace-conflict-and-human-rights/sunni-shia-divide/
   p33176#!/?cid=otr-marketing_url-sunni_shia_infoguide
6. Sunnah literally means a path or way. Hadith, on the other hand, literally means
   something new. Generally, the Quran and Sunnah are on par in terms of authority.
   See Chapter 5, note 7.
7. The Arab Spring is a reference to a period of disenchantment about the various
   governments in the Middle East that caused a series of protests, uprisings, and
   armed rebellion in early 2011. Social media was also used heavily in some of the
   countries concerned.
8. It is estimated that some 20,000 foreign fighters are engaged in the war in Syria
   for ISIS.
9. There are references and narratives on killing and fighting in the Christian text as
   well—the Bible—but scholars point out that these references become less and less
   pronounced in the latter half of the Old Testament and are completely absent in
   the New Testament teaching passages—being replaced with verses such as "… live
   at peace with everyone" (Romans 12:18) ; "Let no debt remain outstanding, except
   the continuing debt to love one another, for whoever loves others has fulfilled the
   law" (Romans 13:8), and "But I tell you, love your enemies and pray for those who
   persecute you" Matthew 5: 44.
10. One of the leading scholars who proposed the case for secularism was Souad T. Ali.
11. This was made possible because Saddam Hussein had earlier organized an Islamic
    Faith campaign designed to give religious legitimacy to his secular totalitarianism.
    In doing so, Saddam created a new category of 'Salafist-Baathists'.
12. While Al-Qaeda focused on the 'far enemy'—the United States, Zarqawi concen-
    trated on Iraq based on his famous words "… if Jihad fails in Iraq, the [Muslim]
    nation will never rise again" (cited in Brooke 2004: para 4).

13. Ramadan is the ninth month of the Muslim year where fasting is observed in daylight hours and Muslims also try to use the month to observe religious activities and make vows to forgo bad habits.

14. The *Shahada* (also spelled Shahadah) is one of the five pillars of Islam. The word is derived from the term testimony. In reciting the *Shahada*, a Muslim verbally testifies that Allah is the only true god, and that Mohammad is Allah's prophet.

15. See https://darvish.wordpress.com/2012/08/10/the-seal-ring-of-the-prophet-saw/

16. Millennialism (from millennium, Latin for 'thousand years') is a doctrine held by some Christian denominations that there will be an age of peace on earth in which Jesus Christ will reign.

17. See http://www.harunyahya.com/en/Allahin-adlari/16737/MALIK-YAWM-AD-DEEN-The-King-of-the-Day-of-Judgment (Surat al-Infitar, 82: 17–19).

18. See also http://www.clarionproject.org/analysis/dabiq-islamic-state-wants-battle-end-days

19. Al-Mahdi is also called, The Imam, The Promised Deliverer, The Khalifatullah (Deputy of God), and Al-Jabir (The Comforter).

20. These duties are taken from two primary sources: *Black Flags from the Islamic State* (EBook), 2015: 93–95, retrieved from http://www.investigativeproject.org/documents/misc/864.pdf and Sunni Documentation on Imam al-Mahdi (as), n.d., retrieved from http://www.al-islam.org/shiite-encyclopedia-ahlul-bayt-dilp-team/sunni-documentation-imam-al-mahdi

21. See https://abusalmandeyauddeeneberle.wordpress.com/the-true-mahdi-and-false-claimants-of-mahdiism/

22. See http://www.abc.net.au/news/2014–06-30/isis-declares-islamic-caliphate/5558508

23. The Montevideo Convention is a treaty signed at Montevideo, Uruguay on 26 December 1933, during the International Conference of American States. The Convention regularizes the theory and practice of statehood as an accepted part of international law.

24. The full name of the author is Abu Bakr Naji and the work is translated by William McCants. See https://azelin.files.wordpress.com/2010/08/abu-bakr-naji-the-management-of-savagery-the-most-critical-stage-through-which-the-umma-will-pass.pdf

25. At its peak, ISIS was in control of 55,000 square kilometers in northern and western Iraq but recently lost 25 percent of its territory (Martinez 2015).

26. The United States and coalition forces need to recognize that the long-term strategy should be to build an Iraq that is inclusive of Sunni, Kurdish, and Shiite. The failed attempts in the former Maliki administration must not be repeated.

References

Abrahamian, E. 1993. *Khomenism: Essays on the Islamic Republic*. Berkeley, CA: University of California Press.

Alexander, Y. and M. Hoening. 2008. *The New Iranian Leadership Ahmedinejad, Terrorism, Nuclear Ambition and the Middle East*. Westport, CT: Praeger Security International.

Ali, S. T. 2009. *A Religion, Not a State: Ali 'Abd al-Raziq's Islamic Justification of Political Secularism*. Salt Lake City, UT: University of Utah Press.

BBC website. 2016. "Dabiq: Why Is Syrian Town So Important for IS?" *BBC News*. 4th October Edition. Accessed on 15 December 2015 from: http://www.bbc.com/news/world-middle-east-30083303

Becker, E. 1973. *The Denial of Death*. New York, NY: The Free Press.

Belanger-McMurdo, A. 2015. "A Fight for Statehood? ISIS and its Quest for Political Domination." *E-International Relations*. Accessed on 12 February 2016 from http://www.e-r.info/2015/10/05/a-fight-for-statehood-isis-and-its-quest-for-political-domination/

Brooke, S. 2004. "The Rise of Zarqawi." In *The Weekly Standard*. June 7th Edition. Accessed on 5 December 2015 from http://www.weeklystandard.com/the-rise-of-zarqawi/article/5385

Caris, C. and S. Reynolds. 2014. "ISIS Governance in Syria, Middle East." *Middle East Security*, Report 22. Accessed on 10 December 2015 from http://www.understandingwar.org/report/isis-governance-syria

Dempsey, M. E. 2014. *Gen. Dempsey Remarks at the Aspen Security Forum 2014*. Accessed on 16 December 2015 from http://www.jcs.mil/Media/Speeches/tabid/3890/Article/571964/gen-dempsey-remarks-at-the-aspen-security-forum-2014.aspx

Di Giovanni, J., L. M. Goodman and D. Sharkov. 2014, 6 November. "How Does ISIS Fund Its Reign of Terror?" *Newsweek*. Accessed on 12 January 2016 from http://www.newsweek.com/2014/11/14/how-does-isis-fund-its-reign-terror-2822607.html

El-Ghobashy, T and A. A. Nabhan. 2017. "Foreign ISIS Fighters Increasingly Isolated in Mosul Battle." *Wall Street Journal*. March 16th Edition. Accessed on 20 May 2017 from https://www.wsj.com/articles/foreign-isis-fighters-increasingly-isolated-in-mosul-battle-1489676887

Engel, P. 2016. "It's Hell: How ISIS Prevents People from Fleeing the 'Caliphate'." *Business Insider*. Accessed on 11 January 2016 from http://www.businessinsider.com.au/how-isis-controls-life-caliphate-raqqa-capital-2015-12

Esposito, J. L. 1991. *Islam: The Straight Path*. Oxford: Oxford University Press.

Fildis, A. T. 2011. "The Troubles in Syria: Spawned by French Divide and Rule." *Middle East Policy* 18(4): 1–4.

Fromson, J. and S. Simon. 2015. "ISIS: The Dubious Paradise of Apocalypse Now." *Survival* 57(3): 7–56.

Furnish, T. 2005. *Holiest Wars: Islamic Mahdis, Their Jihads, and Osama bin Laden*. Westport, CT: Praeger.

Harleem, M. A. S. 2004. *The Qua'ran: A New Translation*. New York, NY: Oxford University Press.

Helfont, S. 2015. *Islam and Islamism: A Primer for Teachers and Students*. Accessed on 10 December 2015 from http://www.fpri.org/article/2015/08/islam-and-islamism-a-primer-for-teachers-and-students/

Hitti, P. K. 1970. *History of the Arabs: From the Earliest Times to the Present*. London: Macmillan.

Kabanni, S. M. H. 2003. *The Approach of Armageddon? An Islamic Perspective*. Washington DC: Supreme Muslim Council of America.

Khan, M. Y. 2008. *Islam Main Imam Mehdi Ka Tassawar* (trans. *Concept of Mahdi in Islam*). Lahore: Jamia Ashrafia.

Landes, R. "Eschatology." *Encyclopaedia Britannica*. Accessed on 11 December 2015 from http://www.britannica.com/topic/eschatology

Lewis, B. 1993. *The Arabs in History*. New York, NY: Oxford University Press.

Lifton, R. J. 1979. *The Broken Connection: On Death and the Continuity of Life*. Washington, DC: American Psychiatric Press.

Lock, H. 2014. "How ISIS Became the Wealthiest Terror Group in History." 15 September 2014 Edition. Independent News website. Accessed on 20 May 2017 from http://www.independent.co.uk/news/world/middle-east/how-isis-became-the-wealthiest-terror-group-in-history-9732750.html

Mallon, E. D. 2014. *Contesting the Caliphate: ISIS and the 'Golden Age' of Muslim Rule*. Accessed on 12 January 2016 from http://americamagazine.org/issue/contesting-caliphate

Martinez, L. 2105. "ISIS Has Lost 25 Percent of Territory It Once Held in Iraq, US Says." ABC News website. May 13 Edition. Accessed on 22 December 2015 from http://abcnews.go.com/Politics/isis-lost-25-percent-territory-held-iraq-us/story?id=29625568

McCants, W. 2015. *The ISIS Apocalypse: The History, Strategy and Doomsday Vision of the Islamic State*. New York, NY: St. Martin's Press.

Mitchell, C. 2013. *Dateline Jerusalem*. Nashville, TN: Thomas Nelson.

Mitchell, R. P. 1993. *The Society of the Muslim Brothers*. London: Oxford University Press.

Mozaffari, M. 2007. "What is Islamism? History and Definition of a Concept." *Totalitarian and Political Religions* 8(1): 17–33.

Mussalli, A. S., G. D. Newby, and A. Mussalli. (n.d.). In *Oxford Encyclopedia of the Islamic World*, edited by J. L. Esposito. Accessed on 12 December 2015 from http://www.oxfordislamicstudies.com/article/opr/t236/e0550

Naji, A. B. 2006. *The Management of Savagery: The Most Critical Stage Through Which the Umma Will Pass*. Translated by W. McCants. Cambridge, MA: Harvard University.

Prusher, I. 2014, 4 September. *What ISIS Flag Says About the Militant Group*. Accessed on 11 December from http://time.com/3311665/isis-flag-iraq-syria/

Commins, D. 1994. "Hassan al-Banna." In *Pioneers of Islamic Revival*, edited by A. Rahnema, 125–53. London: Zed Books.

Rasheed, A. 2015. *ISIS: Race to Armageddon*. New Delhi: United Service Institution of India, Vij Books India.

Raza, W. 2014. *A Study of the Islamic Republic of Iran with Special Reference to the Office of Vali-E-Faqih (the Leader)*. Ph.D. Dissertation. Lucknow: University of Lucknow.

Ranstorp, M. 2007. "Introduction: Mapping Terrorism Research." In *Mapping Terrorism Research: State of the Art, Gaps and Future*, edited by M. Ranstorp. Oxon, UK: Routledge.

Roberts, K. 2015. *ISIS and the Psychology of Terror*. Accessed on 15 December 2015 from http://www.patheos.com/blogs/unsystematictheology/2015/04/isis-and-the-psychology-of-terror/

Rosen, A. 2015. "Africa's Deadliest Terror Group Wants to Team Up with ISIS but Don't Expect Much of an Alliance." *Business Insider Australia* website. March 11th Edition. Accessed on 20 May 2017 from https://www.businessinsider.com.au/africas-deadliest-terror-group-wants-to-team-up-with-isis-2015-3

Steup, M. 2016. "Epistemology." In *The Stanford Encyclopedia of Philosophy* (Fall 2016 Edition), edited by E. N. Zalta. Accessed on 10 December 2016 from https://plato.stanford.edu/entries/epistemology/

Taheri, A. 2016. *Syria: A Checkered Past, Uncertain Future*. Accessed on 15 December 2016 from http://www.gatestoneinstitute.org/7408/syria-past-future

Traub, J. 2015, 14 March. "The Demonic Wellspring." *Wall Street Journal*. Accessed on 10 December 2015 from http://www.wsj.com/articles/book-review-isis-the-state-of-terror-by-jessica-stern-j-m-berger-isis-inside-the-army-of-terror-by-michael-weiss-hassan-hassan-the-rise-of-islamic-state-by-patrick-cockburn-1426280254

Weaver, M. 2006, July–August. "The Short, Violent Life of Abu Musab al-Zarqawi." *The Atlantic*. Accessed on 10 December 2015 from http://www.theatlantic.com/magazine/archive/2006/07/the-short-violent-life-of-abu-musab-al-zarqawi/304983/

Wood, G. 2015, March. "What ISIS Really Wants." *The Atlantic*. Accessed on 15 January 2015 from http://www.theatlantic.com/features/archive/2015/02/what-isis-really-wants/384980/

Conclusion: Globalization of Faith, Faith in Globalization

Introduction

The 11 September 2001 attacks on the United States have been variously interpreted. Nacos (2002) claimed that they depicted how Islamic Jihadists made use of the American and global media for their own ends. The second tower at the World Trade Center was hit approximately 15 minutes after the first one, thus enabling most of the TV network crews to be on the scene to broadcast the destruction of the second tower in real time—something truly unprecedented. This amazing 'media spectacle' was cleverly exploited by the perpetrators through the globalization of media technology (Kellner 2003; Nacos 2002). Globalization has been said to compress time and space and simultaneously shrink distances dramatically (Harvey 1989; Kern 1983). Furthermore, Castells (2000) has argued that the current rise of the 'network society' is due to the rapid development of new information and transportation technologies—all of which are reshaping the landscape of everyday living.

It has also been argued by Kellner (2006) that besides Jihadists, various US administrations have used spectacles of terror to promote their military power and achieve their geopolitical ends via the media, as evidenced in the following wars: Gulf war of 1990–91, Afghanistan war mid-2001, and the Iraq war of 2003 (Kellner 2008). Therefore, globalization, as a contemporary reality, is no respecter of persons; it enables Jihadists and governments alike to fulfil their agendas.

Transnational Religious Movements: Faith's Flows describes the whole gamut of transnational movements—from those that are focused on religion and the upliftment of society, to those that are subversive to the state and people outside the state. Six representative movements were singled out for study: Islamic Relief or IR (Islamic), Gülen-Hizmet (Cultural Islam), Ciji (Buddhist), BAPS (Hindu), Hillsong (Christian), and ISIS (Islamic theocracy). The six case studies show that these movements are both creations of globalization and agents in globalization. All six organizations reveal the interlocking networks of religion, people, spiritual capital, and technologies.

In this concluding chapter, I situate the six transnational organizations within the framework of globalization and reflect on how religious entities encounter today's world. I first show the interplay between globalization and transnational movements and then look at six major trends that arise out of my study.

The classical understanding of religion and globalization articulated by Robertson (1985) and Beyer (1994)—that religious revival was an expression of traditional identities and a reaction against modernity—served as a good starting point, but my study demonstrates that religion and modernity can coexist quite happily. As pointed out by Csordas (2009: 3), the globalization of religion is a multidimensional process in which religion, popular culture, politics, and economics are 'necessarily coeval and intimately intertwined'. Therefore, in my examination of the six transnational organizations, I have argued that as much as these six organizations represent the globalization of faith, they also reflect faith in globalization. On this point, I believe it is helpful to consider Steger's (2009) illustration on the capture and life of Osama bin Laden—at one time, one of the most wanted terrorists in the West (known for his anti-Western rhetoric) and his paradoxical flirtations with globalization.

> A close look at bin Laden's right wrist reveals yet another clue to the powerful dynamics of globalization. As he directs his words of contempt for the United States and its allies at his hand-held microphone, his retreating sleeve exposes a stylish sports watch. Journalists who noticed this expensive accessory have speculated about the origins of the timepiece in question. The emerging consensus points to a Timex product.... After all, Timex Corporation, originally the Waterbury Clock Company, was founded in the 1850s.... Today, the company has gone multinational, maintaining close relations to affiliated businesses and sales offices in 65 countries. The corporation employs 7,500 employees, located on four continents. (Steger 2009: 7)

My exploration of the six transnational religious movements has revealed the following trends:

1. Infatuation with the means and benefits of globalization
2. Reterritorialization

3. No disjunction between faith and fortune, fane and profane
4. Reverse flows
5. Varying approaches to gender
6. Changing modalities and transmodernism

Infatuation with the Means and Benefits of Globalization

All six transnational movements display the aspect of globalization mentioned by Csordas (2009)—they intertwine faith with popular culture, technology, and economics (ISIS intertwines it with politics as well). And the six organizations have adopted the processes and modes of globalization for their own ends. Arguably, there are also points of correspondences between these organizations in so far as they enjoy the benefits of globalization. IR uses the Western model of aid organizations to strengthen its presence in the West and carry out its aid programs to Muslim nations. Furthermore, most of these transnational movements in my study have adopted the modes of imagination and practices of the American entertainment industry, namely Disneyland. For example, BAPS in India has constructed a Disney-like temple in New Delhi (Vijayakumar 2015), thus a tourist-cum-globalization model of the American entertainment industry.[1] Bryman (1995) identified four dimensions of Disneyization:[2] theming, differentiation of consumption, merchandizing, and emotional labor. A brief explanation of these concepts follows with examples drawn from my case studies.

Theming

The BAPS Hindu sect's massive theme park-cum-temple in New Delhi incorporates information, entertainment, and drama mediated by technology. Apparently, a group of high-ranking BAPS gurus visited Disneyland and Universal Studios in the United States during the planning of the New Delhi temple complex; hence, many of the ideas in the temple's exhibition hall reflect these theme parks in the United States. One of the temple officials remarked to Srivastava (2016), "our boat ride [at the BAPS temple] is 12 minutes long, whereas the one at Universal Studios is only 5 minutes" (Srivastava 2016). This is an obvious comparison to point out that the temple is superior to the Western benchmark.

Differentiation of Consumption

This refers to forms of modern consumption of various spheres that are interwoven into each other. For example, Eco describes the Main Street façade at the entertainment theme park in the US Disneyland: "... [it is] presented as toy houses and invite us to enter them, but their interior is always a disguised supermarket, where you buy obsessively believing you are still playing" (Eco 1986: 43). In the same way, BAPS's SAC is built seamlessly as one main structure, but beyond the entrance and the lobby areas, the complex is divided into sections, some of which attract an entry fee. There is a combined ticket fee for the Hall of Values (also known as Sahajanand Darshan, consisting of an 'audio animatrix show' (which depicts various scenes from Swaminarayan's life), Neelkanth Darshan (an IMAX theater), and Sanskruti Vihar (a boat ride through '10,000 years of Indian history'), which cost visitors ₹170[3] (Srivastava 2016: para 6).

Srivastava (2016) explained that the BAPS temple reflects modern-day consumption and middle-class expectations.

> Akshardham's [the BAPS temple's] appeal is related to the fact that its tableau of consumption (of objects and spaces) is understood by its visitors and represented by its promoters as *contiguous* with the world outside. Its self-representation in terms of technological mastery, efficiency, punctuality, educational achievement and the processes of contemporary consumerism link it with the world of toll-ways, highways, shopping malls, city 'beautification', slum-clearance drives, and the creation of spaces of middle-class identity.... (Srivastava 2016: para 12)

Merchandizing

Just as Walt Disney, the founder of the Disney entertainment empire, created the animated character Mickey Mouse,[4] who became the main symbol and product of Disneyland, transnational religious movements have created their own distinctive religious products. Apparently, the products of each group are based on what the group considers its highly valued spiritual capital.

French sociologist Bourdieu (1984) was interested in the ways in which society reproduces itself and how those in power retain their position. For Bourdieu, authority and power cannot be explained only by economics. There are other forces at work such as social and cultural capital, which enable people to reinforce their standing in the hierarchy and cultural signifiers, which enable people being 'above' the rest on the social ladder (Bourdieu 1984). Spiritual capital is an important aspect of life just like social and cultural capital. Spiritual leaders determine what is highly valued per their theological and spiritual foundations. The well-being of society is the main perceived motivation of leaders in religious movements. It must be pointed out that spiritual capital in the eyes of faith leaders is not free. In fact, devotees value it so highly that they are willing to pay for it. Thus, religious groups capitalize on spiritual needs that equate to demand for goods and services and earn millions of dollars (Belk, Wallendorf and Sherry 1989). GHM schools linked with Gülen are high-fee paying schools for students from the middle class and above. Clearly, the provision of educational services constitutes the cultural and spiritual capital of the GHM movement.

Hillsong's spiritual capital is embodied in its music—recognized as a new genre in Christian worship. Hillsong United (a rock band from Hillsong) has successfully made inroads into the United States, filling concert arenas and topping the US charts. Their songs have become part and parcel of US worship music and the band has amassed a huge fan base.

In the case of BAPS and Ciji, their spiritual capital is vested in their current leaders: Pramukh Swami Maharaj (BAPS) and Venerable Zhengyan (Ciji). BAPS's 94-year-old leader is regarded by the community as the incarnation of God, and his successor will likewise be another incarnation of God, thereby ensuring continuity with Swaminarayan, the founder. Ciji's leader is treated as a Bodhisattva, but her successor's status is not so clear cut. ISIS's spiritual capital is its ideology of an Islamic state. It has a Caliph and he will ensure the coming of the Al-Mahdi and the Christ of Islam to usher in the end of days and the destruction of Islam's enemies.

The case studies show that, ISIS, Hillsong, Ciji, GHM, and BAPS, all have taken the liberty to alter or reinterpret traditional religious texts for their own benefit. Ciji, BAPS, and GHM have gone a step further by creating their own spiritual texts—written by their leaders.

It is significant to note that whereas BAPS has created a Hinduism that is monotheistic[5] and exclusive (belief in Swaminarayan and *Akshar* alone), Hillsong has introduced a Christianity that is Unitarian[6] (with more emphasis on the third person in the Trinity) and inclusive —accepting even those who walk in the "broad … road that leads to destruction" (The Holy Bible 1985, Matthew 7:13). On the other hand, ISIS has hijacked Islam for its own ends so that, as mentioned in Chapter 5, it is easy to erroneously identify ISIS as 'Islamic' because ISIS has sneakily embedded significant elements of the Islamic faith into its symbols, theology, and practices. Thus, ISIS has falsified its epistemological underpinnings.

Emotional Labor

Hochschild (1983) defined emotional labor as a trait that "involves an observable display of human emotion by the worker … and this display is intended to elicit emotional responses in others which are desired by the organization" (cited in Sass 2000: 330). Emotional labor is highly controlled and scripted to conform to the values of the organization.

Ciji started with female volunteers basically rural, village women. Women still form the backbone of the whole movement, but since 1990, males have been allowed to serve as well (DeVido 2010). Through the practice of *seva* (voluntary service), BAPS has thousands of volunteers who give their time and share expertise in temple construction, and act as tour guides and security officers in the massive New Delhi theme park-cum temple. This service extends to other aspects in BAPS's multifaceted work. Hillsong also uses volunteers in their mega churches as parking attendants, security personnel, ushers, and a host of other ministries.

So, to summarize the first trend, contemporary transnational religious organizations have exploited globalization's methods to further their objectives, which include successful commercialization of their spiritual capital. BAPS leaders visited US theme park venues like Universal Studios to get inspiration for their temple-building projects and Hillsong has successfully branded itself as a leader of contemporary churches with the help of well-known marketing and public relations firms.[7] Even ISIS has portrayed itself as a global brand in its infamous recruitment videos on social media.[8]

Reterritorialization

The mass migration of people for economic reasons, such as the Gujarati migration patterns from India to Africa, then to the United Kingdom, the United States, and Canada, resulted in a state of deterritorialization or displacement of the new migrants (Vasquez and Marquardt 2003). Scholars have pointed out that one of globalization's main consequences has been its deterritorialization (Basch, Shiller and Blanc 1994; Giddens 1999). However, although globalization may be the main cause of this condition of displacement and loss of identity, globalization may also provide the solace for deterritorialization via interconnections from media and technology. This condition, where groups are connected through a range of ways, is referred to as reterritorialization (Vasquez and Marquardt 2003). Reterritorialization also has taken place within Ciji when community groups and Sunday schools are organized for members in the West. In the same way, BAPS has encouraged reterritorialization by opening temples and organizing women's conferences in the West or wherever its followers are located. Hence, it seems that people who migrate go through three distinct phases: territorialization (where they are comfortable in their homelands), deterritorialization (where they feel unconnected upon migration), and reterritorialization (when they start to connect with like-minded followers of the faith in foreign lands). According to Roy (2004), a third of all Muslims currently live as minorities in non-Muslim communities. Presumably, this predicament has profound implications for both Muslim minorities and host nations and warrants further investigation.

Whilst reterritorialization is potentially a positive phenomenon, it can at times breed tribalism and, in the case of ISIS, induce members of the diaspora to travel from other lands to become part of the Islamic

State; thus, reterritorialization when consummated, may spell chaos and conflict for others. Leech alluded to this issue of fundamentalist groups long before the start of ISIS.

> We believe the fault line is going to lie inside of the great religions, essentially between what are called, in various ways fundamentalists—people who take their position to be very important, and if other people don't share that tradition, then they're infidels, outside the system. (Leach 1999: para 4)

In chapter one, I gave an overview of how in the old world, states and religions were one and the same in two world religions—Christianity and Islam. With the introduction of the modern state, while Christianity seems to have accepted the status of the separation of state and faith, Islam seems to be still fundamentally linked with the state, at least in the extreme example of ISIS.

Reverse Flows[9]

The center–periphery model is a sociological, spatial construct that seeks to understand the link between a highly advanced 'center' (usually the United States) and a less-developed 'periphery' (usually a reference to developing nations; Marshall 1998). The model theorizes the flows of production and distribution from the center to the periphery within a framework of independent and dependent associations between nations based on the classical principle of Western imperialism (Marshall 1998).

Typically, globalization flows have followed the center–periphery pattern—mainly from the United States and the West to the rest of the world. However, all six transnational organizations in my study run counter to this construct. Indeed, it seems that all six are tending to flow to the West and in particular to the United States. BAPS's largest temple was in London, England for many years and now its largest temple is located in New Jersey, USA. IR and IRW have established themselves in the United Kingdom and the United States so the flows originate from the West but the leadership and ideology is mainly Islamic. An interesting observation about IR and IRW is that although most of the donors are citizens of the United Kingdom and the United States, the bulk of the 27 nations/regions mentioned in the list of aid-receiving entities are mainly Muslim.[10] The IR website makes a point that the organization does not 'pay heed to color race or creed', although in reality this seems unlikely.[11] In the case of Kenya, IR boasts that it works among the Mandera ethnic people who are mainly of the Muslim faith.[12]

Hillsong Church in Sydney, Australia has made inroads into the United States starting churches in key cities there. In 2016, Hillsong announced a strategic partnership with the US Global Christian broadcast leader, Trinity Broadcasting Network (TBN), to feature the Hillsong Channel—a 24-hour network—which will include the best from Hillsong's international conferences, worship from groups, singers, and songwriters such as Hillsong United, Young and Free, Reuben Morgan, Joel Houston, and many others.

> [T]here will also be plenty of life-changing teaching from internationally acclaimed Christian leaders like Hillsong Senior Pastor Brian Houston, and wife Bobbi Houston, whose 'Sisterhood' outreach is inspiring and equipping a generation of women to walk in their God-ordained destiny with a planned distribution footprint including broadcast, cable, and nearly a dozen satellites around the world—will combine the best in cutting-edge worship from the most gifted singers, songwriters, and musicians, with dynamic ministry from internationally acclaimed pastors and teachers.[13]

GHM has the largest number of schools in the United States. It established research centers in various US universities. GHM's Rumi Forum is strategically located in Washington, DC, to influence US officials in the Senate (Hendrick 2013).

Eck (2001) revealed that the contemporary United States is now considered the most religiously diverse nation in the world, alluding, in particular to the fact that the United States has welcomed almost every known religion to its shores. Taking the case of Buddhism, the United States has almost every conceivable variety of Buddhism—Sri Lankan, Chinese, Taiwanese, Thai, Myanmar, Tibetan, Vietnamese, Laotian, Cambodian, Korean, Japanese and the like, as well as most of the new and emerging Buddhist movements (Eck 2001). My study of Ciji (Chapter 4) shows how a subset of Buddhism from Taiwan is now a transnational entity with a huge representation in the United States. Each distinct Buddhist community has built its own temple and has established its own habitus—so that its followers have access to the texts, holy men and women, rituals, and ceremonies (Eck 2001). This Buddhist example is but a microcosm of the litany of expressions of the world's religious traditions that have made their home in the United States. Almost all the branches of the orthodox order of Christian churches are also found in the United States, together with all denominations of Islam, and the various Hindu schools of theology—each one focused on the worship of their favorite deity. This phenomenon is also present to some extent in other parts of the Western world especially in Europe (Eck 2001). The cosmopolitan nature of global cities in the West will no doubt continue and be a sociocultural dynamic to be reckoned with. In this regard, van der Veer's (2002) comments need to be taken seriously because he alluded to the fact that religious movements, working with migrants:

> … develop cosmopolitan projects that can be viewed as alternatives to the cosmopolitanism of the European Enlightenment. This raises a number of challenges concerning citizenship, integration and political loyalty for governmentality in the nation-states in which these cosmopolitan projects are carried out. (van der Veer 2002: 95)

Counter trends, such as cultural integration, have also been noticed in my study and therefore there is hope that governments can work with some transnational entities as part of nation building.

No Perceived Disjunction Between Faith and Fortune, Fane and Profane

The transnational religious entities in this study carry out their ministries built on intense materiality. Bourdieu (2000) used the term 'misrecognition' to refer to the social process whereby an action or an aspect of reality is not recognized for what it is because it was previously not placed within the habitus of the person or the group (Bourdieu 2000). Misrecognition relates to the ways in which the underlying processes and structures of the phenomena (what he calls 'fields') are not consciously acknowledged for what they are but made to refer to something noble—such as democracy, equality, or, in our case, spirituality. Hence, the massive, material enterprise of transnational organizations can be attributed to another realm of meaning, concealing the wealth of the group or its leaders. BAPS, Ciji, and Hillsong are wealthy organizations but they do not apologize for the relationship between faith and fortune. However, arguably, this disconnect between faith and fortune, although powerfully visible, is ambiguous because of an equally intense focus on the organization's spiritual 'call' and the unique spiritual expertise that the religious entity is believed to be offering its adherents. Sunni cleric Gülen, the founder of GHM, argued that places of worship should be established to awaken hope and faith in people. He then went on to say, "we may apply the same standards to unions, trusts, political institutions and societies in general" (cited in Hendrick 2013: 1). In other words, political and civil institutions can become sacred with the right religious underpinnings.

An everyday example of misrecognition is our indulgence in mobile phones and Internet platforms. By agreeing to use technological platforms, such as Facebook, we allow companies' access to our private consumption details for their own marketing and business ends. Most people are only vaguely conscious of this invasion of privacy, but that does not stop them from using their mobile phone or the Internet because the perceived need to use these new technologies outweighs their concern for privacy and confidentiality. In the same way, the material, economic, and political interests of transnational organizations tend to override the apparent concern for the spiritual and physical welfare of their flock, clients, or citizens. ISIS, being the wealthiest of the terrorist groups, may be an exception: unlike the other transnational organizations, it does not try to hide its wealth—in fact, it boasts of its resources.

BAPS, Hillsong, GHM, and Ciji share an infatuation with political, business, and media celebrities as well as highly placed public officials. This is a further revelation of the dynamics of realpolitik and the reality that religious organizations are comfortable in both realms—the fane and the profane. This is clearly seen in the example of Hillsong. Hillsong United seems to have extended its parish among the coveted demographic of young Hollywood with movie stars and TV personalities, such as Justin Bieber, Selena Gomez, Ashley Benson, Vanessa Hudgens, and the like who consider the Hillsong LA and New York their spiritual homes (Watson 2015).

Bourdieu's (2000) concept of symbolic violence may be helpful in interpreting the power base of transnational organizations in our study. According to Bourdieu (2000), symbolic violence is a term to represent the concept that powerful individuals, who make decisions for their followers, lead these organizations. Dominant leaders tend to position themselves as God's anointed spokespersons who control the group without resorting to physical violence (Bourdieu 2000). The dominated followers accept this position for various reasons, and hence, the violence is termed symbolic. Symbols such as texts, pujas, attractive websites, rituals, and sermons and the charisma of the leaders may serve as tools to reinforce the power of the leaders. However, this dominance may have a short shelf life for followers. In the case of ISIS, there is both symbolic violence and violence as I pointed out in Chapter 7, which is extreme and gruesome.

Varying Views on Gender

Whereas Hillsong and Ciji embrace a form of feminization, BAPS and GHM are male-dominated entities. Ciji is female-dominated (with a female leader and around 80 percent female volunteers and staff); however, men can be included as volunteers. In 1990, Ciji launched the Compassion Faith Corps for men. Men who wish to join must undertake several vows, such as no stealing, lying, committing adultery, and so on, but more importantly, they are to display feminine traits within Ciji: "Faith Corpsmen are expected to be filial, soft-spoken and have a gentle expression...." (DeVido 2010: 71).

Hillsong churches are usually run by a husband and wife team, which ostensibly shows equality in gender dynamics.

However, Evans (2006) and Chant (2001) are critical of what they term 'intimacy/relational' worship, with regard to the songs that pervade the music ministry at Hillsong.

> These songs have the power to call upon sentimentality and emotionalism without directing the participant's gaze toward God. They also have the power to manipulate the emotions of participants within the gathering, making them feel as though they are experiencing something they are not. (Chant 2001: 1)

Evans (2006) goes so far as to label some Hillsong music as portraying sentimentality and 'feminization'.

> Many males confirmed a sense of isolation or inadequacy being cre-
> ated in their worship due to this 'gendering' of the music. Colloquially
> within the Church, songs of this ilk are known as 'Jesus is my girlfriend'
> songs. (Evans 2006: 138)

It has been reported in the BBC news website that in ISIS, women are subjugated and are often used as sex slaves for soldiers (Gardner 2015). However, these reports also show a dual attitude to women. On the one hand, ISIS treats those it considers heretics (mostly females) as almost subhuman, as commodities to be traded and given away as rewards to Jihadist fighters. Footage from a sex-slave market in Mosul, Iraq, shows militants negotiating prices for young Yazidi girls, captured by ISIS (Gardner 2015). It is believed there are at least 2,000 Yazidi women who are in this situation under ISIS's control; however, the Islamic State also has ambitions for Muslim women to migrate to their territory to play a role in establishing the caliphate (Gardner 2015). Recognizing that women are the building blocks of society, ISIS's long-range plan is for families to be started with women as the nurturers.

> They want women to join them.... They see women as the cornerstones
> of the new state and they want citizens.... What is really interesting
> is that people talk of IS as being a death cult, but that is the opposite
> of what they are trying to create ... they want to create a new state ...
> and they very much want women to join that as part of this utopian
> politics. (Gardner 2015)

Changing Modalities and Transmodernism

Changing Modalities

Modality comes from the word mode, meaning "a quality, attribute, or circumstance that denotes ... mood or manner," or it could mean the way in which something happens or is experienced.[14] In the case of Islam, it is significant to observe the mode or manner in which Islam is changing—the extent to which Islam is being Westernized. The case of Islamic Relief (IR) being situated in the West and acquiring the status of a recognized aid agency is a good example of changing modalities. IR has used Western frameworks of organization and development to place itself on a par with aid agencies such as Christian Aid, Red Cross, and the like. IR changed its way of operating to a more rationalized manner and is the new face of Islam in the West (see Chapter 2). Benthall (2007), who displays a positive stance on Islamic charities, admitted that Islam in the West is changing: "Obviously, there is a considerable difference between a British charity—Muslim or other—and, say, a Saudi charity: for instance, on issues relating to gender" (Benthall 2007: 6). Benthall (2007) also alludes to IR's mode of operation in Britain, which involves Islamic integration with the mainstream non-Muslim aid and development agencies. But other changes are also taking place in the realm of Islam.

According to Roy,

> Patterns of belief and authority are changing, even if the theological content remains the same.... The Westernization of Islam does not mean liberalization, but rather it indicates a process of the individualization of religion and a growing emphasis of faith over knowledge. In a changing Islam religiosity is valued over theology and individual reconstruction of religious behaviors prevails over culturally sanctioned norms. (Roy 2004: 29)

Traditional Islamic theologians are being undermined especially in the West because new teachers who teach a variety of Islamic teachings are springing up through the introduction of Islamic televangelism, the Internet, and social media. This situation is similar to mainline churches who are in decline in some countries because of the upsurge of neo-Charismatic mega churches like Hillsong (James 2010, 2015). Also, BAPS, which is not generally known for its proselytization agenda (because the traditional understanding within Hinduism is that one must be born a Hindu to be considered a Hindu), may be changing. Recent moves within Hinduism, especially in the West, have pointed toward a concept known as 'ethical conversion', which opens the door for outsiders to enter the Hindu fold (Subramuniyaswami 2007). BAPS's strong and growing presence in the West, and the fact that their followers are taking pains to explain Hinduism to people in the West (sometimes even using Western epistemologies), may point to a new development in the dynamics of Hindu conversion.

Transmodernism

A new type of epistemological configuration is taking place, which has caused some scholars to believe a new era has come. For example, Dussel (1998) asserted that a new paradigm or philosophical periodization of our world accounts for the emerging global culture that he termed 'transmodernism'. Transmodernism fuses together the best of modernity with the traditions, indigenous values, and wisdom of religious institutions. Transmodernism is also seen as postmodernity's transition to the next phase—keeping the best of modernity and postmodernity but going beyond it (Luyckx 1999). Dussel (1998) argued that the shift toward transmodernity follows from the period of postmodernism where there was very little room for religion. Transmodernity is a negation of the fragmented life and the privatization of religion dictated by modernity and postmodernity. The paradigm of transmodernity involves an affirmation of indigenous values, wisdom, and traditions while adapting to a changing world. It encompasses social movements and welcomes religious traditions. Thus, transmodernism is both modern and traditional. BAPS, Ciji, Hillsong, GHM, and IR have all adapted to the changing world by taking the best of their traditions and making it palatable for people in contemporary society. As a result, these organizations are attracting more and more high-powered politicians, businessmen, academics, and media personalities into their various endeavors.

I believe that aspects of transmodernism are evident in my study, based on the following realities:

1. The fact that transnational organizations can range from the World Bank to the Mafia or ISIS (Rodrigeuz-Magda 2004).
2. The growth of transnational communities that are based on many varieties of the same religion—BAPS, a subsect of Hinduism is poised to break all records for temple building in the West and its breakaway group, Gunatit Samaj is catching up all over the world. Ciji, a sect of Pure World Buddhism, of

Taiwanese origin, is rapidly creating communities all over the world especially in the West. GHM, based on a form of Sufi Islam (although it is not organized as a traditional Sufi monastic order), is an expanding movement.

3. There is formulation of transnational solutions to problems and stalemates such as Ciji's successful entry into Mainland China and its ability to navigate the difficult political terrain there. Also noteworthy are IR and BAPS' ability to understand the Western habitus and overcome obstacles in the expansion of their organizations in the West.

4. Traditional faiths are changing and accommodating the grammar, epistemologies, and logistics of the West in the formulation of their beliefs and practices. GHM has successfully shown the world that an economically motivated and culturally sensitive form of Islam is compatible in the contemporary world thereby debunking stereotypical conceptions of Islam.

Therefore, our study of the six transnational religious movements supports the philosophical category of transmodernism, albeit on a small scale. This is a new and emerging philosophical periodization (such as premodern, modern, and postmodern); I suggest time will tell whether more transmodern characteristics emerge to intersect with our contemporary world.

Conclusion

The six religious movements presented in this book are creating new transnational spaces in nation-states. Each group globalizes its own version of spirituality. Each movement is different in its spiritual dynamics, and yet there are important similarities and commonalities especially in the way they embrace the modes of globalization. The organizations range from mainly religious organizations that support the upliftment of society, to a theocratic state that threatens the sovereignty of the world.

It behooves scholars of world religions to be aware of the reality of contemporary globalization and the resultant economic, technological, and sociocultural changes. These changes have major implications for faiths operating in the global sphere. History has shown us that world religions do not just simply respond to globalization; they also shape and affect the future dynamics of globalization. Even though some religious organizations are critical of globalization, they still use the modes of globalization for their own benefit. However, because many of globalization's modes and processes are accessible to all groups, there is both an upside and a downside to globalization. On the latter, the focus on religious differences and certain ideologies of transnational entities can have the potential of igniting political con-flicts and religious wars, thereby impeding the progress of globalization or the cosmopolitan values of Western society.[15] Finally, I propose that as the conversation on religion and globalization continues, Eck's (2001) insightful observation needs to be heeded.

> We cannot live in a world in which our economies and markets are global, our political awareness is global, our business relationships take us to every continent, and the Internet connects us with colleagues half a world away and yet live on Friday, or Saturday, or Sunday with ideas of God that are essentially provincial, imagining that somehow the one we call God has been primarily concerned with us and our tribe. (2001: 37)

Notes

1. Mickey Mouse (Disney), Coke, and McDonald's are three of the easily recognized icons of American capitalism and globalization.
2. This is somewhat related to the metaphor 'McDonaldization' introduced by Ritzer (1993), taking the image of America's most well-known fast food restaurant, McDonald's, to show that today's institutions have become organized according to the concepts of efficiency, calculability, predictability, and control. Disneyization takes its metaphor from America's largest and most well-known theme parks, Disneyland, and shows how the Disney theme dominates various sectors of society.
3. This is approximately equivalent to US$3.00 (in mid-2016).
4. Mickey Mouse, an animated cartoon character, was created in 1928 by the Walt Disney Studios and is the unofficial mascot of the company.
5. Hinduism is a theistic religion; however, what is debatable is whether it is a polytheistic, pantheistic, or perhaps even a monotheistic religion. Scholars have noted that this mystery is more difficult for the Western mind to grapple with, as the Indian mind tends to regard divergent views as complementary and not inconsistent. Historically, most scholars and observers have not labelled Hinduism a monotheistic faith because of the preponderance of gods and goddesses.

6. Unitarianism is the doctrine within Christianity, which believes that God exists as one person and not three. It is a denial of the classical doctrine of the Trinity and, in some cases of the full divinity of Jesus. Hillsong's focus on the Holy Spirit in their songs, and worship experience, sometimes to the exclusion of God the Father, is the basis for this observation—not that the Hillsong leadership has outrightly denounced the other two persons in the Trinity.

7. Mercer PR, which provides PR consulting to large Australian corporations, industry groups, and governments in the Pacific region, is Hillsong's PR Company. In addition, Hillsong is a client of US-based BMCFerrell, a church marketing and consulting firm.

8. Sheffield (2015) argued that by using celebrity warriors like 'Jihadi John' and displaying photographs of fighters with familiar products such as Nutella and pizza, in its videos, Isis has branded itself and become adept at attracting young men and women to its cause.

9. The portrayal of religious organizations extending in a 'reverse' direction, from the margins (periphery) to the center, is rather unique. Some might not accept such terminology since the periphery, in the case of BAPS, refers to the birthplace of the Hindu religion (India); hence, India is the center. Still, this is a useful and unique trend that is worthy of our attention.

10. While it is commendable that Muslim organizations are helping fellow Muslims, the issue here is whether the organization has been upfront to the donors as to where the money is going.

11. See http://www.islamic-relief.org/family-governance/

12. See https://www.thereligionofpeace.com/pages/articles/islamic-relief.aspx

13. See http://www.tbn.org/announcements/christian-television-leader-tbn-partnering-with-hillsong-in-launch-of-innovative-worship-network

14. See http://www.collinsdictionary.com/dictionary/english/modality

15. Stackhouse (2000) argued that the Judeo-Christian foundations have underpinned the modern Western culture that has given birth to globalization, technology democracy, and other values today. This view is shared by Friedman (1999) and Spickard (2001).

References

Basch, L. G., N .G. Shiller and C. S. Blanc. 1994. *Nations Unbound: Transnational Projects Postcolonial Predicaments, and Deterritorialized Nation-states.* Langhorne, PA: Gordon and Breach.

Belk, R. W., M. Wallendorf and J. F. Jr Sherry. 1989. "The Sacred and the Profane in Consumer Behaviour: Theodicy on the Odyssey." *Journal of Consumer Research* 16(1): 1–37.

Benthall, J. 2007. "Muslim NGOs: The Overreaction Against Islamic Charities." *ISIM Review* 20(Autumn): 1–7.

Beyer, P. 1994. *Religion and Globalization.* London: SAGE Publications.

Bourdieu, P. 1984. *Distinction: A Social Critique of the Judgement of Taste.* London: Routledge & Kegan Paul.

———. 2000. *State Nobility: Elite Schools in the Field of Power.* Boston, MA: Polity Press.

Bryman, A. 1995. *Disney and His Worlds.* New York, NY: Routledge.

Castells, M. 2000. *The Rise of the Network Society* (2nd edition). Malden, MA: Blackwell Publishers.

Chant, B. 2001. "Retuning the Church." *The Messenger* 39(1): 1–13.

Csordas, T. J. 2009. "Introduction: Modalities of Transnational Transcendence." In *Transnational Transcendence: Essays on Religion and Globalisation,* edited by T. J. Csordas, 1–30. Berkeley, CA: University of California Press.

DeVido, E. N. 2010. *Taiwan's Buddhist Nuns.* Albany, NY: State University of New York Press.

Dussel, E. 1998. "Beyond Eurocentrism: The World-system and the Limits of Modernity." In *The Cultures of Globalization,* edited by F. Jameson and M. Miyoshi. Durham, NC: Duke University Press.

Eck, D. L. 2001. *A New Religious America: How a 'Christian Country' Has Become the World's Most Religiously Diverse Nation.* San Francisco, CA: HarperCollins.

Eco, U. 1986. *Travels in Hyperreality.* London: Pan.

Evans, M. 2006. *Open Up the Doors: Music in the Modern Church.* Sheffield: Equinox.

Friedman, T. L. 1999. *The Lexus and the Olive Tree.* New York, NY: Farrar, Strauss and Girou.

Gardner, F. 2015. *The Crucial Role of Women Within Islamic State.* BBC News. 20th August edition. Accessed on 13 June 2016 from http://www.bbc.com/news/world-middle-east-33985441

Giddens, A. 1999. *Runaway World: How Globalization is Reshaping Our Lives.* London: Profile Books.

Harvey, D. 1989. *The Condition of Postmodernity.* Cambridge, MA: Blackwell.

Hendrick, P. D. 2013. *Gülen: The Ambiguous Politics of Market Islam in Turkey and the World.* New York, NY: New York University Press.

Hochschild, A. R. 1983. *The Managed Heart: Commercialization of Human Feeling.* Berkeley, CA: University of California Press.

James, J. D. 2010. *McDonaldisation Masala McGospel and Om Economics: Televangelism in Contemporary India.* New Delhi and Washington, DC: SAGE Publications.

———. 2015. "Introduction." In *A Moving Faith: Mega Churches go South,* edited by J. D. James. New Delhi and Washington, DC: SAGE Publications.

Kellner, D. 2003. *Media Spectacle.* New York, NY: Routledge.

———. 2006. "War Correspondents, the Military, and Propaganda: Some Critical Reflections." *International Journal of Communications* 2(2008): 297–330.

Kellner, D. 2008. "Globalization and Media Spectacle: From 9/11 to the Iraq War." Accessed on 20 June 2016 from https://pages.gseis.ucla.edu/faculty/kellner/essays/911terrorspectaclemedia.pdf

Kern, S. 1983. *The Culture of Time and Space: 1880–1918.* Cambridge, MA: Harvard University Press.

Leach, M. 1999, June. "Fault-lines for the 21st Century: Interview with Harlan Cleveland." *Share International.* Accessed on 11 January 2016 from http://www.shraeintl.org/archives/political

Luyckx, M. 1999. "The Transmodern Hypothesis: Towards a Dialogue of Cultures." *Futures* 31(1): 971–82.

Marshall, G. 1998. "Centre–periphery Model." *Encyclpedia.com.* Accessed on 1 June 2016 from http://www.encyclopedia.com/doc/1O88-centreperipherymodel.html

Nacos, B. L. 2002. *Mass-mediated Terrorism: The Central Role of the Media in Terrorism and Counterterrorism.* Lanham, MD: Rowman and Littlefield.

Ritzer, G. 1993. *The McDonaldization of Society.* Newbury Park, CA: Pine Forge.

Robertson, R. 1985. "Humanity, Globalization and Worldwide Religious Resurgence: A Theoretical Exploration." *Sociological Analysis* 46(3): 219–43.

Rodrigeuz-Magda, R. M. 2004. *Globalization as Transmodern Totality.* Barcelona: Anthropos.

Roy, O. 2004. *Globalized Islam: The Search for a New Ummah.* New York, NY: Columbia University Press.

Sass. J. 2000. "Emotional Labour as Cultural Performance: The Communication of Caregiving in a Non-profit Nursing Home." *Western Journal of Communication* 64(3): 330–59.

Sheffield, H. 2015. "Isis Has Built a Global Brand Using Nutella, Celebrity and Social Media." *Independent News.* 9th March edition. Accessed 21 May 2016 from http://www.independent.co.uk/news/business/news/isis-has-built-a-global-brand-using-nutella-celebrity-and-social-media-10095915.html

Spickard, J. 2001. "Religion and Globalization." *Newsletter of the American Sociological Association* 8(1): 1–4.

Srivastava, S. 2016. *A Day at a Theme Park Temple.* Accessed on 1 June 2015 from http://www.outlookindia.com/website/story/a-day-at-a-theme-park-temple/294068

Stackhouse, M. L. 2000. *God and Globalization.* Harrisburg, PA: Trinity.

Steger, M. B. 2009. *Globalization: A Brief Insight.* New York, NY: Sterling Publications.

Subramuniyaswami, S. 2007. "How to Become a Hindu: Stories of Ethical Conversion." In *What Is Hinduism? Modern Adventures into a Profound Global Faith,* edited by S. Subramuniyaswami et al., 1–103. Kapaa, HI: Himalayan Publications.

The Holy Bible. 1985. *New American Standard Version (NASB).* La Habra, CA: The Lockman Foundation.

van der Veer, P. 2002. "Colonial Cosmopolitanism." In *Conceiving Cosmopolitanism,* edited by R. Cohen and S. Vertovec, 165–79. Oxford: Oxford University Press.

Vasquez, M. A. and M. F. Marquardt. 2003. *Globalizing the Sacred: Religion Across the Americas.* New Brunswick: Rutgers University Press.

Vijayakumar, S. 2015. "Birth of a Hindu-national Temple: Convergence of Religion and Politics of Swaminarayan Akshardham." *2014–15 Colloquium Series.* University of Berkeley, California. Accessed on 5 May 2016 from http://www.tourismstudies.org/news_archive/VijayakumarShirvani2014.htm

Watson, K. 2015. *Why Does Young Hollywood Love Hillsong So Much?* Accessed on 1 June 2016 from http://www.breathecast.com/articles/why-does-young-hollywood-love-hillsong-church-so-much-29426/

Index

Abu Bakr al-Baghdadi, 134
Adalet ve Kalkinma Partisi (AKP),
  117
ad-Din ar-Rumi, Jalal, 111
Advisory Committee on Voluntary
  Foreign Aid (ACVFA), 94
Afghanistan, 142
  conflicts in, 86
  war of 2001, 162
Akshar Purushottam, doctrine of,
  39, 40
al-Adnani, Abu Muhammad,
  152
al-Baghdadi, Bakr, 142
al-Banna, Hassan, 140
al-Farid, Ibn, 111
Algeria, 155
Al Jazeera, 90
al-Khoei, Hayder, 144
al-Masri, Ayyub, 142
Al-Qaeda, 83, 107, 148, 152, 156
Al-Qaeda in Iraq (AQI), 142
al-Zarqawi, 134
al-Zarqawi, Abu Musab, 142
Amitabha Buddha, 62
Amnesty International, 8
Annan, Kofi, 1
apocalypticism, 147
Arab Doctors, 86
Arabian Islam, 85
Arabi, Ibn, 111
Arab Spring, 137
Arab world, 83
Arif, Muhammd, 150
Assembly of God (AoG), 18
Aston Business School, 92

Australian Christian Churches (ACC),
  18
authority, 166

bayat (to pledge allegiance), 142
Berger, Peter, 9, 11
Bible, 138
Bochasanwasi Shri Akshar
  Purushottam Swaminarayan
  Sanstha (BAPS), 37, 54
  devotees belief on Swaminarayan, 39
  habitus for diaspora Hindus, 52
  Hindu movement, 53
  institutional location, 45
  negotiating with other cultures and
    systems, 53
  opulence and materiality, 50
  organization of, 46
  primary motivation for, 37
  reterritorialization by opening
    temples, 168
  schismatic sect within
    Swaminarayan, 39
  spiritual hierarchy of, 41
  theological basis of, 39
  theology and practices, revised, 41
  visit to US theme park, 168
Bodhisattva, 62, 63, 71, 73, 166
Bodhisattva Gyanyin, 69
Bond for International Development,
  92
Bosnia war (1992–95), 86
Buddhism, 62, 170
  classical, central truths, 61
  division after Gautama Buddha
    death, 61

origin of, 61
reinterpretation of, 71
self-effort, rejection of, 62
Bullock, Geoff, 15
Bush, George W., 16, 134

Cable News Network (CNN), 90
Catholic Church, 64
center–periphery model, 169
centralized secular states, 3
Charity Navigator, 99
Chinese Nationalist Party, 75
Christendom, 3
Christian Aid, 88
Christian/Christianity, 3, 9, 16, 19,
    22, 29, 64, 71, 77, 115, 138, 147,
    149, 169
Christian monasticism, 110
Ciji, Buddhism in, 62
    feminization, 73
    growth and global outreach, 68
    history of, 64
    reinterpretation of, 71
    soft power politics, 77
    spiritual capital, 75
climate change, 97
Combined Federal Campaign (CFC),
    92
conflict transformation, 97
Confucianistic ideas, 71
constructivism, 11
constructivist theory, 11
consumerism, 146
Copenhagen initiative, 92
Core Humanitarian Standard (CHS),
    92
cosmologistical problem, 54
cultural capital, 166
cultural identity, 26
cultural jihad, 108

Dalai Lama's, 1
Da'watist NGO, 86, 87, 99
decline, 4

Diwali festival, 48
democracy, 6, 112, 113, 116, 140, 172
Dempsey, Martin, 149
deterritorialization, 168
developmentalizing Islamic aid, 100
dharma, 70
Dharma Drum Mountain Mission, 70
dictatorship, 140
differentiation, 3
Disneyization, 164

East Windsor Council, USA, 53
Egypt, 151
emotional labor, 168
epistemology, meaning of, 141
Erdogan, Recep Tayyip, 108
European Catholics, 5
European Union (EU), 8

faith, 173
famine in Africa, 86
fane, 173
feminization, 73
Fagushan Mission, 70
Foreign Policy magazine, 107
fortune, 173
Foxtel, 17
FTAA, 7
Fuji-Xerox, 17

G-20, 7
Garudhammas, 63
gender, 87
    justice, 97
georeligion, 95
globalization, 7, 163
    as a contemporary reality, 162
    benefits of, 168
    center–periphery pattern, 169
    impact of, 168
    rise of network society, 162
global security, 10
Greenpeace, 8
Gujarati migration, 168

Gülen, Fethullah, 107, 109, 110
Gülen-Hizmet Movement (GHM)
  controversies and future, 129
  counter radical forms of Islam,
    107
  criticism faced by, 108
  deny relationships between
    member organizations, 108
  evolution of, 115
  Fethullah Gülen role in, 124
  net worth, 107
  organizational aspects, 126
  PR strategies of, 127
  Said Nursi influence on, 114
Gunatitanand Swami, 39
Gunatit Samaj, 40, 176

Hadith, 85, 89, 90, 134, 150
Hamas, 98, 145
hawala, 85
heterosexuality, 26
Hills Christian Life Centre, 15
Hillsong Church, Australia, 15, 170
  criticisms of, 16
  institutional location of, 19
  musical composition, 21
  objectification of body and senses
    in, 26
  political economy, 30
  postmodern nature, 29
  theological position of, 22
Hillsong Music Australia (HMA), 28
Hinduism, 37, 39, 41, 44, 51, 54, 167,
  175
Hezbollah, 145
Hocaefendi (the revered teacher),
  109
Holy Spirit, 20
Houston, Bobbie, 24
Houston, Brian, 16, 19, 22, 24
Human Relief Agency, 86
human rights, 97, 112
Hussein, Saddam, 82, 137
Hyundai, 17

ibn Izzat, Muhammad, 150
ikhlas, 111
IMF, 7
immorality, 146
Improvized Explosive Devices (IEDs),
  155
International Federation of Red Cross,
  92
international nongovernment
  organizations (INGOs), 8, 11
international organizations, 3
international politics, 3, 8, 10
international relations, 2, 6, 9
  assumptions of, 8
  religious organizations approaches
    in, 12
international security, 10
International Whaling Commission
  (IWC), 2
Iran, 82, 137, 150, 151
Iraq, 82, 134, 137
Iraq war of 2003, 162
Islam, 3, 141
  beginning of, 136
  comparative typology of, 84
  dynamics of, 100
  golden age of, 82
  image of, 100
  reinvention in West, 97
  Sunni–Shia division, 139
  theological schools of, 82
Islamic, 83
  fundamentalism, 83
  Jihadists, 162
  meaning of, 83
  terrorism, 143
Islamic aid agencies, types of, 99
Islamic Call Committee, 86
Islamic Relief (IR), 82, 102, 162
  cultural proximity and networks, 91
  Muslim charity, 90
  political links, 94
  secular humanitarian organization,
    93

Islamic Relief Organization of Saudi
   Arabia (IIROSA), 86
Islamic Relief USA (IRUSA), 87, 88,
   91, 94, 98
   special programs for refugees, 95
Islamic Relief Worldwide (IRW), 87,
   92, 94
Islamic Revolution of Iran (1979), 141
Islamic State of Iraq and Syria (ISIS), 10,
   83, 107, 128, 142, 153, 168, 172
   and empire, 155
   emergence of, 134
   eschatology, 151
   origin of, 143
   psychological motivation, 146
   state flag introduction and
     anti-stand against, 147
   true form of Islam, 141
Islamic *Umma*, 87, 95, 100, 101
Islamism, 141
Islamizing development aid, 100
Islamodollars, 97

Japanese Buddhism, 71
Jews, 149
Jihadist NGO, 86, 87, 99
Judaism, 147
Justice and Development Party, 108

Kabbani, Sheikh, 150
Kelman, Ari Y., 27
Khomeini, Ayatollah Ruhollah, 137,
   141
Kubra, Najmuddin, 111
Kuomintang (KMT), 75

Lebanon, 137
Libya, 155
Lindt café terror attack, Australia
   (December 2014), 155
Luckmann, Thomas, 11

Mahayana Buddhism, 61, 63,
   69–71, 77

Mahayana Buddhist, 62, 63, 65
materialism, 146
Mercy Relief, US, 86
Michelle Obama initiative, 88
Microsoft, 17
Middle East, 85, 90
Millennium World Peace Summit,
   New York, 1
modalities, changing, 176
modernism, 12
moksha, 41
Montevideo Convention, 152
music, 27
Muslim, 3
   aid agencies, growth of, 87
   meaning of, 83
   nation, 83
   NGOs, 87
   religious endowment for, 85

Naqshband, Bahauddin, 109
nationalism, 6, 112
National Youth Rock Eisteddfod,
   17
nation-states, 2, 7, 177
NATO, 11, 116, 128, 141
new migrants, displacement of,
   168
new nonstate actors, 2
non-Arab Muslim world, 83
nongovernmental actors, 3
nonreligious transnational actors,
   categories of, 7
non-Western states, Western
   perspective to, 6
North American Global Relief
   Foundation, 86
Nursi, Said, 114
Nursi teachings, 109

Organization of Petroleum Exporting
   Countries (OPEC), 7
Ottoman Empire, 140, 149
Oxfam, 8

Paris terrorist attacks by ISIS
(November 2015), 149
patriarchy, 26
Peace Treaty of Westphalia in 1648,
3, 5
People's Republic of China (PRC), 76
politicized religion, 6
politics, 1, 4, 83, 140, 163
definition of, 3
domestic, 6
of compromise, 92
of soft power, 75
religious, 10
postmodernism, 12, 26
poverty reduction, 97
power, 3, 5, 166
in society, 50
Pramukh Swami Maharaj, 52
privatization, 4
profane, 173
Project Hope, 68
Prophet Mohammad, 135, 136, 140
Prospect magazine, 107
Pure Land Buddhism, 62, 65, 69, 71, 78

Qatar, 137
Quran, 85, 89, 90, 97, 111, 134–37,
147, 150
Qutb, Sayyid, 140

race, 87
racism, 26
Rand Corporation, 83
Ranstorp, Magnus, 144
Red Cross, 88
regimes, interests of, 3
religion, 3, 9, 10, 87, 110, 112, 113,
146, 162, 163, 175, 176
and government, relationship
between, 5
Eastern, 51
European wars of, 4
folk, 70

resurgence of, 10
transnational, 1
religious authority, 6
religious movements, 8, 12, 54, 69,
171
religious organizations, 2, 8, 9, 167
in international relations,
approaches, 12
religious pluralism, 4
religious politics, resurgence in
post–Cold War era, 10
religious revival, 163
religious tolerance, 1
reterritorialization, 169
Risale-i Nur, 111, 112
Roman Catholics, 4

Salafism, 83
Salvation Army, 16
samsara, 41
Saudi Arabia, 83, 137
Sea Shepherd Conservation
Society, 2
secularization theory, 6
aspects of, 4
factors contribute to, 4
secular nation-states, 6
secular state, 5
security theory, 10
Shaivism (Pantha), 38
Shaktism, 38
Shastriji Maharaj, 39
Shia, 136
Shia Islam, 110, 139
Shiites Islam, 82, 83, 136, 137, 141,
142, 151
Shikshapatri, 48
Siddhartha Gautama (Buddha), 61
Siemens, 17
Sinai Peninsula, 155
Smartism, 38
social capital, 166
Society for Social Relief, Kuwait, 86

soft determinism, 100
soft power, concept of, 77
solidarity-based NGOs, 87
Sony, 17
spiritual capital, 166
state sovereignty, 3, 101
Sufism, 111
Sunni Islam, 82, 110, 111, 136, 139
Swaminarayan Akshardham
    Complex (SAC), New Delhi, 47,
    49, 165
Swaminarayan Hinduism, 38
Swaminarayan Sampradaya, 39
Swami or Swaminarayan, 38
Swedish National Defence College,
    144
Syria, 137, 151
    civil war, 137

territorialization, 168
territorial states, 6
Theravada Buddhism, 61
Toshiba, 17
tourist-cum-globalization model,
    164
transmodernism, 12, 177
transmodernity, 176
transnational
    Muslim, 86
    Umma, 100
transnational activist networks
    (TANs), 8, 12
transnational civil society, definition
    of, 2
transnationalism, 2
transnational movements, 45, 54, 163,
    164
    rise of, 8
transnational religion, 1, 10, 11
    as a new actor, 9
transnational religious communities, 3
transnational religious movements,
    164

transnational social movements
    (TSMs), 7, 12
transnational solidarities, 95
tribalism, 168
Trinity Broadcasting Network (TBN),
    170
Turkey, 137
    historical and political sketch of,
    117
    modern, creation of, 119
Turkish Islam, 119
Turkish nationalism, 117
Tzu Chi University, 67

UK Aid, 92
Umayyad Dynasty (661–749), 110
Umma ('community of Muslims'),
    152
UN General Assembly, 92
UNICEF, 88, 92
United Muslim Relief (UMR), 99
United Nations (UN), 1, 7, 11
United States, 91, 107, 120, 122, 127,
    134, 163, 171
U.S. Agency for International
    Development (USAID), 94
USA, terrorist attacks in 2001, 162

Vaishna Hindu School, 53
Vaishnava Hinduism, 38
Vaishnavism, 38
Vajrayana Buddhism, 61

waqf, 85
Western democracy, 85
Western imperialism, 169
Western modernity, 8
WHO, 88
Witty, Michael, 37
World Assemblies of God Fellowship,
    18
World Bank, 7
World Social Forum (WSF), 7

World Trade Center, attack
    on September 2001,
    162
World Vision, 8, 88
World War I, 6
World War II, 116
WTO, 7

Yan, Chen (Zhengyan), 59, 63–65,
    68, 70, 74
Yinshun, 63
Youth Corps, 67

zakat, 85, 89, 99
Zschech, Darlene, 15

About the Author

Jonathan D. James is a researcher and writer on media, religion, and culture. His research interests include cultural globalization, the social effects of new media, new religious movements, indigenization, diaspora Asians in the West, and the image industry in Asia.

With an early education in Singapore, and later trained in Mass Media and Communications in the United States, Dr James is currently an adjunct lecturer at Edith Cowan University, Perth, and well known in the Asia–Pacific region as a consultant, lecturer, and guest speaker. His articles have appeared in refereed journals in Australia, the United Kingdom, and North America, including *The Journal of Religion and Popular Culture, Studies in World Christianity*, and *Continuum: Journal of Media and Culture.*

Widely traveled in Asia, North America, and the Pacific, Jonathan D. James is the author of *McDonaldisation, Masala McGospel and Om Economics: Televangelism in Contemporary India* (SAGE 2010) and the editor of *The Internet and the Google Age* (2014).